Richard Wagner

Self-Promotion and the Making of a Brand

NICHOLAS VAZSONYI

CAMBRIDGE
UNIVERSITY PRESS

CAMBRIDGE UNIVERSITY PRESS
Cambridge, New York, Melbourne, Madrid, Cape Town, Singapore,
São Paulo, Delhi, Dubai, Tokyo

Cambridge University Press
The Edinburgh Building, Cambridge CB2 8RU, UK

Published in the United States of America by Cambridge University Press, New York

www.cambridge.org
Information on this title: www.cambridge.org/9780521519960

© Nicholas Vazsonyi 2010

This publication is in copyright. Subject to statutory exception
and to the provisions of relevant collective licensing agreements,
no reproduction of any part may take place without the written
permission of Cambridge University Press.

First published 2010

Printed in the United Kingdom at the University Press, Cambridge

A catalogue record for this publication is available from the British Library

Library of Congress Cataloguing in Publication data
Vazsonyi, Nicholas, 1963–
    Richard Wagner : self-promotion and the making of a brand / Nicholas Vazsonyi.
        p.   cm.
    Includes bibliographical references and index.
    ISBN 978-0-521-51996-0 (Hardback)
    1. Wagner, Richard, 1813–1883.   2. Composers–Germany–Biography.
    3. Music   trade–Europe–History.   I. Title.
    ML410.W1V29   2010
    782.1092–dc22
    [B]
    2009048047

ISBN 978-0-521-51996-0 Hardback

Cambridge University Press has no responsibility for the persistence or
accuracy of URLs for external or third-party internet websites referred to in
this publication, and does not guarantee that any content on such websites is,
or will remain, accurate or appropriate.

To my parents

Contents

Acknowledgments [*page* viii]
A note on translation and style [xi]
Abbreviations [xii]

Introduction [1]

1 Image [8]

2 Publicity [46]

3 Niche and branding [78]

4 Consumers and consumption [127]

5 Hub [169]

Epilogue: the Wagner industry [205]

Bibliography [208]
Index [219]

Acknowledgments

This book would not have been possible without the help and encouragement of many friends, colleagues, and institutions, whose invaluable support provided financial, intellectual, and emotional sustenance over the approximately six years that it took to bring this project to press. I would like to thank the DAAD (German Academic Exchange Service) and the University of South Carolina for providing grants that funded research in Germany during the summers of 2003, 2004, and 2008 at the State Library in Berlin and the Richard Wagner Archive in Bayreuth. The University of South Carolina covered a variety of incidental costs, including the music examples and the cover art, for which I am truly grateful.

At the Richard Wagner Archive, Kristina Unger was most helpful in providing access to original unpublished documents, especially concerning the formation of the Wagner societies in the early years. Dr. Gudrun Föttinger smoothed the process of obtaining the iconic image on the cover of this book. At Cambridge University Press, I am grateful to Vicki Cooper for believing in this project, and for being such a positive and open-minded force in its completion.

At the earliest stages, when I was the most uncertain about the undertaking, Gregg Horowitz and Greg Forter helped immeasurably to give my wandering thoughts some shape. Shortly thereafter, Mary Sue Morrow generously provided vital guidance in issues of music history. Along the way, I imposed on the patience and goodwill of many. Everyone without exception responded immediately and graciously with their time and expertise: Frank Cooper, Alan Walker, Tom Grey, Hans Vaget, John Deathridge, Mark Evan Bonds, Daniel Chua, my dear friend Eva Rieger, and especially Barry Millington, who encouraged and supported me at a crucial moment. As this project drew to its close, I came to rely in particular on Stephen Brockmann, Peter Höyng, Julie Hubbert, and Sanna Pederson who all gave meticulous and carefully considered feedback at critical stages. They have also been unfailing in their readiness to help me in so many other ways. I hope I can return the favor some day.

Thanks also to the anonymous readers at the *German Studies Review*, Cambridge University Press, and especially to one reader for *Music & Letters*, who probably continues to have misgivings about my project, but whose detailed and highly critical comments were most helpful to me at the time. Thanks also for the opportunity to give talks to the live and lively audiences at the Wagner Societies in Washington DC and New York. I am grateful to my colleagues of the Interdisciplinary German Studies of the South East, especially Sander Gilman, who gave me such a good-humored grilling at the end of a presentation.

I was fortunate to have had the help of several graduate students at the University of South Carolina over the years, starting with Brian Rottkamp, who assisted me with that first attempt at a bibliography, Kristina Brown, who is still helping me as I write these pages, and Peter Kay, who expertly prepared the music examples.

Most of all, I want to thank my friends and family. Bob Bohl, Susan Courtney, Xenia Frenkel, Harald Lazardzig, and Allen Miller have been there through thick and thin in Columbia and Berlin. My parents enveloped me in the world of music and nineteenth-century European culture. Without them, I would never have come to this project. My father was still alive when I began this undertaking. I am sad that he could not see its completion. My mother has faithfully read and re-read every word of every proposal, essay, and chapter and given me the support only a mother can. My wife, Agnes Mueller – who "can't stand Wagner" – saw the potential of this project even before I did. Saying "thank you" to her will never be enough for the unflagging love, encouragement, and honest feedback throughout, including permission to desert the family for a few days every year to go to Bayreuth. Finally my children, Leah and Benjamin, who keep me centered and save me from being sucked eternally into the Wagnerian vortex.

*

Portions of Chapters 1, 2, and 5 have already appeared in earlier versions, and I am grateful to the editors and publishers for permission to reuse some of the material, as follows:

"Beethoven Instrumentalized: Richard Wagner's Self-Marketing & Media Image," *Music & Letters* 89.2 (2008), 195–211.

"Marketing German Identity: Richard Wagner's Enterprise," *German Studies Review* 28.2 (2005), 327–46.

"Selling the *Ring*: Wagner's 'Enterprise,'" *Inside the* Ring, *Essays on Wagner's Opera Cycle*, ed. John DiGaetani (Jefferson, NC: McFarland, 2006), 51–68.

The illustration on the cover, *Richard Wagner* (1871) by Franz von Lenbach, is reproduced with permission of the Nationalarchiv der Richard-Wagner-Stiftung, Bayreuth.

A note on translation and style

In the case of original texts by Richard Wagner, I have used my own translation throughout in consultation with published translations, if they exist. Where the German original is of particular interest, because of Wagner's choice of words, I have included the full text in the footnotes. In some cases, a single word or short phrase is so striking or significant, that I have included the German in parentheses immediately after the English. Titles of Wagner's stage and prose works will be given in English, unless the German version is either identical, or the more commonly used form. Hence, *The Flying Dutchman,* but *Parsifal* and *Die Meistersinger*. Specifically in the case of Wagner's essay "Das Judentum in der Musik," I depart from the standard translation of "Judentum" as "Judaism" and follow instead Barry Millington's more fortuitous and faithful "Jewishness in Music," a version he has used consistently since the publication of his *Wagner* (1984, rev. edn 1992).

In the case of originally German texts by authors other than Wagner, I use the standard English translation (e.g. with Nietzsche and Adorno) unless otherwise indicated. However, most nineteenth-century sources, such as articles from the *Neue Zeitschrift für Musik*, have no published translation, so all translations are again my own. As with the Wagner texts, I include the German original parenthetically or in the footnotes where it seems justified.

In order to facilitate consultation of the German text, I have opted for the aesthetically less appealing footnote, rather than the currently more standard endnote form.

Abbreviations

DHA	Heine, Heinrich. *Historisch-Kritische Gesamtausgabe der Werke*. Ed. Manfred Windfuhr. Düsseldorf: Hoffmann u. Campe, 1973–97.
DS	Wagner, Richard. *Dichtungen und Schriften*. Jubiläumsausgabe. 10 vols. Ed. Dieter Borchmeyer. Frankfurt am Main: Insel, 1983.
ML	Wagner, Richard. *Mein Leben*. Ed. Martin Gregor-Dellin. Munich: List, 1963.
NZfM	*Neue Zeitschrift für Musik*
SB	Wagner, Richard. *Sämtliche Briefe*. Ed. on behalf of the Richard-Wagner-Stiftung in Bayreuth by Gertrud Strobel and Werner Wolf et al. 18 vols. to date. Leipzig: Deutscher Verlag für Musik, 1967–2000; Wiesbaden: Breitkopf & Härtel, 1999–.
SSD	Wagner, Richard. *Sämtliche Schriften und Dichtungen*. Volksausgabe. 16 vols. Leipzig: Breitkopf & Härtel, n.d. [1911].
SW	Herder, Johann Gottfried. *Sämtliche Werke*. 33 vols. Ed. Bernhard Suphan. Hildesheim: Olms, 1994.

Introduction

Richard Wagner (1813–83) was the architect of the industry that today bears his name. At first, this may seem like an unremarkable statement. We have come to expect that anyone intent on a career in the public sphere will engage in self-promotion, or hire specialists for that purpose. During the nineteenth century, however, this was not at all self-evident. Indeed, for certain professions, engaging too obviously in self-promotion might be regarded as inappropriate conduct and serve to tarnish rather than enhance an image.

Admittedly, Wagner was neither the first celebrity in history, nor the only one of his day, nor were most of the techniques and strategies he used to market himself either unique or unprecedented. Nevertheless, the case of Wagner is special. First, as opposed to most of the so-called "great masters" who became commodities, Wagner not only participated in, but pioneered his own merchandizing. Second, beyond creating a recognizable public persona, he also presented his works as distinct creations unlike all others. So dissimilar were these works to anything comparable that he claimed they belonged to a new category; he even invented a vocabulary to describe them. Building a special theater where they were to be performed exclusively constituted only the most visible gesture in a larger enterprise that stamped his works with the markings of a brand. In the realm of art, nothing quite like it had ever been undertaken. Third, and most significantly, he resisted and attacked those very forces of modernity that had set the conditions for self-promotion, celebrity, and product branding in the first place. This is the essential paradox of the Wagner industry, and one that lays bare the pervasiveness and inescapability of the market in modern times. Andreas Huyssen has called this phenomenon "the vortex of commodification," a remark he made specifically in reference to Wagner.[1]

Despite the far-reaching implications of the foregoing, Wagner's enduring significance can still only be explained by his colossal, endlessly fascinating, and powerfully emotional works which seem to offer renewed stimulation

---

[1] Andreas Huyssen, *After the Great Divide: Modernism, Mass Culture, Postmodernism* (Bloomington: Indiana University Press, 1986), 42.

and relevance to every generation. Yet Wagner acted as though quality alone was insufficient, as if to concede that "great art" could not speak for itself, or could no longer do so in the crowded and noisy marketplace of the emerging masses. And so, starting around 1840 when he was not yet thirty, he began to produce a vast body of supplementary texts, all designed in one way or another to increase his visibility in the public sphere, to present a carefully crafted version of himself, and to explain, defend, and promote his works to a variety of different audiences. But he did not stop there. He worked to destroy the standing of his direct competitors and, with the help of his supporters, transformed musical taste for generations. He wrote about himself in such a way that, even today, when we talk about Wagner, we adopt his language and use his imagery. Some of Wagner's writings were scandalous then, and are now; the response to them occasionally horrific. So, in addition to the music and the drama, Wagner the person, the public figure, the discursive agenda, the historical event and its repercussions continue to command the attention of cultural critics, historians, biographers, and journalists to an extent that cannot solely be explained by the magnitude of his theatrical works.

How do we account for Wagner's presence in the public sphere? Several of his contemporaries noted his apparently insatiable need to communicate. The French poet Catulle Mendès captures this with his description of a visit to the composer in Tribschen where he remarks that Wagner "talked, talked, talked ... it was an unending flood."[2] Some interpreted Wagner's inability to stop talking as evidence of a mental illness, aspects of which could be discerned in the stage works themselves, a thesis tenaciously pursued already in Wagner's lifetime, though with unintended comic effect, by psychiatrist Theodor Puschmann.[3] While such a clinical diagnosis of Wagner's loquacious personality may be valid, it isolates the psychological motivation for his writings and other promotional activities from external, social, economic, cultural, or historical contexts and, thus, does not sufficiently address their content.

Friedrich Nietzsche, Wagner's first comprehensive and perhaps still his most perceptive critic, provides a bridge between psychological insight and historical context. Describing the theatricality which infused both his art and life, he epigrammatically called Wagner an incomparable "histrio," someone who "staged" everything, including himself. He diagnosed Wagner

---

[2] "il parlait, parlait, parlait! ... un flot incessant," Catulle Mendès, *Richard Wagner* (Paris: Charpentier, 1886), 14–15.

[3] Theodor Puschmann, *Richard Wagner: Eine psychiatrische Studie* (Berlin: Behr, 1873) (appeared 1872).

as a psychological illness (*Wagner est une névrose*) who made music itself sick. But Nietzsche then makes the case that such is the quality of modernity itself: decadent, hysterical, neurotic, where mass success (*Massen-Erfolg*) is achieved only through showmanship and deception. Wagner is the modern "artist" *par excellence*: "only sick music makes money nowadays; our big theaters subsist on Wagner."[4] For Nietzsche, Wagner is like Franz Liszt and Victor Hugo, a sad comment on the times.

Historically, almost all of Wagner's efforts borrow or adapt practices that had already been in development by about 1800, meaning a generation or more earlier. For instance, the idea of public self-fashioning and the beginnings of celebrity culture are evident in the figures of Lord Byron and Johann Wolfgang von Goethe, to name just two examples. Also around 1800, the habit of not only writing theoretically about the artwork, but anticipating its appearance with the aesthetic manifesto, came into being. The idea that the artist would need to "create the taste by which he is to be enjoyed," as William Wordsworth phrased it, was a direct consequence of what the philosopher Jürgen Habermas has termed the "structural transformation of the public sphere" in the eighteenth century, precipitated by the rise of journalism and the beginnings of what later came to be understood as popular culture.[5] Efforts by Wordsworth and, a generation earlier in Germany, by Karl Philipp Moritz and Friedrich Schiller, were a response to the economic success of what Germans call "Unterhaltungsliteratur" (leisure reading) and what Wordsworth referred to more colorfully as "frantic novels, sickly and stupid German tragedies, and deluges of idle and extravagant stories in verse."[6] The book trade that peddled such works was scorned by a self-selected group of artists who sought to separate themselves from the mainstream by shunning profit and creating aesthetically more challenging literature that offered readers greater spiritual and intellectual rewards. Writing in part for an audience that did not (yet) exist, these authors embodied an "avant-garde" mentality before the term even came into use. In a larger sense, they were resisting emergent consumerist attitudes that had already been awakened by the new fashion industry as well as the phenomenon of the branded product, Wedgwood pottery being perhaps the most

---

[4] Friedrich Nietzsche, *Der Fall Wagner*, ed. Dieter Borchmeyer (Frankfurt am Main: Insel, 1983), §5, §8, and §11; see also *The Case of Wagner*, trans. Walter Kaufmann (New York: Vintage, 1967).

[5] William Wordsworth, "Essay, Supplementary to the Preface (1815)," *The Prose Works of William Wordsworth*, 3 vols., ed. W. J. B. Owen and J. W. Smyser (Oxford: Clarendon, 1974), III: 62–84, here 80. Jürgen Habermas, *The Structural Transformation of the Public Sphere: An Inquiry into a Category of Bourgeois Society*, trans. T. Burger (Cambridge, MA: MIT Press, 1989).

[6] Wordsworth, "Preface to Lyrical Ballads (1800)," *Prose Works*, I: 118–59, here 128.

obvious early case. The sociologist Pierre Bourdieu examined this counter-culture as it emerged in Paris around 1840, the central figures being Charles Baudelaire and Gustave Flaubert.[7] Bourdieu's main argument is that their anti-market pose was in itself a marketing strategy, yet another example of Huyssen's "vortex." Both Bourdieu and Huyssen continue a line of thought already evident in the Marxist cultural criticism of Walter Benjamin – who was also fascinated by the example of Baudelaire – and Theodor Adorno, who saw precisely in Wagner the beginnings of what he termed the "culture industry."[8] In other words, all these thinkers argue that art and artists had become increasingly focused on the consumer.

Even if it is historically too soon to think in terms of consumerism, some economic sociologists like Colin Campbell and, before him, Neil McKendrick have argued convincingly that the late eighteenth century already manifests the practice of consumption, defined as the purchase and use of goods in response to momentary and transitory desires rather than to satisfy basic and permanent needs.[9] Consumption in this context refers to the pursuit of luxury, and self-indulgence in those things that are unnecessary – a long-standing habit of the aristocracy, but new to the growing mass of the middle classes. Similarly, for Donald Sassoon, whose enormous book also begins in 1800, "the story of culture" is the "story of production for a market" for the purpose of "cultural consumption."[10]

All of the above – public self-fashioning, celebrity, the aesthetic manifesto, avant-garde, fashion, the spread of journalism, the expansion of markets, the branded product – are but aspects of the broad changes sweeping England and the European continent, affecting every area of life and culture. Richard Wagner stands out as the artistic figure in the nineteenth century who fused all of these into a comprehensive struggle – ideological, theoretical, rhetorical, and creative – to establish for himself a self-contained niche in the opera market which he alone would control.

It was a tightrope walk. Like the Romantics who preceded him, Wagner vehemently opposed the modern view of the artwork as a commodity for speculation and profit. He, too, would write the aesthetic manifesto, try to

---

[7] Pierre Bourdieu, *The Rules of Art: Genesis and Structure of the Literary Field*, trans. Susan Emanuel (Stanford University Press, 1995).

[8] See Walter Benjamin, *Charles Baudelaire: A Lyric Poet in the Era of High Capitalism* (London: NLB, 1973). Theodor W. Adorno, *In Search of Wagner*, trans. Rodney Livingstone (London: Verso, 1991).

[9] See, for example, Colin Campbell, *The Romantic Ethic and the Spirit of Modern Consumerism* (Oxford: Blackwell, 1987), 17–31 and 60–5.

[10] Donald Sassoon, *The Culture of the Europeans from 1800 to the Present* (London: HarperCollins, 2006), xxi, xiii.

"create the taste by which he was to be enjoyed," and announced that he was composing for an audience that did not as yet exist. In all this, I am convinced that he was completely sincere. But that is not the point. Some of the claims he made, the inflationary language he used, the insistence with which he pressed them home, and the methods he used to promulgate them came precisely from the commercial world he was simultaneously vilifying. The contradiction raised eyebrows already then. One of his many opponents compared his methods to those of a town crier or "carnival barker."[11] Having rhetorically distanced himself from the sphere of profitable art, he nevertheless risked not being taken seriously by those who were nominally on his side of what Huyssen has called the "great divide."

The specter of trivialization continues to haunt Wagner and, I believe, accounts for the absence to this day of any book dealing with his self-promotion. Despite the massive number of works about him, which numbered over 10,000 already at the moment of his death in 1883, Wagner's critics have preferred to dismiss his public demeanor in psychological terms as evidence of megalomania.[12] Rather than viewing his actions as expressions of a flawed personality, I propose that we take seriously Wagner's efforts to craft a persona and to package his works. Most artists in modern times have had to market themselves. Wagner might just have done it better than anyone else.

The reluctance to consider canonical composers in terms of the market – a remnant of nineteenth-century sensibilities – has admittedly begun to erode. A recent book by Dana Gooley about Wagner's contemporary, Franz Liszt (1811–86), is exemplary in that Gooley wishes to resist the notion that Liszt's "virtuoso travels were largely an exercise in self-aggrandizement," noting that "we still lack an interpretation of Liszt's strategizing that does not reduce it to mere vanity."[13] Liszt's story is emblematic of the risks faced by musicians in the nineteenth century who promoted themselves, Niccolò Paganini (1782–1840) and Giacomo Meyerbeer (1791–1864) being two more examples. As opposed to the composer and violin virtuoso Paganini, who went to his death a media sensation albeit regarded as little better than a circus performer, Liszt withdrew from the carnivalesque spotlight that accompanied his public appearances in order to compose and conduct, because he wanted to be taken seriously. Meyerbeer, without question the

---

[11] W. J. S. E. [Julius Schladebach], "Das Palmsonntagsconcert," *Abend-Zeitung* (Dresden) April 16, 1846.
[12] Most recently, see Boris Voigt, *Richard Wagners Autoritäre Inszenierungen. Versuch über die Ästhetik charismatischer Herrschaft* (Hamburg: von Bockel, 2003).
[13] Dana Gooley, *The Virtuoso Liszt* (Cambridge University Press, 2004), 12–13.

most successful opera composer of his day, left himself vulnerable to attack for his calculated triumphs which were engineered by favorable previews in the press and claqueurs in the theater. Meyerbeer's demise in the opera repertoire of the latter nineteenth century may have been directly attributable to the unremitting attacks of Wagner and his allies, yet that did not stop Wagner from using some of the very same tactics. Perhaps one of Wagner's greatest accomplishments was his ability to promote himself and still to be taken seriously.

Meyerbeer, Paganini, Liszt, and Wagner were all responding to the times. Not unlike the eighteenth-century book market, the music market of the nineteenth century went through a similar transformation. Music historian William Weber has chronicled the emergence of the "modern music business" and has argued assiduously that, already in the nineteenth century, it should be examined as a "profit-seeking mass culture." While publication and retailing of printed music was "a burgeoning consumer business," not unlike the book trade, with "crafty merchandizing," the second area of the music industry – public concerts – operated on entirely different economies of scale, especially those performances that required full symphony orchestras, not to mention productions of grand opera. Concurrent with the increase in public concerts came the "commercial exploitation of the masters," meaning "dead great composers," like the recently deceased Ludwig van Beethoven and stretching back to Johann Sebastian Bach.[14] This exploitation is most evident in the stunning shift in concert programming which went from scheduling mainly contemporary to mainly "classical" works, a change in focus that still defines programming today. So, living composers were forced to compete not only against each other, but against the canonized.

Because Wagner chose the most expensive of musical genres – opera – he would lifelong be beholden to its economic imperatives. Nevertheless, because of his equally urgent literary aspirations, he in many ways brought the sensibilities of the author – both aesthetically and as a critic of modernity – to the table. So he united in ways that continue to seem contradictory, if not paradoxical, the public and necessarily publicized persona of a celebrity performer with that of the private, more introspective and contemplative author who shuns the world of media manipulation to preserve the integrity of the work, a persona which Wagner then shamelessly publicized

---

[14] William Weber, "Mass Culture and the Reshaping of European Musical Taste, 1770–1870," *International Review of the Aesthetics and Sociology of Music* 8.1 (1977), 5–22, here 6 and 15–16.

as such. Equally paradoxical, his works themselves: on the one hand meant to realize the Romanticist dream of unified art that would make man whole again, but on the other, works marketed as one-of-a-kind products that would guarantee precisely this effect – if you want to heal the world and feel good about it, buy Wagner.

How did Wagner go about making such claims, and what techniques did he use to make them so effectively? The following isolates five intersecting areas of activity – creation of a persona, public relations, development of a niche and brand, marketing embedded in the theatrical works themselves, and establishment of a hub and global network. One chapter is devoted to each of these, with special emphasis on a specific set of examples or episodes. To give the book a sense of structure, the examples and episodes are arranged chronologically over the five chapters. But this is not to suggest that one set of activities replaced the other. Wagner's efforts were ongoing in all areas, though some were emphasized over others at different times in his career. Despite the chronological arrangement, this is also not a biographical study, and biographical detail surfaces only when it is of particular relevance. Instead, the following engages in careful textual analysis of selected works by Wagner: prose essays, some correspondence, his autobiographies, journalism, as well as two of his operas.

These works reveal the extent to which Richard Wagner was his own press agent, his own manager, his own public-relations consultant. He pioneered his image as a leading cultural figure, creative genius, true German, inventor of a brand new form of aesthetic product. The Wagner industry today continues to rely on the astounding wealth of themes conceived, images shaped, and issues developed by Wagner in order to assert and retain the exclusivity of his brand.

1 | Image

"I believe in God, Mozart and Beethoven."[1] These words begin the deathbed confession of "R ... ," a fictional character of Richard Wagner's creation, the central figure in the novella "A Death in Paris." "R ..." is a poor German expatriate musician who, in an earlier novella, had made "A Pilgrimage to Beethoven." Between these two short prose works, written and first published between 1840 and 1841, the twenty-seven-year-old Wagner fuses contemporary ideas and topoi with characteristics deeply ingrained in German cultural discourse to produce a figure both familiar and new. The poor, honest, German musician, who composes for the love of music rather than for monetary gain. Music as the transcendental art form. The great composers (Germans, of course) forming a divine succession. All these ideas, rich in signs, were then circulating. With sleight of hand, Wagner concentrates them into a single character, has him die on the printed page, only to reappear as the nucleus of the public persona Wagner adopted for the remainder of his career: therein lies the novelty. Richard Wagner's public image is a literary creation. Moreover, it is one of such complexity, so full of meaning, that it demands the careful unpacking to which the remainder of this chapter will be devoted.

The term "image" can be understood both visually and conceptually. Because the advent of photography coincided with Wagner's adult life, we have an even more accurate idea of how Wagner looked than we do of his illustrious predecessors like Mozart and Beethoven. Reproduced countless times on postcards, concert programs, posters, book and record covers, iconic and carefully posed photographs of Wagner, no less than the ubiquitous portraits of Mozart and Beethoven, determine our mental picture of the composer. Nevertheless, in the case of Wagner, these photographs cannot reflect some of the most enduring aspects of his public image: as "the most German of all composers," Beethoven's only legitimate successor, a misunderstood and embattled victim of libelous intrigues engineered

---

[1] "Ich glaube an Gott, Mozart und Beethoven," Richard Wagner, "Ein Ende in Paris," *Sämtliche Schriften und Dichtungen*, popular edution, 16 vols. (Leipzig: Breitkopf & Härtel, n.d. [1911]), I: 114–36, here 135 (hereinafter *SSD*).

by a hostile, Jewish-controlled press, too good for Paris, the savior of European art, communicating only with friends of his art – the initiated – yet creating an art which would speak to the entire German Folk. These conceptual components of Wagner's image – too intricate to be conveyed by pictures alone – were all established textually and, more importantly still, by Wagner himself. This is where the case of Wagner is different from that of any composer, any artistic figure, predecessors and contemporaries alike, even those who wrote a great deal, like Carl Maria von Weber or Hector Berlioz. Wagner wrote and rewrote, enough to fill ten volumes in his own lifetime, later expanded to sixteen. His collected letters pack dozens more volumes, the project to publish a complete edition begun in 1967 and still underway. Attributed most often to a psychological need, the continuous flow of words from Wagner's mouth and pen has been described alternately as an urge to communicate (*Mitteilungsdrang*) or as the desire and ability to make a spectacle of himself (*Selbstdarstellungsvermögen*). Contemporary eyewitness accounts suggest that this was indeed a fundamental part of his personality. However, such verboseness also indicates the need to generate and control a discourse, what Robert Gutman refers to as Wagner's creation of "his own myth," but which is actually a far more involved issue and goes to the heart of this study.[2]

Wagner's musical-dramatic works have certainly become associated with the "myth" he created, making them possibly the most over-determined set of artworks in modern times. Wagner was the primary engineer of this association. However, rather than "myth," it would be more accurate to describe the result of Wagner's prose writings as a complex and disturbingly seductive amalgamation of poses, aesthetic theory, social commentary, ideology, woven amidst a colorful and suggestive autobiographical narrative. Many consumers of his artworks, then and now, have both identified and been identified with the ideas accompanying them, foremost the claim that his music dramas are exemplary expressions of the German spirit, a claim haunted by the specter of anti-Semitism. This is what has made enjoying Wagner such a forbidding exercise in the wake of the Holocaust. The lingering Wagner problem of the post-War period is a negative example which nonetheless testifies to Wagner's astonishing success at setting and controlling the discourse about his work. Wagner studies are beset by what I call "permalore," the Wagnerian version of permafrost: a narrative web of such glacial density that impedes alternative accounts. Wagner's version of

---

[2] Robert Gutman, *Richard Wagner: The Man, His Mind, and His Music* (New York: Harcourt, Brace & World, 1968), xi.

his story and explanation of his work have traditionally been the starting points for anyone wishing to write about him.

Thus Gutman's term "myth" certainly addresses an aspect of the issue, but there is more to it. The same goes for his misperception that Wagner first began to go about inventing himself at the age of fifty-two, in 1865, with the dictation of his autobiography to his second wife, Cosima. This misses the mark by a quarter-century and suggests implicitly that Wagner was mainly interested in dominating how posterity viewed him. On the contrary, Wagner was in the first place concerned with controlling his own environment, his present. Moreover, while wanting like most people to influence how others perceived him, issues of control for Wagner were framed by specific and largely practical objectives. As a public figure and creative artist, control meant the suitable performance of his works together with commensurate recognition and acceptance by an audience: success in the marketplace. In this respect, Wagner's desires were no different from those of any other modern composer or artistic creator. However, the sum total of the ways in which he went about the task of generating, ensuring and maintaining his success were both unprecedented and, intuitively perhaps, remarkably sensitive to the market he was attempting to negotiate. Rather than "myth," the terms "persona" and "image" seem a more appropriate description of what Wagner undertook to construct, terms which denote the marketing rather than the psychological or literary dimension of his activities.

Without dwelling excessively on the murky science of long-distance psychoanalysis, it is hard to miss the personal and professional significance for Wagner of the approximately two and a half years he spent in Paris between September 1839 and April 1842 shortly before he turned thirty. Beset by failure, disappointment, and loss of control, this period is also witness to an exponential increase over previous years in the quantity of Wagner's prose writings and publications to levels he would sustain for the remainder of his life. Wagner's attempt to assert and maintain control through writing is as clear as is his move to use available media deftly to market himself, his ideas and, eventually, his works. Admittedly, nothing could have been further from his mind when he abandoned his conducting post and set forth from the provincial town of Riga to travel with his first wife, Minna, to the opera capital of the world.

The Paris music industry and its detractors

For a German, especially a German composer, going to Paris raised a number of issues. Since the late seventeenth century, the indisputable French cultural hegemony projected by the court of Louis XIV and his successors had haunted the German imagination and, in large measure, gave the early search for a German national identity in the eighteenth century its original impetus. Despite the fact that music – especially opera – was principally the domain of the Italians, the opera world was still centered around the French courts. Thus, whether they looked south or west, it seemed to Germans that all they could do was imitate. Hence the increasing German preoccupation in the late eighteenth century with instrumental (non-operatic) music, and the development of a corresponding discursive apparatus filled with projections of national superiority.

Beyond the symbols of cultural dominance, Paris's superior infrastructure and institutional traditions also satisfied highly practical financial needs for opera composers and librettists. The famed Paris Opéra paid royalties for each performance, while German opera houses offered only a one-time licensing fee for performance rights no matter how successful the work turned out to be. Success in Paris not only guaranteed performance back in the German provinces, but opened up ancillary markets substantially augmenting potential earnings for the successful musician.[3] Wagner's models were the inordinately prosperous German-Jewish composer Giacomo Meyerbeer – originally Jacob Liebmann Beer – and the librettist Eugène Scribe. They reigned over the opera scene of 1840s Paris, the metropolis Wagner's eminent biographer Ernest Newman describes as a "combination of Mecca and Klondyke," a fortuitous mixed metaphor referring both to the relatively recent ascension of music to the religious sphere, as well as to the potential for profit which success in the world of music offered.[4]

Money and profit were the primary motivators for Wagner's journey to Paris. While the immediate timing for his escape from Riga was a response to the increased pressure from his numerous creditors, he had long hoped that in Paris he would achieve his big break as a composer, become "rich and famous," and "no longer be a German philistine," dreams he unabashedly announced to his friend Theodor Apel already in 1834.[5] For Wagner at that time, success began with a disavowal of his Germanness which was inseparable from philistinism: a reflection of his culture's provincialism and relative lack of sophistication when compared with that of the French. Like his fellow countryman Meyerbeer, he set his eyes on cosmopolitan Paris to

---

[3] Ernest Newman, *The Life of Richard Wagner*, 4 vols. (London: Cassell, 1976), I: 258.
[4] *Ibid.*
[5] "Ruf u. Geld gewinnen … kein deutscher Philister mehr," Letter to Theodor Apel, October 27, 1834. Richard Wagner, *Sämtliche Briefe*, ed. Gertrud Strobel and Werner Wolf (Leipzig: Deutscher Verlag für Musik, 1979), I: 167–8 (hereinafter *SB*).

compose a "French opera for the French" – not only to satisfy existing taste and market expectations, but because German opera as a genre was still a work-in-progress.

Despite his apparent willingness to conform, Wagner's stay in Paris turned out to be a complete disaster because, despite his persistent efforts and even the support of Meyerbeer, his operas were never performed. So the big break he sought eluded him. The desperate financial plight in which the Wagners found themselves as a consequence fills the correspondence of those years, is described subsequently in every one of Wagner's several autobiographies, and was reportedly the subject of dinner conversation with colleagues, friends, and admirers for decades to come.

According to Ernest Newman, Wagner failed in Paris because he "forgot that there was a business side to art," a rationale many Wagner biographers echo.[6] But this seems unlikely, since Wagner went to Paris explicitly for business reasons: "money was his goal."[7] Failure in Paris was normal, just as it is for those trying to break into Broadway or Hollywood today. So, dwelling on why Wagner failed may be less interesting than examining his response.

Wagner instrumentalized his failure. He presents himself as precisely the kind of artist who would indeed forget "that there was a business side to art," an image Newman perhaps unwittingly facilitates by perpetuating and legitimizing a legend Wagner created about himself. Actually, Wagner not only remembered the business side to art, he was consumed with it, a fact he masks so skillfully and thoroughly that this aspect of his image persists. Financial disinterestedness – as opposed to pecuniary need – was but one aspect of the complex persona Wagner began to create in Paris between 1840 and 1842. Other enduring issues like "Wagner-as-victim," even his anti-Semitism, also find their first expression during this time. Above all, Wagner's self-fashioning as most German of the Germans begins here, where genuine "Germanness" is no longer coupled with philistinism, and where, ultimately, the province becomes the virtuous and wholesome antidote to the corrupt and decadent metropolis. It would be presumptuous to ponder how genuine Wagner was about these sentiments; instead, the following examines the ways in which each of these rhetorical positions appropriated and responded to existing cultural discourses and thus contributed to the specific market position Wagner created for himself.

---

[6] Newman, *Life of Richard Wagner*, I: 269.
[7] Gutman, *Wagner*, 69.

Wagner's total reversal both on his wish to become "rich" as well as to "no longer be a German," may have reflected his inability to conquer Paris but also played on its moral vulnerability. While the music business of mid-nineteenth-century Paris began to reveal the enormous economic potential of sonic diversion for the masses, some observers, like the composer Hector Berlioz (1803–69), perceptively and contemptuously described it as an "industry."[8] Ten years Wagner's senior, Berlioz made a deep impression on the young German, with his innovative musical ideas but especially the figure he cut as a maverick artist. In one of Wagner's reports for the *Abend-Zeitung* (Dresden), he explains:

Whoever wishes to hear Berlioz's music, must go to Berlioz specifically, because nowhere else will they come across any of it. One hears Berlioz's compositions only in those concerts that he himself organizes once or twice a year; these concerts are exclusively his domain; his works played by an orchestra which he has put together specially, and for a public that he has won over as the result of a ten-year campaign.[9]

It is quite stunning to consider how closely Wagner would come to emulate the way Berlioz managed himself in public: his separation from the conventional market, the idea of exclusivity, iconoclasm, even pilgrimage; the purpose-created orchestra and venue, the struggle to gain an audience and requisite recognition. Failure to break into the industry is reinterpreted as heroic independence. Berlioz's supposed inability to profit from his work – a failure Wagner could identify with – is transformed into one of Berlioz's chief moral virtues, namely "that he doesn't write for money."[10] More recent Berlioz scholarship has begun to question the myth of Berlioz as the chronically outcast and financially destitute composer.[11] But, for whatever reason, it was expedient for Wagner to accept and propagate the

---

[8] "L'industrialisme de l'art," Hector Berlioz, *Memoires*, 2 vols., ed. Pierre Citron (Paris: Garnier-Flammarion, 1969), II: 312. Gutman describes it as "bringing the Industrial Revolution to music" (69).

[9] Richard Wagner, "Bericht an die *Dresdener Abendzeitung* 5. Mai 1841," *Der junge Wagner: Dichtungen, Aufsätze, Entwürfe 1832–1839*, ed. Julius Kapp (Berlin: Schuster & Loeffler, 1910), 179–90, here 179–80. See also Philippe Reynal, "Richard Wagner als Pariser Korrespondent 1841: Neun *Pariser Berichte* für die Dresdener *Abend-Zeitung*: Reportage oder Vorwand?" *"Schlagen Sie die Kraft der Reflexion nicht zu gering an": Beiträge zu Richard Wagners Denken, Werk und Wirken*, ed. Klaus Döge, Christa Jost, and Peter Jost (Mainz: Schott, 2002), 21–31. Reynal reports on Wagner's Paris articles written for a German readership, but offers minimal analysis.

[10] "daß er nicht fürs Geld schreibt" ("Bericht an die *Dresdener Abendzeitung* 5. Mai 1841," 183).

[11] Peter Bloom talks of Berlioz's "orchestration" of his life which was "often brighter than the dark colors of so many reminiscences, including his own," *The Life of Berlioz* (Cambridge University Press, 1998), 1–2; and D. Kern Holoman argues that the tone of "misery and defeat" in Berlioz's

image of failure, misunderstanding, and financial loss. This relationship between art and money constitutes a critique of the money-driven music industry that defines Berlioz's and, by extension, Wagner's moral stature as artists.

Nor were composers alone in criticizing the music "industry." The German-Jewish poet, thinker, social commentator, and journalist Heinrich Heine (1797–1856), then also living in Paris, was one of the most eloquent critics of the new entertainment culture. He referred to the prolific Eugène Scribe as the "the libretto manufacturer" (*Librettofabrikant*), in other words, as:

[t]he man of money and jingling reality, who never loses his head in the unproductive clouds of romanticism, but holds fast onto the earthly reality of a marriage of convenience, of the industrial bourgeoisie, and royalty payments.[12]

Heine and Wagner were in frequent contact during this time, the latter even admitted to copying Heine's popular style in his own journalistic work,[13] so Wagner's contemporaneous reference to opera houses as "institutions of the art industry" reflected an ongoing conversation with his peers.[14] Heine was especially critical of the piano, a mechanical device representing the "victory of machinery over spirit," and he condemned both virtuosos and middle-class girls for playing an instrument which "kills thinking and feeling."[15] The virtuoso was instrumental in driving the lucrative domestic music market, which William Weber has called "intensively – often deviously – entrepreneurial in its economic practices, probably as much so as any other consumer business."[16] Exhibiting unheard-of technical mastery

---

Mémoires is "demonstrably false," that "the old notion of Berlioz as a failure is the greatest myth of all," *Berlioz* (Cambridge, MA: Harvard University Press, 1989), 5. On Berlioz's success at putting on his concerts, see Holoman, *Berlioz*, 231 and 234.

[12] "der Mann des Geldes, des klingenden Realismus, der sich nie versteigt in die Romantik einer unfruchtbaren Wolkenwelt, und sich festklammert an der irdischen Wirklichkeit der Vernunftheurat, des industriellen Bürgerthums und der Tantième," Heinrich Heine, *Lutezia*, II. Teil, LVI, *Historisch-Kritische Gesamtausgabe der Werke* (hereinafter *DHA*), ed. Manfred Windfuhr (Düsseldorf: Hoffmann u. Campe, 1990), XIV.1: 53 and Anhang – Musikalische Saison 1844, Zweiter Bericht, May 1, 1844, XIV.1: 141.

[13] Richard Wagner, *Mein Leben*, ed. Martin Gregor-Dellin (Munich: List, 1963), 208 (hereinafter *ML*).

[14] "kunstindustrielle Anstalten," Richard Wagner, "Halévy und die *Königin von Cypern*," *Der junge Wagner*, 271–306, here 274. A different version, originally printed in the *Abend-Zeitung* (Dresden), was reprinted as "Bericht über eine neue Pariser Oper (*La Reine der Chypre* von Halévy)" in *SSD* I: 241–57.

[15] Heine, *Lutezia*, LV, March 20, 1843, *DHA* XIV.1: 45.

[16] William Weber, "Wagner, Wagnerism, and Musical Idealism," *Wagnerism in European Culture and Politics*, ed. David C. Large and William Weber (Ithaca: Cornell University Press, 1984), 28–71, here 33.

in combination with astute showmanship and charismatic appearance, these virtuosos – perhaps most notably the violinist Niccolò Paganini – created a sensation wherever they performed; they beguiled and seduced audiences, and inspired amateurs to try the same at home. Virtuosos were consummate self-promoters: their "success a function of journalistic advertising and good press coverage," as much as they provided "the cultural reporter with subject matter."[17] In other words, "the virtuoso and the journalist mutually exploit each other," essential participants in the new media-and-sensation-driven entertainment business.[18] So it is surely a bit hypocritical when Heine attacks the pianist Franz Liszt, whose concerts arouse "Lisztomania" (*Lisztomanie*), no longer art but a "pathology" – "madness … unheard of in the annals of frenzy," creating an effect Albrecht Betz has described as "structurally" akin to today's rock concerts.[19] Heine sees through the manipulation: "no one in the world knows better how to organize his successes, or much more their mise-en-scène, than our Franz Liszt."[20] Liszt is the "general manager of his fame" (*Generalintendant seiner Berühmtheit*), second only to Meyerbeer in self-promotion.[21] Inspired by and envious of the Liszt and Meyerbeer publicity machines, Wagner would later perfect similar techniques, made more insidious because they were couched in the rhetoric of "pure art."

In fairness, Liszt was ultimately an inappropriate target as much as Heine, the journalist who depended on the likes of Liszt for his material, was being disingenuous. The most celebrated piano virtuoso of his time, considered by some a charlatan in the mold of Paganini, Liszt was nevertheless committed to the idea of the serious musician as creative genius. In a lengthy and remarkable series of articles about the "Situation of Artists and Their Condition in Society," published 1835 in the *Gazette musicale de Paris*, he complains that not much had changed since the days when Mozart was forced to eat with the servants.[22] Tinged with Saint-Simonian ideas, the article declares that, though now charged with a "grand mission both

---

[17] Susan Bernstein, *Virtuosity of the Nineteenth Century: Performing Music and Language in Heine, Liszt, and Baudelaire* (Stanford University Press, 1998), 11.

[18] *Ibid.*, 79.

[19] Heine, *Lutezia*, 1. Bericht, April 25, 1844, *DHA* XIV.1: 132. Also Albrecht Betz, *Der Charme des Ruhestörers: Heine-Studien – Ästhetik und Politik II* (Aachen: Rimbaud, 1997), 75. Betz's citations are often inaccurate.

[20] "niemand auf dieser Welt seine Successe, oder vielmehr die *mise en scène* derselben so gut zu organisieren weiß wie unser Franz Liszt" (*ibid.*).

[21] *Ibid.* on Meyerbeer, see also Heine, *Lutezia*, *DHA* XIV: 245–6.

[22] Franz Liszt, *Sämtliche Schriften*, ed. Rainer Kleinertz (Wiesbaden: Breitkopf & Härtel, 2000), I: 2–75 (parallel French and German versions).

religious and social," artists still suffered a low social status.[23] Liszt used his own example to assert his post-revolutionary, more expansive definition of aristocracy: of birth, of fortune, and of ability. He reformulated the feudal motto "noblesse oblige" to "génie oblige!" – tantamount to declaring that the gifted artist was the aristocrat's equal.[24] Liszt was consistent, his aristocratic disdain of money suggesting that art – in order to retain its nobility – should not be demeaned by mercantilist considerations. Hence the amusing anecdote in which Princess Metternich asked Liszt after a concert tour: "did you do good business?" and Liszt's reply: "Princess, I make music, not business."[25]

Disinterestedness and being German

Liszt was articulating an attitude to money and entrepreneurship shared by a segment of the artistic community throughout Europe. The expansion and proliferation of the mass market threatened to make art just another commodity, subject to the laws of supply and demand. Already in the eighteenth century, some authors and thinkers, especially in Germany, resisted the imperative to produce works that would sell. Alternately, they needed to devise a means of justifying why their works did not sell.[26] Either way, they claimed that true art, genuine art, was not created with a view to profit. In a reverse argument, popular, hence profitable art was a sure sign of its inferiority, its creation based on economic calculation. This rhetorical position, theorized most powerfully by Immanuel Kant, brought serious, disinterested art into proximity with religion as well as its institutionalized form, the Church – on the face of it, the only remaining enterprise untouched by the economic imperatives of the modern marketplace. Establishing a connection between art and religion was not difficult, since certain branches like sculpture, painting, and music had long been adopted by the Church to propagate its mission, just as art had served the aristocracy's desire to

---

[23] "nous crions sans relâche … qu'une grande MISSION religieuse et sociale est *imposée* aux artistes" (Liszt, *Sämtliche Schriften*, I: 62). See also Ralph P. Locke, *Music, Musicians and the Saint-Simonians* (University of Chicago Press, 1986), esp. 104 and, more recently, his "Liszt on the Artist in Society," with a translation into English of the last installment of "de la Situation," *Franz Liszt and His World*, ed. Christopher Gibbs and Dana Gooley (Princeton University Press, 2006), 291–302.

[24] Alan Walker, *Franz Liszt*, 3 vols. (New York: Knopf, 1983), I: 290–1.

[25] *Ibid.*, I: 289.

[26] See Martha Woodmansee, *The Author, Art, and the Market: Rereading the History of Aesthetics* (New York: Columbia University Press, 1994).

project its wealth and sophistication. With the rise of the secular, bourgeois state and the concurrent demise of religious and aristocratic institutions in the wake of the Enlightenment and the French Revolution, artists too declared independence from their former masters and the servile role art had played. Nonetheless, like Franz Liszt, they sought to retain both the spiritual and aristocratic aura of the artwork. These principles, albeit formulated with greater subtlety, lay at the heart of the Romantic movements from England to Germany.

Richard Wagner took this Europe-wide aesthetic discourse, aligned it narrowly with German characteristics, making the Romantic attitude to art an expression of national typology, to which he then tied his personal identity. Already the title of one of his essays, "The Disastrousness of Being German in Paris" (*Pariser Fatalitäten für Deutsche* [1841]), published in August Lewald's journal *Europa*, proclaims Wagner's regained national pride. Apparently, it required going abroad and coming into contact with the "other" to reawaken one's patriotism: "In Paris, Germans learn renewed appreciation of their mother tongue … Their often weakened patriotism gains new strength here."[27] Wagner even repeats this sentiment ten years later in his autobiographical *Communication to my Friends*, transforming the earlier generic statement into a personal confession: "It was the feeling of homelessness in Paris that awakened the longing for my German homeland."[28] Clearly no longer embarrassed to be a German, Wagner instrumentalizes his origins by making claims of national moral superiority which necessarily also apply to him: "The greatest, most authentic Germans are poor."[29] The money-centered exigencies of French society, most evident in the corrupt metropolis of Paris, predestine Germans for failure: "In *Paris* being *German* is truly the most irksome."[30] Germans in Paris are victims, their inescapable poverty proof of intact integrity and honesty which, in turn, become markers for true Germanness: "Poverty is the greatest vice in Paris," consequently: "a German and a dumb, wretched – meaning honest and poor – person have come to mean one and the same."[31]

From the outset of Wagner's journalistic work in Paris, the relationship between money and art functions as a leitmotif in his assessment of aesthetic quality and moral virtue: "One can thus judge how dangerous a virtue

---

[27] Richard Wagner, "Pariser Fatalitäten für Deutsche," *SSD* XII: 44–62, here 59.
[28] *SSD* IV: 268.
[29] "Die vortrefflichsten, echtesten Deutschen sind die Armen" (*SSD* XII: 59).
[30] "im ganzen ist es das Ennuyanteste, in *Paris Deutscher zu sein*" (*SSD* XII: 44).
[31] "ein Deutscher und ein dummer, schlechter – nämlich ehrlicher, armer – Mensch [ist] zu einem und demselben Begriffe geworden" (*SSD* XII: 45).

honesty is in Paris."[32] Money becomes the characteristic that distinguishes Berlioz from Liszt. Albeit aesthetic "brothers" – given their admiration of Beethoven – they are morally poles apart: "Liszt makes money without having any expenses, whereas Berlioz has expenses and earns nothing."[33] Wagner condemns Liszt as an immoral profiteer, a virtuoso who sells out by "playing the part of the fool."[34] Berlioz (like Wagner) is a loser in what Wagner, a century before Theodor Adorno and the Frankfurt School, denounces as "the art industry" (*die Kunstindustrie*), where "losing" denotes a moral victory.[35]

Here, as elsewhere, Wagner's association of artistic disinterestedness with an almost genetic national virtue is not his own invention but rather synthesizes discourses deeply embedded in the Christian-German traditions. The link between Christianity and Germanness, established in the Middle Ages with the so-called "Reichsmythos" (myth of the Empire), was based on the claim that the Holy Roman Empire of the German Nation was the rightful successor to the Roman Empire, meaning that it was now the guarantor of Christianity. Disinterestedness in money seemed common to both the Germanic and Christian traditions. The biblical admonition that "it is easier for a camel to pass through the eye of a needle, than for a rich man to enter into the kingdom of God"[36] glorifies the poor and damns the wealthy. It also explains Christendom's strained relationship with money, and perhaps even accounts in part for the anti-Semitism of the Middle Ages and beyond, given that money-lending was an activity pursued by Jews who in turn were often accused of usury. Independently, Tacitus's *Germania* (AD 98) thematizes ignorance of gold and silver amongst Germanic tribes as an indication of their wholesomeness, and as a foil to critique the more decadent, corrupt Romans. These two discursive lines merged with the rediscovery in 1455 of Tacitus's text, and Martin Luther's protest against papal fiscal abuses in 1517. Luther lived what he preached. He condemned publishers for profiting from the sale of books, and presented himself as the model of disinterestedness, selflessly proclaiming in his "Warning to Publishers" (1541): "I received it for nothing, gave it away for nothing, and seek nothing for it,

---

[32] "Man möge somit urteilen, welche gefährliche Tugend in Paris *Ehrlichkeit* sei" (*SSD* XII: 45).
[33] "Doch ist einiger Unterschied unter ihnen zu machen, vor allem der, daß Liszt Geld gewinnt, ohne Kosten zu haben, während Berlioz Kosten hat und nichts gewinnt" (Wagner, *Der junge Wagner*, 185).
[34] See, for example, Wagner's letter to Robert Schumann, January [*recte*: February] 3, 1842 (*SB* I: 573–9).
[35] Wagner, *Der junge Wagner*, 274.
[36] Gospel According to St. Matthew 19:24.

Christ my Lord has repaid me for it many hundred thousand times over."[37] Luther's status as exemplary German seemed to confirm Tacitus's observations about the virtues of the Germanic folk, observations which became crucial in the extended effort to (re-)construct a German national identity during the eighteenth century. Luther's status as an exemplary author who did not seek to profit from his creative work was no less influential.

Wagner simply combined existing discourses: one which claimed disinterestedness was a distinctly German trait, with another Europe-wide assertion that genuine art could only be produced in the spirit of disinterestedness. He would later define Germanness as "doing something for its own sake … whereas utilitarianism turns out to be unGerman."[38] Only Germans create genuine art: "Italians are singers, the French virtuosos, the Germans – musicians."[39] Wagner clarifies:

> The German has an exclusive right to be called "musician," – because one can say of him: he loves music for music's sake, – not as a means to impress, or to earn money and reputation, but rather because it is a divine and beautiful art which he worships and which, when he gives himself over to it, means everything to him.[40]

The French and the Italians commodify art for personal gain. Germans do not. Structurally, this argument is reminiscent of Luther's much earlier critique of the Church, whose fiduciary abuses he protested in the famous Ninety-Five Theses. There, too, even before the formal advent of the nation state, the quarrel became one between geographically distinct cultures. Papal Rome was the unChristian seat of debauchery, thievery, and decadence, robbing and thus victimizing the inhabitants of German lands in order to finance costly building projects and generally subsidize

---

[37] "Denn ich habs umb sonst empfangen, umb sonst hab ichs gegeben, und begere auch dafur nichts, Christus mein Herr hat mirs viel hundert tausentfeltig vergolten" ("Warnung an die Drucker von 1541," Martin Luther, *Die gantze Heilige Schrifft Deudsch*, 2 vols. [Munich 1972], n.p.).

[38] Richard Wagner, *Deutsche Kunst und deutsche Politik*, SSD VIII: 96–7: "was Deutsch sei, nämlich: die Sache, die man treibt, um ihrer selbst … willen treiben; wogegen das Nützlichkeitswesen … sich als undeutsch herausstellte." Wagner's definition matches an earlier formulation by Carl Maria von Weber: "dem deutschen Künstler sei vorzugsweise der wahre Eifer eigen, im Stillen die Sache, eben um der Sache willen, zu tun," Carl Maria von Weber, "*Die Bergknappen*, Oper von Ludwig Hellwig (1820)," *Kunstansichten. Ausgewählte Schriften*, ed. Karl Laux (Leipzig: Reclam, 1969), 215–18, here 216.

[39] "der Italiener ist Sänger, der Franzose Virtuos, der Deutsche – Musiker" (*SSD* I: 151).

[40] "Der Deutsche hat ein Recht, ausschließlich mit 'Musiker' bezeichnet zu werden, – denn von ihm kann man sagen, er liebt die Musik ihrer selbst willen, – nicht als Mittel zu entzücken, Geld und Ansehen zu erlangen, sondern, weil sie eine göttliche, schöne Kunst ist, die er anbetet, und die, wenn er sich ihr ergiebt, sein Ein und Alles wird" (*SSD* I: 151). Wagner later tied this notion to his person: "Eines hielt mich aufrecht: meine Kunst, die für mich eben nicht ein Mittel zum Ruhm- und Gelderwerb, sondern zur Kundgebung meiner Anschauungen an fühlende Herzen war" (*SSD* IV: 304).

an extravagant lifestyle. Luther's reform proposed to restore the direct relationship between believers and God, and allow the faithful to worship for its own sake. His unprecedented translation of the Bible into a German language understandable to all conveys the impression that the "faithful" he was in the first place addressing were his fellow Germans.

That even non-religious art could transform and transcend – and should thus be treated religiously – was based on claims advanced by several thinkers, most notably perhaps Friedrich Schiller who set out his moralistic redemptive vision of art in his seminal *On the Aesthetic Education of Man in a Series of Letters* (1795). Instrumental music, not bound by the limitations of language, seemed the most transcendent, a potential enhanced once the privileged position formerly held by the performer was shifted to the composer,[41] rendering the composer's creation – the "musical work"[42] – the centerpiece of deliberation. Wagner was not alone in connecting such generic aesthetic issues to the emerging nationalist discourse. Even before 1800, German-speaking music critics associated German music with manliness and French–Italian music with femininity, the German emphasis on instrumental music reflecting that nation's more complex and sophisticated intellect when compared with the apparent superficiality of French and Italian vocal music.[43] Since these attributes merely confirmed existing assertions about national characteristics, they fueled the aspiration of German culture to one of universal significance and value,[44] and the promotion of instrumental (necessarily German) music as a "universal" language.[45]

Where Wagner differed from his predecessors and peers was in his ability to identify his persona and ultimately his works with the national mission. As if he had wrapped himself in the as yet non-existent German national flag and placed a "made in Germany" label on his compositions. However

---

[41] Michael Talbot, "The Work Concept and Composer-Centredness," *The Musical Work: Reality or Invention?* ed. Michael Talbot (Liverpool University Press, 2000), 168–86.

[42] Lydia Goehr, *The Imaginary Museum of Musical Works: An Essay in the Philosophy of Music* (Oxford: Clarendon, 1992). See also Mark Evan Bonds, *Music as Thought: Listening to the Symphony in the Age of Beethoven* (Princeton University Press, 2006).

[43] See Mary Sue Morrow, *German Music Criticism in the Late Eighteenth Century: Aesthetic Issues in Instrumental Music* (Cambridge University Press, 1997).

[44] "Unsre Sprache wird die Welt beherrschen" (our language will rule the world), writes Friedrich Schiller in the unpublished fragment subsequently titled, "[Deutsche Größe]," *Werke* (Weimar: H. Böhlaus Nachfolger, 1983), II.1: 431–6, here 432.

[45] E. T. A. Hoffmann wrote that music "ist die romantischste aller Künste" (is the most romantic of all the arts), in "Beethovens Instrumental-Musik," from his *Kreisleriana. Phantasiestücke in Callots Manier (1.Teil)*, *Sämtliche Werke in 6 Bdn*, ed. H. Steinecke and W. Segebrecht (Frankfurt am Main: Deutscher Klassiker, 1993), II.1: 52; and Friedrich Schlegel: "Die romantische Poesie ist eine progressive Universalpoesie" (Romantic poetics is a progressive

genuine his feelings of homesickness and consequent patriotism may have been, it was nevertheless an inspired marketing maneuver, considering the surge of patriotic sentiment in German lands generally in the nineteenth century, but especially during the period of the so-called Rhine Crisis of 1840–41.

Marketing and the avant-garde

Wagner complained life-long that, in order to survive financially during the Paris years, he was "compelled" to write journal articles and short stories. This aspect of his chronic self-portrayal as victim has been perpetuated by his biographers. One of the earliest, Carl Friedrich Glasenapp, described Wagner's journalistic work as "compulsory labor" (*Frondienst*), a tendentious word conveying the sense of feudal bondage.[46] In fact, Wagner loved to write, and continued to do so even when it was no longer a financial necessity. Not that this stopped him from complaining, however. Ten years later, in his *Communication to my Friends*, he once again verbalized the necessity yet his "reluctance" to write.[47] Even if Wagner penned more commentary than most of his peers, it was no longer unusual for artists to do so.

Already a generation earlier, authors began to understand the importance of accompanying their creative work with explanatory prose and theoretical justification in order to create "taste," as Wordsworth put it, meaning an audience – a market – for their often difficult or at least unfamiliar work. Among Wagner's contemporaries, the most prolific writer-composer – other than Wagner himself – was Robert Schumann (1810–56). Founder and first chief editor of the *Neue Zeitschrift für Musik* (henceforth *NZfM*), the prestigious music journal which began in 1834 and still runs today, Schumann's impact as a music critic rivals his work as a composer. Schumann had multiple objectives: to rejuvenate an art form whose development seemed to have stalled since Beethoven's death in 1827; to counter the aesthetic conservatism embodied in the sterile worship of the classic masters, and to oppose the opportunism of popular composers like Meyerbeer. Most of all, Schumann battled what he and his peers called "philistinism" in all its forms: bourgeois

---

universal poetics), the first sentence of his "Athenäums-Fragment Nr. 116," *Kritische-Friedrich-Schlegel-Ausgabe*, vol. II/1, ed. Ernst Behler (Munich: Schöningh, 1967), 182.

[46] Carl Friedrich Glasenapp, *Das Leben Richard Wagners in sechs Büchern dargestellt*, 4th edn (Leipzig: Breitkopf & Härtel, 1905), I: 388.

[47] *SSD* IV: 330.

consumers who used music to display social status, as much as virtuosos who served up music to satisfy middle-class tastes for entertainment and distraction. To assist in what he presented as a solitary struggle, Schumann formed an imaginary circle of friends, resistance fighters called the "League of David" (*Davidsbund*), front-line defenders of true art – art for the sake of art, not for profit or to achieve some other objective. Speaking in the voices of these characters, Schumann wrote a series of articles for his journal and depicted his gang musically in the *Davidsbündlertänzen* and *Carnaval* whose musical "mignons" of individual league members culminate in the rousing martial finale, appropriately titled: "Marche des Davidsbündler contre les Philistins." To borrow from Matei Calinescu, Schumann's "Art for Art's Sake is the first product of aesthetic modernity's rebellion against the modernity of the philistine."[48] Living what he preached, Schumann's renegade and unconventional early piano compositions seem all but designed to fail in the marketplace.[49] Ironically perhaps, these pieces today form the core of the Schumann repertoire.

For Wagner, Schumann's example must not be ignored, though too often it is. Aside from the fact that Schumann published some of Wagner's Paris writings in the *NZfM*, it is not by accident, as Robert Gutman points out, that Wagner named Hans Sachs's apprentice "David," the character who beats the philistine Beckmesser in the pivotal Act II riot, the dramatic seed around which *Die Meistersinger von Nürnberg* was originally conceived.[50] Schumann ushered in "the age … when artists undertook to write about their creations so that what had earlier been the exception now became the rule," an accomplishment recognized already then, as this comment by Franz Brendel, Schumann's successor as chief editor of the *NZfM*, on the occasion of the journal's twenty-fifth anniversary celebration in 1859, testifies.[51] Though Wagner may have complained over the years about being compelled to write essays instead of music, Schumann's example made it respectable, even normal, for a composer to do so. Nevertheless, they differed because, while Schumann wrote in general about music and usually about other composers and performers, Wagner almost invariably wrote about himself.

[48] Matei Calinescu, *Faces of Modernity: Avant-Garde, Decadence, Kitsch* (Bloomington: Indiana University Press, 1977), 45.
[49] See Anthony Newcomb, "Schumann and the Marketplace: From Butterflies to *Hausmusik*," *Nineteenth-Century Piano Music*, ed. R. Larry Todd (New York: Shirmer, 1990), 258–315.
[50] Gutman, *Wagner*, 95; Gutman pairs Walther and Sachs with Florestan and Meister Raro, two of Schumann's *Davidsbund*.
[51] Franz Brendel, "Zur Anbahnung einer Verständigung: Vortrag zur Eröffnung der Tonkünstler-Versammlung," *NZfM* 50.24 (June 10, 1859), 265–73, also published in Richard Pohl, *Die*

Just the same, there is no small paradox in Schumann's work and the journal he founded. Dedicated to the future direction of "serious" music, the *NZfM* was nonetheless an entrepreneurial venture of its own, attentive to the marketplace, intent on creating demand for non-commercial music and for those composers it championed. Nor was Schumann alone in making a disavowal of the market the centerpiece of his marketing effort.

The French sociologist Pierre Bourdieu has examined this phenomenon amongst authors working in Paris around 1840, specifically the poet Charles Baudelaire (1821–67) and the novelist Gustave Flaubert (1821–80), who emerge as founding figures of a movement which reacts to the "industrialism [that] has penetrated literature itself after having transformed the press."[52] Building on the conception of the autonomous artist who was putatively independent of all forces – feudal, ecclesiastical, political, economic, and social – which had either traditionally or recently determined the form and content of the artwork, Baudelaire took the lead in resisting industrial modernity by means of aesthetic modernism. But, as Bourdieu shows, and Walter Benjamin before him insinuates, the imperative of a "pure" art, resistant to the market and broadly rejecting bourgeois culture and morality, was problematic from the start. Baudelaire's *flâneur* is the lone stroller who stands at the margins of society ostensibly to gaze, "but in reality … to find a buyer."[53] Equally paradoxical was the new nonconformist "bohemian" lifestyle which would put this resistance on public display. The shabbily clothed, often amoral, "starving artist" soon became a vulgarized literary figure, dramatized in Henri Murger's *Scènes de la vie de bohème* (1853), immortalized in Giacomo Puccini's operatic adaptation *La Bohème* (1896), and theorized by Benjamin. In Paris, certain districts like Montmartre and the Latin Quarter came to be identified with bohemian living, a convention later adopted in other urban centers. Over time, Bohemian "artsiness" has itself become an institution, a cliché obliging its own conformism including the performance of a certain political stance always in opposition to the establishment. Bourdieu's claim that there is no such thing as a "*right-wing* intellectual" perhaps involuntarily reveals the perfunctoriness of the "*left-wing* intellectual."

The choreographed lifestyle of the anti-establishment artist is part of an image which also entails, even requires, a certain attitude to aesthetics

---

Tonkünstler-Versammlung zu Leipzig am 1. bis 4. Juni 1859 (Leipzig: Kahnt, 1859), 75–95, here 76.

[52] Albert Cassagne, *La Théorie de l'art pour l'art en France: chez les derniers romantiques et les premiers réalistes* (Paris: Dorbon, 1906), 155, cited by Bourdieu, *Rules of Art*, 53.

[53] Benjamin, *Baudelaire*, 170–1.

perhaps best understood under the rubric "avant-garde." Originally used by the military to denote that part of the army which ventured first into harm's way, often at great personal cost, the term "avant-garde" as used in the aesthetic sphere continues to elude conclusive definition. Applied narrowly, as Peter Bürger has done, it refers to the post-Expressionist and Dada movements of the 1920s and 30s.[54] However, Bürger's approach fails to acknowledge the existence of the "avant-garde" as an ongoing set of artistic attitudes and practices with roots substantially predating the early twentieth century. Understood more broadly as an idea rather than as a distinct period, "avant-garde" denotes a position claimed by artists in the "field of cultural production" since the 1840s (Bourdieu), or a concept based in the radical politics of post-revolutionary France of the 1790s (Calinescu),[55] or an offspring of Romanticism (Poggioli).[56] The problem with these broader approaches is that they fail to discern the often significant differences between distinct avant-gardist movements. Nevertheless, common to all these definitions is the idea of avant-garde as a mode of opposition to the numerous transformations – social, political, economic, philosophical, technological – following the French Revolution and characteristic of modernity.

The military connotation of "avant-garde" is preserved in the notion of resistance, in the practice of aesthetic risk-taking, as well as in the locational sense of being at the forefront. The self-appointed role of the avant-garde to suggest new directions is evident in the explicit future-orientedness of its practitioners. Claiming the future became a beloved rhetorical position in the first half of the nineteenth century, evident in countless invocations: "new wine demands new bottles" (Franz Liszt);[57] Liszt is "pianist of the future" (Berlioz);[58] "l'art d'avenir" (art of the future – Joseph d'Ortigue); "Neue Bahnen" (New Paths – Schumann's 1853 review of Johannes Brahms); "the philosophy of the future" (Ludwig Feuerbach, 1843), not to mention Wagner's own "the Artwork of the Future" (1849) a concept which earned his works the misnomer "Zukunftsmusik."

[54] Peter Bürger, *Theory of the Avant-Garde* (Minneapolis: University of Minnesota Press, 1984). For a critique of Bürger and a broadening of the term "avant-garde," see, for example, *European Avant-Garde: New Perspectives*, ed. Dietrich Scheunemann (Amsterdam and Atlanta: Rodopi, 2000), especially Ian Revie, "Apollinaire and Cubist Innovation: Resetting the Frontiers, Changing the Paradigm," 83–95.
[55] Calinescu, *Faces of Modernity*, 101, and Bourdieu, *Rules of Art*, 158.
[56] Renato Poggioli, *The Theory of the Avant-Garde*, trans. Gerald Fitzgerald (Cambridge, MA: Harvard University Press, 1968), 15 and 46.
[57] Quoted in Walker, *Franz Liszt*, II: 309. Attributed to Liszt by his pupil August Stradal in the latter's *Erinnerungen an Franz Liszt* (Berne, 1929) the German original was "Neuer Wein bedarf neuer Schläuche." My thanks to Alan Walker for the additional insight.
[58] Walker, *Liszt*, I: 236.

Politically, the avant-garde is often misunderstood as an anti-modern (not to be confused with anti-modernist) movement, but instead avant-garde regards modernity as an incomplete project, imperfectly executed. It is modernity's partner, its conscience, distinguished, like modernity itself, by "its permanent instability."[59] Paradoxically, perhaps, the avant-garde mimics Marx's critique of the "bourgeois mode of production" and capitalism. Indeed, one possible definition of the avant-garde can be obtained by citing the *Communist Manifesto* and replacing the words "bourgeois" and "social" with "avant-garde" and "aesthetic" (my amendments are in italics):

The *avant-garde* cannot exist without constantly revolutionizing the instruments of production … Constant revolutionizing of production, uninterrupted disturbance of all *aesthetic* conditions, everlasting uncertainty and agitation distinguish the *avant-garde* from all *other art*. All fixed, fast-frozen relations, with their train of ancient and venerable prejudices and opinions are swept away, all new-formed ones become antiquated before they can ossify.[60]

Permanently dissatisfied with the status quo, the political wing of the avant-garde, aligned with so-called progressive ideologies and social movements, produces art in service of a political agenda rather than for profit. In this sense, "Avant-gardism often offers no other guarantee of its conviction than its indifference to money."[61]

While indifference to money is a pose adopted almost uniformly by the avant-garde, the art for art's sake movement within the avant-garde distinguishes itself by renouncing all other agendas – political, philosophical, sociological – save for the artwork itself. Like "avant-garde," art for art's sake can be understood historically as *l'art pour l'art* – a French literary movement of the late nineteenth century – or as an idea common to several generations of artists, including composers, beginning in the late eighteenth and continuing into the twentieth century.

From about 1840, Richard Wagner's newly defined artistic persona takes up its rhetorical position at the murky nexus of ideas permeating the avant-garde and "art for art's sake" movements – nationalized – where disavowal of the market and money become markers for both Germanness and a broad rejection of industrial modernity. Given Wagner's investment in the Germanization of his position, it is paradoxical that French artists of the historical *l'art pour l'art* were among the most significant Wagner enthusiasts, or *Wagnériens*. And yet the degree to which they overlooked Wagner's

---

[59] Revie, "Apollinaire and Cubist Innovation," 93.
[60] Karl Marx and Friedrich Engels, *The Communist Manifesto* (London: Penguin, 1980), 83.
[61] Cited in Bourdieu, *Rules of Art*, 162.

nationalist appropriation of what was a Europe-wide movement bespeaks his own ability to fashion distinct images for particular audiences.

Marketing martyrdom

Is it just coincidence that one of the areas in Paris known for its colony of starving artists was Montmartre, literally "martyr's hill"? Self-sacrifice, denial of earthly rewards (money) in the name of spiritual fulfillment or intangible future recognition, is a rhetorical position of the avant-garde structurally equivalent to the Christian topos of martyrdom. Not just a rhetorical position, however, it is also a marketing pose with a distinct economic philosophy.

Bourdieu refers to this as an "upside-down" economy, one which claims victory in defeat, a gesture which mimics the Christian conviction that the "poor shall inherit the earth," a corollary to the notion of *Kunstreligion* (religion of art) that music in particular appropriated at the beginning of the nineteenth century. The anti-market pose plays a "game of 'loser takes all,'"[62] shunning worldly success in order to gain canonical immortality – modernity's version of salvation. The bohemian lifestyle where "immediate success [is] the mark of intellectual inferiority" comes with a set of assumptions taken directly from Christian dogma, like: "the artist cannot triumph on the symbolic terrain except by losing on the economic terrain," "temporal failure a sign of election," "success a sign of compromise."[63] Just as "good" Christians shun money, so too the real artist performs disinterestedness. Like martyrs and saints, the genuine artist must be poor, a "Christ-like" figure "sacrificed in this world and consecrated in the one beyond."[64] "Great" artists, the new priesthood, can never profit from this "symbolic capital"[65] – like the saints they emulate – renouncing short-term gain to have a chance at "canonization." Ironically, the impoverished intellectual class which today questions the validity of a canon has historically had the greatest "interest" in creating and maintaining it. "Canonization" yields long-term economic benefits denied the creator, but from which the intellectual class draws dividends through teaching, scholarship, publication, and performance. Bourdieu shows diagrammatically how sales over time of "canonical" works outperform the

---

[62] *Ibid.*, 21.
[63] *Ibid.*, 83 and 217.
[64] *Ibid.*, 83.
[65] *Ibid.*, 148.

short-term success of popular artists.[66] Like the world it represents, art is no less divided into secular (popular) and sacred (canonical).

The institutionalization of the avant-garde mimics that of the culture industry it demonizes; *l'art pour l'art* is an "enterprise" of artistic creation with its own market, a fact "always overlooked."[67] An anomalous market, "foreign to the ordinary logic of the ordinary economy," the work of art has no commercial value (Flaubert), cannot be paid for, thus "has no market."[68] Art for art's sake entails a double-bind: the absence of marketability becomes a marketing angle; the anti-market pose a central selling point. There is no escape from the market.

Wagner's market position borrows heavily from "art for art's sake" rhetoric, but is no less informed by the tactics of more popular, commercial artists such as his eventual nemesis Meyerbeer, whom he shunned yet emulated. No doubt, Paris was the turning point when "the great Wagner of history took his first steps," as most Wagner biographers agree.[69] But such comments refer exclusively to Wagner's aesthetic turn away from French Grand Opera and towards what he would claim as his own distinct and individual style. Biographers usually overlook the equally significant turn in his occasional prose writings about musical life in Paris, music in general, as well as the remarkable set of short stories and novellas he penned. In these works, Wagner adopts the "starving artist who suffers for his art" pose, instrumentalizing his failure by capitalizing on it. In these often ignored or at best superficially treated works, Wagner takes advantage of the access he was given to the media to reach a wider audience at the time than he could through his music. When read attentively, they turn out to be rich in evocative and provocative imagery. Most of these writings, critical of the Parisian music world, serve simultaneously as the foundation for his subsequent and highly elaborate justification for his own aesthetic project. Leaving the theory aside for a moment, the tactic of disparaging the competition in order to promote one's own product is a classic advertising strategy.

Journalism, the market, and anti-Semitism

Print media, primarily journalism, provided the means and the forum in the struggle to win public attention. Despite their stated rejection of the

---

[66] *Ibid.*, 144.
[67] *Ibid.*, 58.
[68] *Ibid.*, 81.
[69] Gutman, *Wagner*, 70.

market, artists of the avant-garde made as much use of the media as their more overtly commercial rivals because, as they also realized, "to talk about art becomes equivalent to making it."[70] "The work's value is defined above all by its power to generate discourse about it … The real value is circulation itself."[71] From the eighteenth century on, newspapers and periodicals not only led the "structural transformation of the public sphere," they also established "imagined communities" of people no longer connected by physical location but rather by ideas and information.[72] No longer a mere means, control of the media became an end in itself already in the nineteenth century, a lesson Wagner seems to have understood intuitively. Where Franz Liszt often tried to influence what was written about him, Wagner went a step further by writing it himself, whenever possible.[73]

In this respect, Maurice (orig. Moritz) Schlesinger (1798–1871), the Paris publisher of German-Jewish descent, becomes the key figure for Wagner during his stay in the French capital. Schlesinger was best known as publisher of *La Revue et Gazette musicale de Paris* which, in 1835, combined two existing publications: the *Revue musicale* (1827–35) published by François-Joseph Fétis, and Schlesinger's own *Gazette musicale de Paris* (1834–5). Fétis sold his longer-running journal to the more speculative, business-minded Schlesinger. As music publisher and editor of "the most important and influential music journal in France until its closure in 1880," Schlesinger became a central figure, immortalized in Flaubert's novel *Sentimental Education* (1869).[74] Set in Paris of 1840, Schlesinger appears thinly disguised in the fictional figure of Jacques Arnoux, proprietor of *L'Art industriel*, "a hybrid establishment, comprising both an art magazine and a picture shop."[75] Flaubert captures the contradiction of the "arts entrepreneur" when Arnoux begins to dabble in the pottery business and declares to the novel's hero: "You know how devoted I am to the cause of beauty! I must take you to see my factory one of these days."[76] Flaubert's amorous feelings

---

[70] Marjorie Perloff, *The Futurist Moment: Avant-Garde, Avant Guerre, and the Language of Rupture* (University of Chicago Press, 1986), 90.

[71] Paul Mann, *Theory-Death of the Avant-Garde* (Bloomington: Indiana Universiy Press, 1991), 23.

[72] Benedict Anderson, *Imagined Communities: Reflections on the Origin and Spread of Nationalism*, rev. edn (London: Verso, 1991).

[73] See "Ludwig Rellstab's Biographical Sketch of Liszt," intro. and trans. Allan Keiler, in *Franz Liszt and His World*, ed. Gibbs and Gooley, 336.

[74] Katharine Ellis, *Music Criticism in Nineteenth-Century France:* La Revue et Gazette musicale de Paris, *1834–80* (Cambridge University Press, 1995), 1 and 33.

[75] Gustave Flaubert, *Sentimental Education*, trans. and intro. by Robert Baldick (London: Penguin, 1964), 17.

[76] *Ibid.*, 116.

toward Schlesinger's wife, Elisa, only made personal what constituted the classic confrontation between art and money or, more properly, between the reality of one age and the idealized memory of another. The new "feudalism of money" now appeared "far worse than the old feudalism,"[77] a "naïve nostalgia" Flaubert documents, which idealizes the "aristocratic patronage in the manner of the eighteenth century."[78] No small irony, given the immense struggle waged by artists to liberate themselves from that particular yoke, yet a yearning from which even the revolutionary Wagner suffered.

While Flaubert chiefly describes the new art world as a socio-historical phenomenon with economic consequences, the historical Schlesinger's "chronic unwillingness to pay contributors for their work" seemed to confirm long-standing prejudices about Jews and money.[79] Composer and pianist Frédéric Chopin referred to him on several occasions in his 1839 correspondence as "le Juif" (the Jew) making further anti-Semitic comments about Schlesinger's business practices and the "Jewish habit" of putting "profits before artistry."[80] Is it possible that the avant-garde's adoption of Christian rhetoric in its resistance to the modern marketplace, and the assumed pose of martyrdom in its self-denial of financial reward, was simultaneously informed by a fundamental and deep-seated anti-Semitism, albeit unspoken in most cases?

With Richard Wagner, nothing remained unspoken. Anti-Semitism became essential to his public image. During the Paris years, his anti-Semitism – not yet as virulent – combines with anti-French and anti-English rhetoric to reject the modern market, to express distaste for international cosmopolitanism, and to provide the foil for his dichotomy of German "self" and non-German "other." Wagner's antipathy for the "Parisian intrigue and con racket" extended to the music industry, "prostituted" to the dictates of (Jewish) money: an accusation echoed in Chopin's comment about Schlesinger.[81] Financial backing is essential to success in the new music industry: "Only as a banker can one become an influential composer of Grand Opera, like Meyerbeer, because a banker can do everything in

---

[77] *Ibid.*, 143.
[78] Bourdieu, *Rules of Art*, 66.
[79] Ellis, *Music Criticism*, 54.
[80] Diana R. Hallman, *Opera, Liberalism, and Antisemitism in Nineteenth-Century France: The Politics of Halévy's* La Juive (Cambridge University Press, 2002), 272.
[81] "*Pariser Intrigen- und Schwindelsystem*" ("Pariser Fatalitäten," *SSD* XII: 57). See also Dieter Borchmeyer, *Richard Wagner: Ahasvers Wandlungen* (Frankfurt am Main: Insel, 2002), "Wie Paris so verkörpert auch das Judentum für Wagner den Geist der Moderne" (377). "[B]anquier-musikhurerei," Letter to Ferdinand Heine, September 14, 1850 (*SB* III: 408).

Paris, even compose and perform operas."[82] Success is for sale; sufficient capital guarantees access to the media and oils the publicity machine. From Wagner's perspective, Jews were at the hub of this nexus. If he could not become a part of it, he wanted to condemn it and separate himself entirely.

Schlesinger and Meyerbeer, both German-Jews, both inordinately successful in Paris, both of whom helped Wagner, both become "morally unfit" to be considered German precisely because of their financial success. Like Rothschild in banking, each of them becomes "more international Jew than German."[83] Meyerbeer and Schlesinger are cosmopolitans like "German bankers" who "don't count as Germans anymore; they transcend nationality; they belong to the world and the Paris stock exchange."[84] Wagner's anti-Semitism is evident well before his public campaign began with the anonymous publication of "Jewishness in Music" (1850).

The Schlesinger episode also exposes the anti-Semitism that pervades Wagner studies, illustrating again both Wagner's control of the discourse, and the often unreflected work of his biographers. Initially, Schlesinger did employ Wagner to copy parts and make piano arrangements of operas by other currently popular composers, like Halévy and Donizetti. Admittedly exploitative, poorly paid, exhausting work, and maybe a waste of time for someone with Wagner's abilities, biographers have rarely missed the opportunity to describe how degrading such work was, thus reproducing Wagner's own correspondence and autobiographical spin on his plight at the hands of mercantile Jews.[85] Such commentaries often exceed even Wagner's own inflammatory account in *My Life*, where he describes the relationship with Schlesinger as a "monstrous acquaintance," twice specifically mentioning his Jewishness, first in an encounter most likely from 1841, followed by Wagner's report of a brief Paris visit in June 1849 when he met Schlesinger's "even more Jewish" successor.[86]

Wagner lifelong reiterated the claim that he was the misunderstood, slandered victim of a Jewish-controlled press, fueling an antagonistic relationship with its roots in Paris. But to portray Wagner as a victim is at best only half the story. He also used the press masterfully, exploiting it for his purposes and to his advantage. By his own admission this, too, began in Paris.

---

[82] *SSD* XII: 58.
[83] "mehr Universaljude, als Deutscher" (*SB* III: 59).
[84] "Die *deutschen Bankiers* … gelten nicht mehr als Deutsche; sie sind über alle Nationalität … sie gehören dem Universum und der Pariser Börse an" (*SB* III: 58–9).
[85] See, for example, Bryan Magee, *The Tristan Chord: Wagner and Philosophy* (New York: Henry Holt, 2001), 344–6.
[86] "monströsen Bekanntschaft" (*ML* 184); See also *ML* 219, and "ein noch bei weitem dezidierterer Jude, Herr Brandus, mit schmutzigster Persönlichkeit als Nachfolger eingetreten war" (*ML* 431).

The Wagner persona drafted

Hector Berlioz once wrote: "my life is a novel which greatly interests me."[87] In the case of Wagner, a more apt version would be: "My life is a drama I wrote." Nietzsche accused Wagner of being nothing more than an actor, an intuition which lives on in statements like: "No doubt, Wagner was always playing the role of his life."[88]

But why the note of disapproval in all such comments? Public figures have a persona which is not identical with their private selves and which, nowadays, is an image carefully crafted by a PR firm, calculated to sell products or win public approval. Is there not a double standard when we accept the subterfuge in the case of pop stars, but not in the case of so-called "serious" artists or politicians? As if the implied dishonesty of the media image is acceptable in one instance but not in the other. We want our politicians to be honest, and we want "serious" art to be genuine. This is Nietzsche's point, when he laments that: "great success, success with the masses no longer sides with those who are genuine – one must be an actor to achieve that."[89] But isn't Nietzsche's "no longer" a sentimentalization of a past which never existed? It is merely the appearance of honesty and genuineness that remains crucial, today as before. Wagner made genuineness – a trait already integral to his definition of Germanness – central to his public persona, an image and a role which he designed and then acted out using all the media then available.

To this end, Wagner seized opportunities which Paris – as opposed to his earlier haunts of Magdeburg or Riga – provided him. In addition to the menial work as copyist and arranger, Schlesinger commissioned Wagner to write articles for the *Gazette musicale*, a task Wagner confesses he completed "with expedient latitude."[90]

His essays, generally commentaries on the music scene, include works of fiction the most striking of which is a novella titled "A Pilgrimage to Beethoven."[91] Relatively unoriginal in its conception, Wagner's work is nevertheless fascinating because of the way he appropriates pre-existing

---

[87] Letter to Humbert Ferrand, June 12, 1833, Hector Berlioz, *A Selection from his Letters*, selected and trans. Humphrey Searle (New York: Vienna House, 1973), 53.
[88] Claudius Reinke, "'Die Kunst des Übergangs.' Richard Wagners Selbstinszenierungen zwischen Ästhetik und Politik," *Zukunftsbilder: Richard Wagners Revolution und ihre Folgen in Kunst und Politik*, ed. Hermann Danuser and Herfried Münkler (Schliengen: Argus, 2002), 74–88, here 83.
[89] Nietzsche, *Case of Wagner*, 179. I have slightly amended Kaufmann's translation.
[90] *ML* 197.
[91] Richard Wagner, "Eine Pilgerfahrt zu Beethoven" (*SSD* I: 90–114).

forms, conventions, and topoi to serve as a uniquely self-serving vessel. "Pilgrimage" belongs to a subgenre called "Musiknovelle" (music novella), a recent innovation starting with an experimental work by Wilhelm Heinrich Wackenroder c.1797 and reaching its zenith with E. T. A. Hoffmann's short stories two decades later. Wagner's immediate model may have been a "conte fantastique" titled "Le Dîner de Beethoven" by Jules Janin which appeared in the first issue of the *Gazette musicale*. By 1840, several accounts of visits to Beethoven, factual, embellished, or fictitious had been published.[92] The standard *Musiknovelle* rehearses several familiar tropes: music as a religious experience, music as "earthly manifestation of the Absolute," the starving artist who lives for his art, who resists the commercial world of philistine consumers, the dichotomy of easy "enjoyable" popular thus superficial music versus the deep, complex, and esoteric – a dichotomy which suggests always that the artist who writes or performs "difficult" music necessarily suffers financial ruin.[93] This literary-musical discourse develops concepts from the earlier "Cult of Genius" (*Geniekult*) of the *Sturm und Drang*, itself influenced by Shaftesbury's elevation of the author to "second *Maker*, a just Prometheus under Jove" (1711).[94] E. T. A. Hoffmann synthesized these discourses, writing both works of fiction about music, musicians and composers, as well as inaugurating a literary style of music criticism, centered around the person and work of the then living composer Ludwig van Beethoven (1770–1827).

Wagner's novella participates in the emergent "cult of Beethoven" reflected in numerous published "pilgrimages," but also differs from all its predecessors and models. To borrow a phrase from Hollywood, it is a public relations vehicle, produced, directed and starring Richard Wagner, with a special guest appearance by Ludwig van Beethoven. Wagner quite brilliantly adopts the ongoing Beethoven discourse and insinuates his persona into it.

[92] Jules Janin, "Le Dîner de Beethoven – *conte fantastique*," *Gazette musicale* 1.1–2 (Jan. 1834), 5–12, cited in Ellis, *Music Criticism*, 262. For detailed discussion of Janin, see Matthias Brzoska, *Die Idee des Gesamtkunstwerks in der Musiknovellistik der Julimonarchie* (Laaber: Laaber, 1995), 70ff. See also K. M. Knittel, "Pilgrimages to Beethoven: Reminiscences by his Contemporaries," *Music & Letters* 84.1 (2003), 19–54.
[93] For an overview, see Karl Prümm, "Berglinger und seine Schüler: Musiknovellen von Wackenroder bis Richard Wagner," *Zeitschrift für deutsche Philologie* 105.2 (1986), 186–212. After Wagner, the genre continues with Grillparzer's *Armer Spielmann* (1848), Mörike's *Mozart auf der Reise nach Prag* (1855), reaching its diabolical apotheosis with Thomas Mann's full-scale novel *Doktor Faustus* (1947). See also Bonds, *Music as Thought*, 26–7.
[94] Anthony Earl of Shaftesbury, "*Soliloquy* or Advice to an Author," *Characteristics of Men, Manners, Opinions, Times, etc*, ed. with intro. by John Robertson (Gloucester, MA: Peter Smith, 1963), I: 136.

Nevertheless, there is no end to the discussion of Wagner's borrowings and thus implied lack of originality. Peter Bloom surmises that the subtitle of the French translation: "Épisode de la vie d'un musicien allemand" alludes to Hector Berlioz's first symphony titled "Épisode de la vie d'un artiste." K. M. Knittel shows how most of the published "pilgrimages" to Beethoven are structurally and motivically similar. Matthias Brzoska argues that Ludwig Rellstab's "Tableau des Souvenirs de ma vie" provided the model for the novella.[95] Then, there is also Beethoven's own story. Deified during his lifetime, Beethoven was blessed early on by Count Waldstein who combined the "invented tradition" (Hobsbawm) of great composers with a form of "anticipatory canonization" (my term) by writing that the young composer would "receive Mozart's spirit from Haydn's hands."[96] This pantheon of the great (German) composers was again confirmed in the funeral oration written for Beethoven by the Austrian poet Franz Grillparzer, who described the deceased composer as "heir to the eternal fame of Handel and Bach, Haydn and Mozart."[97] For Grillparzer, Beethoven represents the end of an epoch, the last in a divine succession of composers. But such declarations of endings, common in early nineteenth-century German culture where Hegel theorized the "end of History"[98] and Heine predicted the "end of art" (*Ende der Kunstperiode*)[99] were often simply a way to assert new

---

[95] See Peter Bloom, "Berlioz and Wagner: Épisodes de la vie des artistes," *The Cambridge Companion to Berlioz* (Cambridge University Press, 2000), 235–50; also Knittel, "Pilgrimages to Beethoven"; and Brzoska, *Idee des Gesamtkunstwerks*, 173. Brzoska also prefers citing the French translation "for reasons of accuaracy." William Ashton Ellis has compared all three versions: the French translation (*Gazette musicale*), the German original (*Abend-Zeitung*) and the final version (*Gesammelte Schriften und Dichtungen*). According to him, the German versions agree entirely "saving for two or three minute emendations of style and the omission of a tiny clause." All variances between the French and German versions are noted in Ellis's English translation. None of them affect the substance of my analysis. See "A Pilgrimage to Beethoven," *Richard Wagner's Prose Works*, trans. William Ashton Ellis (London: Kegan Paul, 1898), VII: 21–45, here 21.

[96] Tia De Nora, *Beethoven and the Construction of Genius: Musical Politics in Vienna, 1792–1803* (Berkeley: University of California Press, 1995), 83–4. See also Eric Hobsbawm and Terence Ranger, eds., *The Invention of Tradition* (Cambridge University Press, 1983).

[97] "Grillparzer's Grabrede 29. März 1827," *Ludwig van Beethoven: In Briefen und Lebensdokumenten*, selected by A. Würz and R. Schimkat (Stuttgart: Reclam, 1961), 212–14, here 212. The canonized succession of Handel, Haydn, Mozart, etc. had already begun by 1799, see Weber, "Wagner, Wagnerism," 39.

[98] "Europa ist schlechthin das Ende der Weltgeschichte," Georg Wilhelm Friedrich Hegel, *Vorlesungen über die Philosophie der Geschichte, Sämtliche Werke in 20 Bdn*, ed. Hermann Glockner (Stuttgart: Frommann, 1961), XI: 150.

[99] Heine formulated the concept first in his 1828 review of Wolfgang Menzel's *Die deutsche Literatur* where he talks of the end of the Goethean "Kunstidee," see "Die deutsche Literatur von Wolfgang Menzel," *DHA* X: 239 and 247 and notes X: 620–4. The term "Ende der

beginnings, a device characteristic of the avant-garde movements already discussed.

Several nineteenth-century composers proclaimed themselves or were deemed to be Beethoven's successor, a proposition which simply reproduced Beethoven's own appointment as heir to Haydn and Mozart.[100] Amongst Wagner's generation, Liszt allegedly received a "public embrace" – the so-called "Weihekuss" – from Beethoven following one of his concerts. Even the term itself – *Weihekuss* (consecrating kiss) – again conveys the sacred dimension music had acquired. The truth of what happened is still in doubt. Beethoven apparently never attended the concert. Instead, the eleven-year-old Liszt had visited Beethoven in his home where he received the blessing in question.[101] Alan Walker gives credence to this version, while Allan Keiler has argued that no *Weihekuss* ever took place. Nevertheless, Liszt did nothing to deny the story whose foundations were already laid in Joseph d'Ortigue's 1835 Liszt biography and amplified in Ludwig Rellstab's version of 1842.[102] And this is the point. Whether true or not, the legend circulated and, in Liszt's mind, "set the seal on his career."[103] Keiler explains Liszt's interest in the legend psychologically as representing the kind of fatherly approval denied him in reality.[104] He might well have a point, but from a marketing and promotional perspective, the benediction from Beethoven would have been an endorsement of the kind that, as they say, money cannot buy.

There was no *Weihekuss* for Wagner: neither from Beethoven, who died when Wagner was thirteen, nor from Carl Maria von Weber, who was acquainted with the Wagner family in Dresden. Nor was there anyone in Wagner's life who would have spread such a story. So Wagner fabricated one. In the novella, "A Pilgrimage to Beethoven," "R …" (hereinafter *R*),

---

Kunstperiode" appears subsequently in *Französische Maler* (1831), *DHA* XII: 47, and *Die romantische Schule* (1835), *DHA* VIII: 125.

[100] See also Nicholas Vazsonyi, "Beethoven Instrumentalized: Richard Wagner's Self-Marketing & Media Image," *Music & Letters* 89.2 (2008), 195–211.

[101] For a complete account, see Walker, *Franz Liszt*, I: 80–5. More recently, Alan Walker devotes the first chapter of his *Reflections on Liszt* (Ithaca: Cornell University Press, 2005) to "Beethoven's *Weihekuss* Revisited" (1–10). For a rebuttal, see Allan Keiler, "Liszt Research and Walker's *Liszt*," *Musical Quarterly* 70.3 (1984), 374–404, esp. 380–96, and "Liszt and Beethoven: The Creation of a Personal Myth," *19th-Century Music* 12.2 (1988), 116–31.

[102] Joseph d'Ortigue, "Franz Liszt: Étude biographique," *Revue et gazette musicale* (June 14, 1835). See "The First Biography: Joseph d'Ortigue on Franz Liszt at Age Twenty-Three," intro. and ed. Benjamin Walton, trans. Vincent Giroud: 303–34, and "Ludwig Rellstab's Biographical Sketch of Liszt," intro. and trans. Allan Keiler, 335–60, both in *Franz Liszt and His World*, ed. Gibbs and Gooley.

[103] Walker, *Franz Liszt*, I: 85.

[104] Keiler, "Liszt and Beethoven," 130–1.

a fictionalized Wagner-figure, meets an imagined Beethoven. Even better than Liszt's meeting with Beethoven, Wagner scripted his version, loaded it with powerfully suggestive referents and adapted the existing Beethoven discourse for his own purposes. Speculation about Wagner's model for *R* has included Johann Friedrich *R*eichardt and the same Ludwig *R*ellstab, who was to write the Liszt biography of 1842.[105] But, irrespective of his sources, to read *R* as *R*ichard Wagner makes the most sense, not least because *R*, like Wagner, was born in a "medium-sized city in the heart of Germany" with first letter "L" (Leipzig).[106] Klaus Kropfinger has noted that "with his Beethoven novella, Wagner took the first step towards consciously fashioning his own myth, his self-image."[107] Sadly Kropfinger does not pursue this. However, his remark comes the closest so far in addressing the issue of self-marketing which is, I submit, the work's primary function. Wagner's novella demands thorough and attentive reading because its portrayal of a fictitious meeting with Beethoven presents a multi-layered *Weihekuss* which formalizes Wagner's persona and sets the public relations agenda for the remainder of his career.[108]

The publication history of the novella reveals how Wagner was increasingly aware of and instrumentalized its potential for self-promotion. First appearing in French translation under the blander title "Une visite à Beethoven, épisode de la vie d'un musicien allemand" (1840), it consists solely of a first-person account by a German musician living in Paris named *R*. Its apparent success prompted Schlesinger to offer another commission. The second novella, titled "Un musicien étranger à Paris," again features *R*, but is narrated by yet another unnamed German musician living in Paris, who has befriended *R*. The story recounts *R*'s final days and includes an emotional deathbed scene at which the Narrator is present. Although the title "Un musicien étranger à Paris" refers to *R*, the presence of the Narrator

---

[105] For the Reichardt thesis, see Martin Gregor-Dellin, *Richard Wagner: Sein Leben – Sein Werk – Sein Jahrhundert* (Munich: Piper, 1980), 153. For the Rellstab thesis, see Brzoska, *Idee des Gesamtkunstwerks*, 174–6.

[106] *SSD* I: 91 and 107.

[107] Karl Kropfinger, *Wagner and Beethoven: Richard Wagner's Reception of Beethoven*, trans. P. Palmer (Cambridge University Press, 1991), 15. See also William Meredith, "Wagner's Beethoven: A Posthumous *Pilgrimage to Beethoven* in 1840," *The Beethoven Newsletter* 8.2 (1993), 46–53. Meredith suggests that writing the essay gave "Wagner the opportunity to fulfill – at least in his imagination – a long-held dream" to meet Beethoven. This is based on a remark he made to Cosima; see also Cosima's diary entry for May 26, 1871 (not August 27, 1872, as per Meredith's note 24) (*ibid.*, 48).

[108] K. M. Knittel suggests that Wagner's novella presents "a *Weihekuss* of sorts," but her interest is in what the novella as a piece of "historical evidence … tells us about Beethoven's posthumous status as an icon" instead of its value for Wagner as a means to self-promotion (Knittel, "Pilgrimages," 21, also 35–8).

means that there are now two German musicians in Paris. Even though it is not wise to identify fictional characters too closely with their authors, aspects of Wagner are present in both. This was neither the only time Wagner would present an aestheticized version of himself, nor the only time he would divide himself between two characters: the most notable example being the pairing of the elderly and experienced Hans Sachs with the youthful and naturally gifted Walther von Stolzing in *Die Meistersinger von Nürnberg*, to be examined more closely in Chapter 4.

In 1841, a few months after the French publication, the German original of both novellas appeared together in the *Abend-Zeitung* (Dresden), under the collected title: "Zwei Epochen aus dem Leben eines deutschen Musikers" (Two Episodes from the Life of a German Musician). The first piece, with the religiously more loaded title "Eine Pilgerfahrt zu Beethoven," was augmented with an introductory note by the fictitious Narrator, who presents the "Pilgrimage" as one of the writings found amongst the papers of the recently deceased *R*.

"These works helped me considerably to become known and noticed in Paris," Wagner admits shortly thereafter in his "Autobiographical Sketch" (1842), clearly aware of their PR value.[109] Three decades later, Wagner included both novellas in volume I of his *Gesammelte Schriften* and combined them with five additional essays most of which had been printed separately in French in the *Gazette musicale* between 1840 and 1841. Now presented as "posthumous works by *R*," assembled and published by his friend, the Narrator, they appeared in the *Gesammelte Schriften* collectively as *Ein deutscher Musiker in Paris: Novellen und Aufsätze*. The transfer of authorship from Wagner to the fictitious *R* begs the question of the multiple identities of *R*, Narrator, and Wagner, as well as the relationship between these three and the unifying theme of the essays: the person and works of Ludwig van Beethoven.

Beethoven's "kiss"

R is not just any musician. Like Beethoven, he is "also a poor German musician."[110] Each of these words requires scrutiny. "Also" signals the protagonist's identification with Beethoven in apparent contradiction to the

---

[109] "Diese Arbeiten haben mir nicht wenig geholfen, in Paris bekannt und beachtet zu werden" (*SSD* I: 17).

[110] "auch ein armer, deutscher Musiker" (*SSD* I: 92).

religious awe suggested by the title "Pilgrimage," and confirmed on a number of occasions throughout the novella. By making himself Beethoven's equal, the protagonist grants himself the possibility of joining the hallowed. "Poor" is crucial, indicating honesty and genuineness – composing music for its own sake and not for profit – and because it is coterminous with "German." Wagner, *R*, and Beethoven, "poor German musicians" all.

In order to raise the necessary funds to make his pilgrimage possible, *R* must prostitute himself and his ideals by composing hits for the new music industry: "I shuddered, but my longing to see Beethoven won out; I composed galopps and potpourris, but during this time, out of shame, I could never bring myself to look over at Beethoven [his bust], because I was afraid to desecrate [*entweihen*] it."[111] Later, Beethoven even refers to such music as "commodities" (*Ware*).[112] Once on the road, *R* happens on a group of traveling musicians gathered under a tree playing Beethoven's Septet Op. 20. An Englishman passing by throws them a gold coin, which none of them takes. The English, the wealthiest and – according to Wagner's logic – the least musical, are the antithesis of Germans.[113] The amateur musician from what Adam Smith and later Napoleon called the "nation of shopkeepers" tries to buy his way into the arts. Reminiscent of E. T. A. Hoffmann's works, the Englishman is the demon who haunts the plot of the novella and its protagonist. That evening, he turns up at the inn where *R* is staying and, again throwing him money, asks him to play some more. "That annoyed me," reports *R*, "I explained that I didn't play for money."[114]

R eventually reaches Beethoven, but must overcome enormous hurdles first, not least getting rid of the Englishman who, using his unlimited financial resources, insinuates himself into the meeting, leaving only after he deposits the score of one of his compositions with Beethoven for critical review. Finally alone, *R* begins talking about *Fidelio* which he had seen performed the evening before. Beethoven quickly concedes: "I am no opera composer" but adds:

At least I know of no theater in the world for which I would gladly write another opera! If I were to compose an opera according to my wishes, everyone would flee, because there would be no arias, duets, terzetts and all the stuff they use nowadays

---

[111] *Ibid.*
[112] *Ibid.*, 112.
[113] For Marc Weiner, the novella is "redolent with Francophobic and anti-Semitic sentiment," but Wagner made the nemesis figure an Englishman because the novella was initially published for a French readership. For Wagner, Weiner asserts, French, English and Jewish was all the same, but his French readers would not have known this, see his, *Richard Wagner and the Anti-Semitic Imagination* (Lincoln, NB: University of Nebraska Press, 1995), 156–7.
[114] "Das verdroß mich; ich erklärte, daß ich nicht für Geld spielte" (*SSD* I: 95).

to patch operas together. What I would do instead no singer would want to sing and no public would want to hear.[115]

Beethoven despairs at the practical impossibility of composing a real "music drama" (*musikalisches Drama*). *R* is eager to know more about this new term that Dieter Borchmeyer has shown does not originate with Wagner, but rather in a short story by E. T. A. Hoffmann.[116] True, Wagner appropriated ideas from a variety of sources. This is not where his originality lies. But there is a distinction between Hoffmann's and Wagner's use of "music drama." For Hoffmann, the story is the end in itself. For Wagner, the novella is a means to distance himself from the existing opera world by having Beethoven dream of the ideal "dramatic composer" (*dramatischer Komponist*) whose work would achieve the "union of all elements" (*Vereinigung aller Elemente*), a dream that would ultimately be fulfilled by Wagner the composer.[117]

Let me be clear. At the time he wrote the "Pilgrimage" novella, Wagner had not yet conceived of the *music drama* or the *Ring* project as it later developed. Nevertheless, even though he was still trying to get his "conventional" French Grand Opera *Rienzi* performed, Wagner's transformation had begun. Provoked by his failure to succeed in Paris, Wagner has Beethoven create the conditions which only he, Wagner, will be able to realize. Though the theory is not yet worked out in the kind of detail of his groundbreaking book-length essay *Opera and Drama* written a decade later, the essentials of Wagner's new direction are introduced here in a handful of sentences: the obsolescence of opera with its set pieces, the necessity to reconceptualize the genre and, with it, to conceive a new kind of theater and audience. Attracting and educating that audience will become a central concern of Wagner's project. In "A Pilgrimage to Beethoven," Wagner skillfully creates the shelf-space and potential demand for a new, as yet unavailable product, and even has none other than Beethoven endorse it.

This is only the first of the three-part *Weihekuss*. The second is the "sneak preview" *R* is granted of Beethoven's Ninth Symphony. Within the novella's timeframe, the Ninth Symphony is yet to be published or performed,

---

[115] "Ich bin kein Opernkomponist, wenigstens kenne ich kein Theater in der Welt, für das ich gern wieder eine Oper schreiben möchte! Wenn ich eine Oper machen wollte, die nach meinem Sinne wäre, würden die Leute davon laufen; denn da würde nichts von Arien, Duetten, Terzetten und all dem Zeuge zu finden sein, womit sie heut' zu Tage die Opern zusammenflicken, und was ich dafür machte, würde kein Sänger singen und kein Publikum hören wollen" (*SSD* I: 109).

[116] Dieter Borchmeyer, *Das Theater Richard Wagners. Idee – Dichtung – Wirkung* (Stuttgart: Reclam, 1982), 100.

[117] *SSD* I: 109 and 111.

so the protagonist is privy to information available only to the select and initiated (the German for "initiated" – ein*gewih*t – contains the same root as "*Weih*ekuss"). Beethoven concedes the ultimate poverty of "absolute music" (Wagner's later term), explaining the final movement of his Ninth Symphony as an attempt to transcend its limitations through language. Wagner's subsequent theoretical writings are in part founded on ideas first articulated here by "Beethoven" himself, a revelation of biblical proportions in which the master of instrumental music anticipates Wagner's "artwork of the future" by conceding that this is the only reasonable direction remaining for musical composition to take.[118] If opera, "liberated from its feudal bondage" had now become "suspect of capitulating to market forces," it was imperative for Wagner to rescue the genre by integrating it with the German symphonic tradition which had been discursively associated with self-sufficiency.[119]

In these first two parts of the *Weihekuss*, Wagner offers evidence that his own aesthetic project continues the trajectory inherent in Beethoven's development, as Beethoven himself understood it. Had Beethoven lived longer, so the argument goes, this is the direction he would have taken. Wagner becomes nothing less than the executor of Beethoven's musical will as well as the ultimate authority on Beethoven's last symphony. No longer a mere "interpreter," Wagner makes himself privy to Beethoven's "intentions," a self-appointed expertise, imagined in a work of fiction that he will subsequently claim in reality.

The third part of the *Weihekuss* confirms the first two by making *R* quite literally Beethoven's apostle. Taking the Englishman's score, Beethoven remarks: "Let's deal with that musical Englishman!"[120] He then examines the composition with evident disdain and, instead of marking each problematic area with a cross as the Englishman had requested, puts the entire work unmarked inside an envelope which he covers with a giant "X." Handing the envelope to *R*, he says: "'Return this masterpiece back to that lucky man! He's an ass, but I envy him for his long ears!'"[121] Now officially Beethoven's intermediary, *R* the "poor German musician" has received the priceless gift all the Englishman's money could not buy. Wagner's imaginary world is the

---

[118] For a more detailed account of the significance of the Ninth Symphony in Wagner's theoretically most sophisticated and extensively mounted argument for his aesthetic project, consult Thomas S. Grey, *Wagner's Musical Prose* (Cambridge University Press, 1995).
[119] Thomas S. Grey, "Commentary: Opera in the Age of Revolution," *Journal of Interdisciplinary History* 36.3 (2006), 555–67, here 566.
[120] *SSD* I: 113.
[121] *Ibid.*

inverse of the money-driven Parisian establishment; yet what kind of an apostle is *R*? I quote the following passage in full:

> I had to laugh out loud as I examined the cross on the envelope of the Englishman's composition. Nevertheless, this cross was a memento of Beethoven and I begrudged giving it to the evil spirit of my pilgrimage. In an instant, I made up my mind. I put my own galopps into the damning envelope. The Englishman's composition was returned without envelope, accompanied with a little note in which I reported that Beethoven envied him and didn't know where to put a cross.[122]

Though devoted to preserving the memory of his "master," *R* deliberately falsifies it. He grants himself knowledge of a greater good, and gives himself leave to alter the message. From a psychoanalytic perspective, this particular twist in the story raises interesting issues concerning Wagner's own awareness of the veracity of his claimed aesthetic pedigree.

In this respect, the "cross" (*Kreuz*) on the envelope is also significant: a memento of *R*'s meeting with Beethoven, thus a symbol of Beethoven, the composer who suffered for his music. By placing his own works inside the marked envelope, *R* crucifies himself for composing utilitarian works.[123] In the process, he dons the holy symbol both as penitent and as newly ordained priest.

Death and transfiguration

The self-identification between Wagner and *R* becomes more complex in the following novella, whose German title "Ein Ende in Paris" points directly to *R*'s death as opposed to the generic "Un musicien étranger à Paris," which refers both to *R* and to the Narrator. Like Wagner, *R* is the dreamer who comes to Paris hoping in vain for fame and success. Unlike Wagner, *R* dies, penniless, unrecognized, in a dingy Montmartre apartment, the address itself emblematic of his martyrdom.[124] Meanwhile, the Narrator, no less a German musician, appears more practical, having understood the realities of the Paris scene well enough to survive: like Wagner.

---

[122] *Ibid.*
[123] Music critic Joseph d'Ortigue (1802–66) also drew parallels between Beethoven and crucifixion, see Brzoska, *Idee des Gesamtkunstwerks*, 161–2.
[124] "Willkommen hieß ich den Berg der Martyre und beschloß auf ihm zu sterben. Auch ich starb ja für die Einfalt meines Glaubens, auch ich konnte mich daher einen Martyr nennen" (*SSD* I: 133).

Moments before his death, *R* receives a visit from the Narrator who performs the role of father confessor. *R*'s lengthy credo begins quite shockingly with the declaration: "I believe in God, Mozart and Beethoven, and also in their disciples and apostles; – I believe in the Holy Ghost and in the truth of one indivisible Art."[125] Echoing Grillparzer's funeral oration of Beethoven and E. T. A. Hoffmann's famous review of the Fifth Symphony, musical experience has a sacred power; the greatest composers – Germans, of course – are on a par with God. But Wagner remaps Grillparzer's divine succession, which had originally ended with Beethoven, and alters Hoffmann's "progressive triumvirate" of Haydn, Mozart and Beethoven, which functioned as a "closed system," with "no room for a fourth composer."[126] Instead, Wagner removes Haydn and opens up a future beyond Beethoven. Rather than being the end of the line, Mozart and Beethoven now become founders of a new church, the select, charged with receiving and spreading the Holy Spirit of Music. Like Christ clearing the money-lenders from the temple, *R* condemns those who commodify and thus prostitute music, who dare "to profit from lofty chaste art, which they would defile and dishonor."[127] *R* dies, a victim of the newly commercialized, market-driven middle-class musical culture, martyred for his faith in the new religion of the German Romantics: Music. Deeply moved, the Narrator beholds the transfigured expression on the face of his now deceased friend, and "prays to God for a similar death."

Read autobiographically, the novella suggests that Wagner the idealist died in Paris, leaving only the realist. But this is not autobiography. Wagner the idealist did not die in Paris; he was created there. Recall that Wagner came to Paris seeking fame and fortune, not as a believer in Mozart and Beethoven, instead wanting to satisfy French taste to secure his success. *R* – the literary creation – dies on the printed page but is resurrected as Wagner's public persona. This is the veneer behind which Wagner scripts and narrates the drama that became his public life, a persona designed to elicit sympathy, to achieve moral victory, to proclaim a cause.

In his autobiography, Wagner presents his novelistic work light-heartedly, as if to suggest that it was of little consequence, at most an opportunity to take "revenge" both against specific persons as well as against an entire

---

[125] *SSD* I: 135.
[126] Mark Evan Bonds, *After Beethoven: Imperatives of Originality in the Symphony* (Cambridge, MA: Harvard University Press, 1996), 22–3.
[127] "Wucher mit der hohen keuschen Kunst zu treiben, die sie schändeten und entehrten" (*SSD* I: 135).

establishment and system of practices which denied him even the opportunity at entry.[128] But these works are much more than an exposé of superficial Paris life or merely an exercise in short-term revenge. If we take Wagner's confession seriously, revenge is the motivation for his entire subsequent endeavor. As Katharine Ellis and Matthias Brzoska point out, of those who failed in Paris, Wagner "remains the only one who made a career by constructing his little Paris (petit Paris) outside of France but nevertheless peopled by the Parisian elite."[129] A true, yet misleading statement. Wagner's "little Paris," i.e. Bayreuth, was designed to stand for the opposite of Paris. Far from being a "little Paris," Bayreuth is its inverse.

The prodigal son returns[130]

With an economy of means uncharacteristic for the mature Wagner, the series of essays subsequently assembled under the title *A German Musician in Paris*, specifically the first two pieces in the collection – "A Pilgrimage" and "A Death in Paris" – serve as pre-publicity. They introduce Wagner's aesthetic agenda and establish his persona: the starving "German" musician, apostle of (Mozart and) Beethoven, a messiah chosen to be the salvation of art. Wagner's essays are different from the host of other Beethoven- and music-related novellas of the period, because his works of fiction serve to support his real life as a composer.

This link between imagined and real existence is established in Wagner's "Autobiographical Sketch" of 1842,[131] written and published at the invitation of Heinrich Laube, editor of the influential magazine *Zeitung für die elegante Welt*. Structurally congruous with the story of the prodigal son,

---

[128] "Mit einer Fortsetzung der Novelle unter dem Titel 'Das Ende eines Musikers in Paris,' französisch 'Un musicien étranger à Paris,' nahm ich Rache für alle mir widerfahrene Schmach" (*ML* 201) and, for its echo in biographies, see, for example, Curt von Westernhagen, *Wagner* (Zurich: Atlantis, 1968), 67.

[129] Katharine Ellis and Matthias Brzoska, "Avant-propos méthodologique," *Von Wagner zum Wagnérisme: Musik, Literatur, Kunst, Politik*, ed. A. Fauser and M. Schwartz (Leipzig: Leipziger Universitätsverlag, 1999), 35–7, here 36.

[130] Tom Grey also uses this biblical allusion to describe Wagner's return to Germany. However, he does not show how Wagner structurally appropriates the biblical narrative to frame his life. See Thomas S. Grey, "The Return of the Prodigal Son: Wagner and *Der fliegende Holländer*," *Richard Wagner: Der fliegende Holländer*, Cambridge Opera Handbooks (Cambridge University Press, 2000), 1–24, esp. 12 and 20–1.

[131] "Autobiographische Skizze," *Zeitung für die elegante Welt* 1.5 (1843), 114–19 and 1.6 (1843), 135–9. See also Joseph Kürschner, "Varianten und Ergänzungen zu Richard Wagners 'Autobiographischer Skizze,'" *Richard-Wagner-Jahrbuch*, ed. Joseph Kürschner (Stuttgart 1886), 286–2, which includes Laube's introductory remarks.

its clearly marked stations lead away from and back to a geographic and spiritual home, what Germans refer to untranslatably as "Heimat." Born in Leipzig, the young Wagner is drawn to works like Weber's *Der Freischütz* and Mozart's *Magic Flute*; Beethoven becomes the twenty-year-old's "leading role model" (*Hauptvorbild*).[132] As he begins his professional career, Wagner – attracted by the easy and pleasing music of the French and Italians – turns his back on Beethoven and Germany which "seemed to me only a very small part of the world."[133] His trip to Paris bodily enacts this intellectual journey: "With very little money, but the best of hopes, I now entered Paris."[134] The failure of the Paris venture is sealed with Wagner's aestheticized suicide:

> This period was the culmination of my extremely pitiful state: I wrote a little novella for the *Gazette musicale*: "The End of a German Musician in Paris," in which I had the unfortunate hero die after uttering the following credo: "I believe in God, Mozart and Beethoven."[135]

"I believe in God, Mozart and Beethoven" becomes a refrain seamlessly uniting his fiction and non-fiction, a connection reinforced by the threefold use of the colon, syntactically joining the real Richard Wagner with the image he fashions for himself, between life and the artwork.

Notice that, within the narrative structure of the "Autobiographical Sketch," it is not the original Wagner as Beethoven worshipper who dies, but Wagner the prodigal son who abandoned house and home and whose death-bed born-again avowal of Beethoven echoes the biblical realization: "Father, I have sinned, against God and against you."[136] The living Wagner now leaves Paris and returns to a Germany which can exclaim: "For this son of mine was dead and has come back to life; he was lost and is found."[137] The final sentence of the "Sketch," often quoted during Wagner's lifetime to confirm his visceral Germanness, encapsulates the union of culture, national identity, and art rehearsed in his previous essays. Wagner, acknowledged sinner, reborn as poor German musician, writes: "For the

---

[132] *SSD* I: 4–8.
[133] "Deutschland schien mir nur ein sehr kleiner Teil der Welt ... Ich gab mein Vorbild, Beethoven, auf" (*SSD* I: 10).
[134] *SSD* I: 14.
[135] "Diese Zeit war der Kulminationspunkt meiner äußerst traurigen Lage: ich schrieb für die *Gazette musicale* eine kleine Novelle: 'Das Ende eines deutschen Musikers in Paris,' worin ich den unglücklichen Helden derselben mit folgendem Glaubensbekenntnis sterben ließ: 'Ich glaube an Gott, Mozart und Beethoven'" (*SSD* I: 18).
[136] Luke 15:21.
[137] *Ibid.*, 15:24.

first time, I saw the Rhine – my eyes glistening with tears, I, poor artist, swore eternal loyalty to my German fatherland."[138] These words from the first, but not last, of his autobiographies launch Wagner's public persona.

Wagner's staged death and transfiguration is emotional and dramatic in part because he folds his life story into a narrative structure emblazoned into the cultural consciousness of the Western reader. No wonder Heinrich Laube changed his original plan that Wagner send "a sketch of his life … so that I could expand on it." Instead he published the "Sketch" as is, because he realized: "I would only ruin it if I attempted any changes."[139]

No one wrote better about Wagner than Wagner himself. Through sheer repetition, his version so dominates that it is ubiquitously repeated, beginning already with Heinrich Laube's introductory remarks to the "Sketch." Is it Laube talking, or rather Wagner the ventriloquist, when Laube complains that Paris is a city: "where everything is bought or has to be paid for, even the most worthwhile, if it is to succeed in the marketplace." Or when he describes Wagner as the financially poor but spiritually rich German musician: "well, it didn't work out, but also wasn't a failure; outwardly poorer, but inwardly richer, the wandering minstrel was back home in Saxony after a couple of years."[140] Even French accounts decades later perpetuate this image: "One must remember those first years of Richard Wagner's youth, spent in Paris in misery and neglect. Dying of hunger."[141]

One of Friedrich Nietzsche's last utterances about his friend, mentor, and demon, is that "Wagner is just a misunderstanding amongst the Germans."[142] This idea is cited often to de-emphasize his Germanness and thus deflate Hitler's appropriation of him.[143] While the motivation to "denazify" Wagner is legitimate, to efface the image of Germanness from Wagner itself constitutes a deep misunderstanding. During the years in Paris and his subsequent

---

[138] "Zum ersten Male sah ich den Rhein, – mit hellen Tränen im Auge schwur ich armer Künstler meinem deutschen Vaterlande ewige Treue" (*SSD* I: 19).

[139] Laube, in Kürschner, "Varianten und Ergänzungen," 288.

[140] "wo alles erkauft, wenigstens bezahlt werden muß, auch das Verdienstvollste, wenn es auf den Markt und // dadurch zu Geltung kommen will … Nun es gelang nicht, ist aber auch nicht mißlungen, und außen ärmer, innen reicher, war nach zwei Jahren der fahrende Musikus wieder in Sachsen" (Kürschner, "Varianten und Ergänzungen," 287–8).

[141] Mendès, *Richard Wagner*, ii.

[142] "Wagner unter Deutschen bloß ein Mißverständnis ist," Nietzsche, *Ecce Homo* (1889), §6 (in *Fall Wagner*, 242).

[143] For example Dieter David Scholz, *Ein deutsches Mißverständnis: Richard Wagner zwischen Barrikade und Walhalla* (Berlin: Parthas, 1997), 302. Most recently, Udo Bermbach, "'Reine Kunst, persönliche Lebensmacht, nationale Kulturmacht.' Wagner, seine Epigonen und die Instrumentalisierung einer großen Idee," in *Zukunftsbilder*, ed. Danuser and Münkler, 61–73. The fact that Bermbach misquotes Nietzsche does not strengthen his case.

return to Germany, Wagner embarked on becoming *the* German composer of the nineteenth century: clearly as much an act of conviction as it was a bold marketing strategy. Yet he remained critical of the German political landscape and of contemporary German culture, enduring years of self-imposed exile to elude a warrant for his arrest as an activist.

Given his suffering in Paris and the emblematic Germanness which resulted, it is no small irony that Paris is a constant reference point throughout Wagner's writings, and a city he repeatedly visited. For Nietzsche, Paris was where Wagner "belonged."[144] Paris was certainly the seminal experience. Even at the end of his life, Wagner would write of the "exciting and undeniable influences that came from the remarkable intellectual boom in France during the two decades either side of the year 1830," admitting that it was the "stimuli unified in that time and place" which were like "productive motors."[145] Set in motion by these "productive motors," Wagner traveled back to Germany where he soon became Hofkapellmeister at the Royal Court of Saxony in Dresden. The next chapter focuses on two media events orchestrated by Wagner during this period between 1842 and 1849, but beholden to ideas conceived and lessons learned in Paris. These two events, designed for broad public appeal, instrumentalize the image of the poor, honest, genuine German musician, now conveyed with an increasingly sophisticated knack for publicity.

---

[144] "daß Paris der eigentliche *Boden* für Wagner ist" (*Nietzsche contra Wagner*, in *Fall Wagner*, 139); and *Ecce Homo* §5: "wohin Wagner gehört … ist die französische Spät-Romantik" (*Fall Wagner*, 241).

[145] Richard Wagner, "Das Publikum in Zeit und Raum," *SSD* X: 101.

2 | Publicity

As if nothing had changed, Wagner still refers to himself in an 1845 letter to Franz Liszt as a "poor German opera composer."[1] In fact, everything had changed. The extraordinarily successful world premiere of *Rienzi* in Dresden on October 20, 1842, was followed shortly thereafter by Wagner's appointment in February 1843 to the Royal Court of Saxony as Hofkapellmeister, a well-paid post he now shared with Carl Gottlieb Reissiger, who had served alone in this capacity since 1828, succeeding Carl Maria von Weber. Reissiger, who conducted the sensational *Rienzi* premiere, would have been less than human had he not been at least annoyed having to share the limelight with this new, more flamboyant, younger colleague. Wagner sensed this and, in a letter to the Berlin music critic Karl Gaillard, noted that, while he had arrived in Dresden as "the unknown, impoverished musician," his success since had begun to cause him difficulties, including "envy" (*Neid*) from his peers and superiors.[2]

A remarkable letter Reissiger wrote in 1843 to Joseph Fischhoff in Vienna not only confirms Wagner's claims but, more significantly, documents the degree to which Wagner's careerist publicity-consciousness and media-manipulation tactics were clearly apparent to those in his orbit. The letter is worth quoting at length:

> There is constant adulation of Wagner here in the newspapers … As little as I care about such things, it is nevertheless difficult for me to suppress my rage over Wagnerian arrogance and his constant scribbling in all the papers. As you know, Wagner lived in Paris for quite a while before coming to Dresden, and he occupied himself there solely with musical reportages … He is even suspected of writing against himself and his oddities, only to answer and thus furnish the opportunity for even more adulation. – What a rumpus is being made of Wagner's operas in the papers! And except for the *Wiener Musikzeitung* [*Allgemeine Wiener Musik-Zeitung*] as yet no even-tempered impartial appraisal has been published.[3]

---

[1] Letter to Franz Liszt, October 5, 1845 (*SB* II: 448), "arme(r) deutsche(r) Operncomponist."
[2] Letter to Karl Gaillard, June 5, 1845 (*SB* II: 432), "der unbekannte, arme Musiker."
[3] Letter from Carl Gottlieb Reissiger to Joseph Fischhoff, November 11, 1843, in Ernst Rychnowski, "Reissiger über Wagner," *Der Merker* 1.9 "Wagner Heft" (Feb. 1910), 379–81 (*Richard Wagner Archiv*, Nr.: A 3016 I-3). "Hier liest man immerwährend in den Journalen

Reissiger's suspicions that, already in Paris, Wagner manipulated the press to engineer his own publicity contains an element of truth. But it is during the Dresden period that Wagner would go even further to generate publicity, to make a spectacle of himself and his causes, activities to which most biographies pay insufficient attention.

The Dresden years

Instead, Wagner biographies typically stress the same handful of motifs from the so-called Dresden years (1842–9), a phase of Wagner's life framed at the beginning by the successful *Rienzi* premiere, and at the end with the failed uprising of May 1849. While the musical success of *Rienzi* was ultimately overshadowed by the mature Wagner's more significant aesthetic achievements, the mix of sensation and scandal associated with his later participation in the political uprising and its consequences became essential and permanent features of Wagner lore; a founding myth of Wagner's life. The exact nature of Wagner's activities during the Dresden revolution remain blurred by an impenetrable assemblage of conflicting accounts running the gamut from Wagner's own protestations of innocence – themselves inconsistent – to more incriminating reports of friends, eyewitnesses, as well as the indictment of state authorities. Whatever his activities may have been, the outcome is undisputed. Wagner fled Dresden only moments before a warrant was issued for his arrest. He barely escaped imprisonment; some of his fellow revolutionaries received a death sentence, albeit subsequently commuted. The result for Wagner was more than a decade of self-imposed exile from Germany. Not unlike the episode in Paris, Wagner's suspenseful night-time escape from the authorities, forged papers, and illegal border crossings, lent him the heroic air of the political fugitive. His forced exile simply augmented the image of desperation, misery, and scandal which beset him. From 1849 on, there would be a grim conformity between Wagner the political and operatic outlaw.

> Lobhudelein über Wagner … So wenig ich mich um dergleichen kümmere, so unterdrücke ich doch manchmal meinen Ingrimm über die Wagnerischen Arroganzen und seine beständigen Schreibereien in alle Blätter mit Mühe. Du weißt, daß W. vor seiner Ankunft in Dresden lange Zeit in Paris lebte und sich dort lediglich mit musikal. Berichten beschäftigte … Man vermutet sogar, daß er oft gegen sich und seine Kuriositäten schreibt, um nur wieder zu antworten und Stoff zu weiteren Lobhudeleien über sich zu haben. – … Welcher Spektakel ist mit den Wagnerischen Opern in öffentlichen Blättern getrieben worden! und außer der Wiener Musikzeitung ist noch keine ruhige unparteiische Würdigung erschienen" (380).

Biographies also tend to dwell on Wagner's trip during the summer of 1845 to the Bohemian resort town of Marienbad. This one summer was perhaps Wagner's single most fertile time. In Marienbad, he began to conceive the thematic content for almost all his mature works – from *Lohengrin* to his last opera, *Parsifal*. The significance of this summer and his turn towards Germanic myth cannot be overestimated, a crucial stage in the development of the innovative theoretical work Wagner would write during his later exile in Switzerland. But the biographical focus on this idyllic summer away from the daily tedium of a civil service post serves another purpose dear to the Wagner mystique. Even though it brought the financial and thus existential security for which Wagner, and especially his wife Minna, had yearned during the years of hardship in Paris, the composer would characterize his Kapellmeister position with increasing exasperation. In keeping with the carefully honed image of the creative artist, it was important to convey the idea that quotidian routine and the pettiness of office politics were incompatible with Wagner's genius, a claim legitimized by the productive Marienbad summer away from the court. (The fact that his Dresden and earlier Riga experience running an operatic establishment would prove invaluable in the later Bayreuth venture – which required all of Wagner's bureaucratic and managerial skills – is never mentioned.) So the forced flight into exile – and the consequent loss of the Kapellmeister position – is presented as a liberation, freeing the post-Beethovenian composer genius from the demeaning bonds of eighteenth-century servitude and nineteenth-century philistine bureaucracy. The fact that Minna disapproved of Wagner's recklessness, and never forgave him for the loss of the post, only served to highlight Wagner's chronic claim that he was misunderstood – even by his unimaginative first wife – that his genius was insufficiently recognized.[4] This self-fulfilling prophecy – that he was too big for petty-minded bourgeois conventionality – eventually provided grounds not only for his separation from Minna and the scandalous erotic encounters that followed, but legitimized also his demand that he be funded by patrons, not to mention the aesthetic revolution he was trying to sell.

There is a certain degree of disingenuousness in Wagner's mounting disdain for his civil service job. Just as there had been advantages to be reaped from access to print media provided by the otherwise "humiliating" and exploitative association with Maurice Schlesinger in Paris, so too did

---

[4] See the exhaustive account of this episode and its consequences from both Minna's and Richard's perspective in Eva Rieger, *Minna und Richard Wagner: Stationen einer Liebe* (Düsseldorf and Zurich: Artemis & Winkler, 2003).

Wagner now exploit the public platform of the Dresden court position to maximize his notoriety. Just as he had drawn on the Paris stay to throw his Germanness into relief, so too did he take advantage of his close encounter with state bureaucracy to underscore his artistic "otherness" and quasi genetic inability to conform. In Paris, Wagner had begun to construct his media image; in Dresden, he developed his amazing knack for publicity which he would perfect over the remainder of his professional career.

The untranslatable German word "Selbstinszenierung" (self-staging, making a production of oneself) has often been used to describe Wagner's activities. The term conveys the idea of making a public spectacle of oneself, producing oneself as a carefully constructed persona, often causing a mixture of sensation and scandal, usually as a vacuous ego-trip. I do not object to using the term "Selbstinszenierung," because it does describe Wagner's activities accurately. But we need to understand its usage as describing a purposeful – i.e. not at all vacuous – exercise in self-management in order to establish a clear position in the marketplace. The potent combination of sensation and scandal – engineered nowadays by high-priced PR firms – is a constant feature of Wagner's professional life, and continues to fuel the Wagner industry today.

It was during this time in Dresden, 1847 to be precise, that the word "Wagnerianer" was used for the first time.[5] Wagner was a polarizing figure who excited a following as totally committed to him as his enemies were implacable. Though he often complained that he was misunderstood and maltreated by the press, he nevertheless seems to have comprehended – intuitively at least – that in the media-dominated world, there is no such thing as "bad" publicity.

Two episodes in particular from the Dresden period exemplify the coherent connection between the image Wagner fashioned for himself in Paris and his "Selbstinszenierung" in Dresden. Even though most biographical studies pass over them rapidly, Wagner's involvement in the ceremonies marking the return of Carl Maria von Weber's remains from London to Dresden in December 1844, and his performance of Beethoven's Ninth Symphony at the Palm Sunday concert in April 1846 are important to study in some detail, because they underscore how Wagner's public championing of the German musical legacy is inseparable from his championing of himself. Moreover, these two episodes reveal Wagner's uncanny ability

---

[5] *Signale für die musikalische Welt* (May 19, 1847), quoted in Helmut Kirchmeyer, *Situationsgeschichte der Musikkritik und musikalischen Pressewesens in Deutschland*, Teil 4: *Das zeitgenössische Wagner-Bild*, 4 vols. (Regensburg: Bosse, 1967–72), III: 260. See also Gregor-Dellin, *Richard Wagner*, 223.

to mount what, for the time, was a publicity campaign of breathtaking inventiveness.

Remains of the day

Carl Maria von Weber (1786–1826) died from tuberculosis during an extended visit to London, where he was buried. Fourteen years later, in January 1841, an anonymous Frenchman reported in the *Gazette musicale* on his efforts to locate Weber's coffin, urging that it be removed to a more suitable location.[6] Almost immediately thereafter, a committee was formed to return Weber's remains to Dresden, not his birthplace, but the city where he served as Kapellmeister for the last and most successful decade of his career.[7] The committee's efforts continued in 1842 and 1843, but all without success.[8] The resistance principally from the court came in part because, as one newspaper at the time reported, there were concerns over the similarity to the return of Napoleon's ashes from St. Helena in 1840 and the nationalistic furor the event had unleashed in France.[9] While the comparison between Napoleon and Weber might be a bit overdrawn, there were nationalist repercussions in both cases which the admittedly declining restoration powers wanted to contain. Indeed, given Weber's status as one of Germany's leading musicians, if not its foremost opera composer, and given the increased emphasis since the early nineteenth century on the national characteristics of music and those who composed it, one wonders why it took so long to even consider returning his remains to Germany, not to mention the irony that the idea was apparently initiated by a Frenchman at the height of the so-called "Rhine Crisis."

The attempt finally succeeded in 1844. The funds necessary for transporting the remains, burial costs, and seed money for an eventual Weber statue, were raised through a series of benefit concerts. After some delay caused by the frozen waters of the Elbe River, Weber's remains were transferred from ship to a train which arrived in Dresden on December 14, 1844.[10] The coffin was accompanied by a torchlight parade, with funeral music

---

[6] See John Warrack, *Carl Maria von Weber*, 2nd edn (Cambridge University Press, 1976), esp. 363–4.
[7] For a detailed description of the efforts in Dresden, see Max Maria von Weber, *Carl Maria von Weber. Ein Lebensbild*, 3 vols. (Leipzig: Ernst Keil, 1864), II: 714–18.
[8] See Kirchmeyer, *Situationsgeschichte*, I: 678–9.
[9] *Deutsche Allgemeine Zeitung* (Leipzig) (December 18, 1844), 520.
[10] *Tagebuch des Königl. Sächs. Hoftheaters auf das Jahr 1844*, January 1, 1845; repr. in Kirchmeyer II: 699–704.

Wagner composed from strains of Weber's *Euryanthe*, to the Old Catholic Cemetery in Dresden-Friedrichsstadt.[11] There, the great singer, Weber's friend, Wilhelmine Schröder-Devrient placed a wreath on the casket. At the burial the next day, December 15, three eulogies were delivered, the first by Dr. Heinrich Wilhelm Schulz (chairman of the committee), followed by Wagner, and lastly a poem in honor of Weber recited by Hofrath Winkler. The music for the occasion – a hymn for male chorus – was again composed by Wagner.

Immediately after the event, on December 16, 1844, a new committee was formed to organize the Weber statue. On December 21, it printed a large appeal for donations in the *Deutsche Allgemeine Zeitung*, listing its seven principal members arranged non-alphabetically, i.e. in order of importance: first is Dr. Heinrich Wilhelm Schulz and last is Richard Wagner, described as "königlich sächsischer Kapellmeister."[12]

The series of events from the 14th to the 16th received extensive newspaper coverage both in Dresden and elsewhere. Wagner's participation was duly reported, namely that he composed the funeral music, a male chorus for the burial, and that he held a speech at the graveside. Some reports devote a good deal of attention to his speech for reasons discussed later on. However, neither Wagner nor any other individual is credited either for the idea or for organizing the event as a whole. Nevertheless, today, it is hard to find an account of the Weber translocation that does not in the first place credit Wagner and Wagner alone for the feat. Why the difference between perceptions in 1844 and since? How did the (hi)story come to be reshaped and why did that reshaping become fixed?

The answer to the first question is that Wagner wrote the definitive account of the event; he inscribed himself indelibly into Weber's biographical narrative, overwhelming and eventually silencing the putatively more balanced reports published in newspapers. According to Wagner, "Wagner" was the prime mover. Descriptions today invariably repeat Wagner's retelling of the story perhaps because, in our star- and celebrity-driven culture, we need to attribute events to a single, identifiable, recognizable figure. For Wagner, the event satisfied his general desire for attention while also providing the opportunity to consolidate several elements of his persona: to appear as Weber's successor both in his capacity as Dresden's next world-famous Kapellmeister and, even more, as the next great composer of German opera.

---

[11] *Trauersinfonie* WWV 73 (*Funeral Music on Motifs from Weber's* Euryanthe).
[12] Repr. in Kirchmeyer II: 528.

In his memoirs, Wagner claims he became the head (*Vorstand*) of the committee, a claim Helmut Kirchmeyer suggests cannot be verified.[13] According to Wagner, court resistance to the translocation had not yet subsided when he joined. It was Wagner who maneuvered around it. His boss, von Lüttichau, had implored Wagner to desist from participating. "What if Reissiger would die some time soon on a spa trip," Lüttichau supposedly argued, "then his wife could demand the return of his body with all pomp and circumstance, just like Weber's wife is doing now."[14] Apparently, Wagner's efforts to "explain the differences" between Weber and Reissiger were not successful. In fairness, Wagner does seem to have been instrumental in raising the necessary funds, making an end run around the Dresden Court by involving the Prussian Court and Theater in Berlin. Ironically, the benefit performance of *Euryanthe* in Berlin which launched the fundraising was arranged by none other than Meyerbeer!

Weber's Germanness

Once again, the issue of Germanness is central to Wagner's involvement in and presentation of Weber's return to Dresden. Already in 1841, while in Paris, Wagner published two essays on Weber, specifically *Der Freischütz*: one for a French readership, the other for Germans back home in Dresden.[15] Not unlike his appropriation and construction of Beethoven, Wagner – the self-conscious patriot and self-appointed interpreter of things German – uses Weber and *Der Freischütz* in order to augment his own Germanness.

Quite provocatively, the review addressed to the French audience suggests that, despite its popularity in France, Weber's opera is not and cannot be properly understood by the French for whom it is so difficult "to explain this German nature which is so foreign to you."[16] "We really are a strange [*sonderbares*] people,"[17] he writes. The use of "sonderbar" is ambiguous. While it underscores otherness and separateness, the word can also mean "special" or simply "weird." It also alludes to the later and much-debated concept of the *deutscher Sonderweg* (German special path) in German historiography, a concept used to explain the "deviant" nature of German

---

[13] *SSD* II: 42.
[14] *SSD* II: 43.
[15] "*Der Freischütz*: An das Pariser Publikum," and "*Le Freischutz*: Bericht nach Deutschland," *SSD* I: 207–19 and 220–40.
[16] "diese euch so fremdartige deutsche Natur zu erklären" (*SSD* I: 214).
[17] "Wir sind wirklich ein sonderbares Volk" (*SSD* I: 214).

national developments when compared to the normative trajectory of France and Britain, a painful issue for Germans since the late seventeenth century.

To the German readership, Wagner stresses not only the Germanness of Weber's opera but his own sentiments as well: "Oh my wonderful German fatherland, how I love you, how I dote on you … how wonderful it makes *me* feel that I am German."[18] *Der Freischütz* was a milestone in the development of a German national operatic form, both thematically and musically, even though its roots lie in French *opéra comique*. One of the few German operas to become an international success, even in Paris, its "ideological transformation" into a work of specifically German character occurred soon after its 1821 world premiere in Berlin.[19] So Wagner's appeal to its national character in the early 1840s was nothing new.[20] Still, Wagner's description of its "specifically German character" and "unparalleled success" is not "merely codifying various strains of Weber's reception,"[21] as Michael Tusa claims, but instead is a masterful and complex appropriation of existing discourses, tailored to serve a media image he was creating for himself at the time.

Two issues are particularly important to Wagner. First, the opera's theme is a product of the "Volk" that has lost its sense of identity, victim of the social transformations of modernity. A composer of genuine sensitivity (*geistvoller Tondichter*) was needed to bring this tale-of-the-*Volk* back to life to create an artwork which would in turn be understood by the *Volk*.[22] This narrative of a genuine, organic *Volk* culture, effaced by historical development, then revived in an organic work of art, models a triadic movement of cultural history dear to German idealists around 1800 (Schiller, Novalis, Hegel). Structurally mirroring the Christian prophetic historiography of Grace – Fall – Redemption, the artwork now becomes a

---

[18] "O, mein herrliches deutsches Vaterland, wie muß ich dich lieben, wie muß ich für dich schwärmen … Wie ist *mir* wohl, daß ich ein Deutscher bin!" (*SSD* I: 220).

[19] See Annegret Fauser, "Phantasmagorie im deutschen Wald? Zur *Freischütz*-Rezeption in London und Paris 1824," *Deutsche Meister, böse Geister? Nationale Selbstfindung in der Musik*, ed. Hermann Danuser and Herfried Münkler (Schliengen: Argus, 2001), 245–73; and Ludwig Finscher, "Weber's *Freischütz*: Conceptions and Misconceptions," *Proceedings of the Royal Musical Association* 110 (1983–4), 79–90, here 82.

[20] Michael C. Tusa, "Cosmopolitanism and the National Opera: Weber's *Der Freischütz*," *Journal of Interdisciplinary History* 36.3 (2006), 483–506; see also Wolfgang Michael Wagner, *Carl Maria von Weber und die deutsche Nationaloper* (Mainz: Schott, 1994).

[21] *SSD* I: 212, and Tusa, "Cosmopolitanism," 485.

[22] Henceforth, I use the German spelling *Volk* because it is conceptually different from the English "folk." For a discussion of *Volk* and *Volkston* in eighteenth- and nineteenth-century German discourse, see Chapter 3 of David Gramit, *Cultivating Music: The Aspirations, Interests, and Limits of German Musical Culture, 1770–1848* (Berkeley: University of California Press, 2002), 63–92. I return to this issue in Chapter 4. See *SSD* I: 207 and 213.

means of restoring a utopian *Volk* spirit (*Volksgeist*). Wagner borrows this idea for his aesthetic theory and, later, builds it into his "most German of operas" *Die Meistersinger von Nürnberg* – an idea Weber, the most German of opera composers (before Wagner), anticipates in *Der Freischütz*.

The second issue for Wagner follows from the first. Weber's visceral Germanness is proved by the culturally unifying effect *Der Freischütz* has on the as yet non-existent German nation: "Fellow countrymen from the North and South … from readers of Kant to those of the Viennese fashion periodicals … from every political persuasion all came together in this one matter: from one end of Germany to the other, *Freischütz* was listened to, sung and danced."[23]

Even Wagner's enemy, the Dresden critic Julius Schladebach, echoes this same image of Weber as an aesthetically unifying force in German culture: "Germany *loves* him; Germany claims him with the most heartfelt feelings, and 'as far as the German tongue is spoken' (*soweit die deutsche Zunge klingt*), from north to south, from east to west, his melodies resound."[24] The nation which as yet lacks the means to unite politically is made whole through the work of art, a possibility specifically articulated by Schiller around 1800 in his poem fragment "German Greatness."[25] Conceptually, the modern nation state requires and compels unification behind a single purpose which cuts across geographic, social, educational, even political and religious differences. For German-speaking thinkers and authors of the late eighteenth century, the artwork became a substitute for the absent centrifugal political force. Schladebach's citation of Ernst Moritz Arndt's hugely popular chauvinistic poem from 1813 reinstrumentalizes the artwork for exactly this purpose.[26] After more than a century of such rhetorical gestures, the eminent historian Friedrich Meinecke coined the term *Kulturnation* (cultural nation) in 1907 to differentiate the German national corpus from the *Staatsnation* (nation state) which characterized France and England. Perhaps the most intense period during which a united German state was imagined culturally was between 1800 and 1840, when many such patriotic poems were written and set to music as "Lieder." The most famous was Hoffmann von Fallersleben's "Deutschland, Deutschland über alles" (1841) set to Haydn's "Emperor" quartet which

---

[23] *SSD* I: 213.
[24] *Dresden. Beiblätter zu den Correspondenz-Nachrichten der Abend-Zeitung*, December 19, 1844 (repr. in Kirchmeyer II: 524–8, here 525).
[25] Schiller, "[Deutsche Größe]," *Werke*, II.1: 431–6.
[26] "As far as the German tongue is spoken" (*soweit die deutsche Zunge klingt*) is perhaps the most cited line from the poem: *Was ist des Deutschen Vaterland?* (1813) by Ernst Moritz Arndt.

eventually became the national anthem. So Wagner's intervention here was timely.

While the Lied is a more portable form, the reception of *Der Freischütz* proved that the large-scale musical-dramatic work contained no less potential to capture and represent this national aspiration in what we of the cinematic age understand to be the complex, powerful and seductive combination of dramatic text, visual image, and music. For Wagner's purposes, this model of the patriotically rousing potential of opera is as important a precedent as "Beethoven" and the Ninth Symphony.

To underscore the point about the inherent power of a complex aesthetic representation of a unified Germany, I refer to a stirring cinematic realization in one of the most often played scenes from Leni Riefenstahl's seminal propaganda film, *Triumph of the Will* (1934). Uniformed men from distant parts of Germany individually call out their place of origin and then, at the end, in chorus chant: "Ein Volk, Ein Reich, Ein Führer: Deutschland!" (One people, one empire, one leader: Germany!) I am precisely not suggesting a direct link between Wagner and the Nazi movement, as so many have done before me. Instead, I point to the connection between the way Weber's *Freischütz* was broadly received in the nineteenth century on the one hand and, on the other, the way this same idea is visualized in a Nazi propaganda film, to explain the emotional and emotive power of both Wagner's appeal to German unity and this cathartic moment in Riefenstahl's film. Riefenstahl's masterstroke was to make visual and palpable an idea well prepared in German cultural history. One hundred years earlier, Wagner had already understood how to appropriate this same deeply embedded and widely articulated national fantasy. My point is that, what in the political sense functioned for Hitler as propaganda was, for Wagner, a way of addressing a market for aesthetic products not only "made" in Germany, but also thematically reflective or evocative of Germany.

The speech

Wagner's memoirs describe the Weber translocation in great detail: his composition of the funeral music, how he organized the performance and the timing to achieve maximum theatrical effect. He reports that witnesses told him of the sublime experience.[27] According to Wagner, his graveside

---

[27] "Mir wurde von Zeugen, welche an den Fenstern den Zug kommen und verübergehen sahen, versichert, daß der Eindruck der Feierlichkeit unbeschreiblich erhaben gewesen ist" (*SSD* II: 44).

speech had an even more powerful effect. In later years Wagner would speak extemporaneously, but on this his first occasion for a public speech, Wagner memorized his lines, apparently delivering them with such effectiveness that his friend the actor Emil Devrient was allegedly "astonished."[28]

Newspapers reported the events widely, though Wagner's role was given differing weight. The *Leipziger Zeitung* published two lengthy articles, one on the December 14th arrival, the other reporting on the burial. It mentions the speeches by Dr. Heinrich Schulz ("Committee Chair") and Wagner (described as "also a committee member"), who gave a "deeply moving speech."[29] Even Julius Schladebach describes the speech in positive terms, and the *Deutsche Allegemeine Zeitung* reprints it – as opposed to the other two speeches – in its entirety as the closing portion of its exhaustive report.[30]

Wagner's speech emphasizes the German national dimension of both the event and the composer it honors. In this, he is no different from Schulz, the preceding speaker, who had allegedly already spoken of Weber "as *German* artist, as composer of the people."[31] But Wagner's speech is more universal, more romantic than Schulz's and richer in signs and motifs. Wagner's delivery may have been powerful, but the content demands more careful scrutiny than it has been given, because it transcends the momentariness of the event and explains both why some newspapers reprinted it and why Wagner included it in his collected works.[32]

The opening exhortation: "Let this be the plain site [*prunklose Stätte*] which will preserve your precious remains for us," immediately plays on the issue of German modesty and genuineness, which Wagner then reaffirms in the following sentence. Even if Weber had been buried in the

---

[28] SSD II: 45. See also Eduard Devrient (1801–77), *Aus seinen Tagebüchern, Band 1. 1836–1852*, ed. Rolf Kabel (Weimar: Böhlaus Nachfolger, 1964): entry for December 15, 1844: "Dr. Schulz sprach am Grabe eine Art Abhandlung über den Verstorbenen, recht in deutscher Gelehrtenweise. Vortrefflich war des Kapellmeisters Wagner Rede, ein Meisterstück an Feinheit, Takt, richtiger und schöner Empfindung und Gedankenreichtum."

[29] "tief zum Herzen gehender Rede," *Leipziger Zeitung*, December 18, 1844 (repr. in Kirchmeyer II: 518–20).

[30] Schladebach (signed W. J. S. E.), *Dresden. Beiblätter zu den Correspondenz-Nachrichten der Abend-Zeitung* December 19, 1844 (repr. in Kirchmeyer II: 524–8). *Deutsche Allegemeine Zeitung* (Leipzig), December 18, 1844 (repr. in Kirchmeyer II: 520–4).

[31] "als *deutschen* Künstler, als Volkscomponisten," *NZfM*, December 23, 1844 (repr. in Kirchmeyer 533–6, here 535).

[32] See Eckart Kröplin, *Richard Wagner: Theatralisches Leben und lebendiges Theater* (Leipzig: Deutscher Verlag für Musik, 1989), 154–5. Kröplin discusses the Weber translocation only as far as it represents Wagner's "discovery of himself as a theatrical hero" (and "Inszenierung des 'Ich'"). He does not analyze the content of the speech, or question how Wagner's actions and account of them serve the goal of fashioning a public personality.

most magnificent of circumstances in England, he surely would still have preferred "a modest grave on German soil."[33] This first section of the speech is devoted to Weber's character which in turn defines him as German. His German qualities become all the clearer when compared with "those cold fame seekers, who have no fatherland, who love those countries which provide the most fertile soil for their ambition to blossom."[34] Though unnamed, it is the stateless Meyerbeer-type he describes: German maybe, but actually a Jew who abandons his homeland to seek fame and fortune in Paris and who thus becomes a global player, a put-down rehearsed already in Wagner's Paris essays. Modernity's seductive powers are so strong that even Weber had been pulled by a "fateful urge" (*verhängnißvoller Drang*) to that place where "even genius must bring itself to the market in order make its mark."[35] The difference between Meyerbeer and Weber was that the latter regained his moral compass "in enough time to turn his longing gaze back to the homeland hearth [*heimathlichen Herde*]."[36] As the historical Weber's health deteriorated in London, he apparently did speak of little else than returning to Germany. Even on the night of his death, and against his doctor's wishes, he had continued making plans for the trip back. Wagner plays on this verifiable biographical detail – that he would have known from his close connection to the Weber family – in order to make a larger point about Weber's association with and faithfulness to Germany.[37] It also rehearses the same image Wagner paints at the conclusion of his *Autobiographical Sketch*. Not unlike Weber, Wagner too had trekked to Paris in search of success, only to reconnect with his Germanness while abroad. The difference was that Wagner had lived to make the "tearful" journey back across the Rhine, an experience denied Weber. The parallelisms need to be noted. *R* (i.e. "Wagner") had "also" been a poor German composer like Beethoven. Wagner like Weber experiences similar life trajectories, pulled in one direction by the market and in the other by feelings of national belonging.

This first section of the speech emphasizes morally loaded terms. Weber is alternately: "modest, pure, chaste, manly" (*bescheiden, rein, keusch, männlich*), is "childlike" and "virtuous" (*Kindlichkeit, Tugend*): these in turn make him "the people's favorite" (*zum Liebling Deines Volkes*). It is a reciprocal relationship, because he has in turn remained consistently

---

[33] "ein bescheidenes Grab in deutschem Boden" (*SSD* II: 46).
[34] "jenen kalten Ruhmsüchtigen an, die kein Vaterland haben, denen das Land der Erde das liebste ist, in welchem ihr Ehrgeiz den üppigsten Boden für sein Gedeihen ist" (*SSD* II: 46).
[35] "Genie sich zu Markte bringen muß um zu gelten" (*SSD* II: 46).
[36] *SSD* II: 46–7.
[37] See also Max Maria von Weber, *Weber*, II: 690 and 714.

"bound to the heart of the German *Volk*."[38] The climax of this sequence, and subsequently the most often quoted sentence from the speech is Wagner's declaration: "Never has a *more German* musician lived, than you!" (*Nie hat ein* deutscherer *Musiker gelebt, als Du!*).[39] As we already know from Paris, this Germanness has as much to do with Weber's morality and aesthetics as it does with his actual music.

The next section traces Weber's reception at home and abroad. While he may have enjoyed fairness (*Gerechtigkeit*) in England and awe (*Bewunderung*) in France, only the German can "love" him (*aber* lieben *kann Dich nur der deutsche* [emphasis RW]). This accentuation on the word "lieben" harks back to Luther's use of the word in defense of his iconoclastic translation of the Bible into German.[40] Again, the Germans as a people are, like Weber himself, more human because, of all living creatures, only humans have the capacity to love. Building on national differences Wagner had already enumerated in his Paris essay, "Über deustches Musikwesen," he again emphasizes cultural differences that go deep: the legalistic and unemotional English have a capacity for fairness, the French an irrational need to be amazed, but only Germans have the uniquely human capacity for "love."

Wagner concludes this middle part of his speech by asking almost pathetically, "who can blame us for wanting your ashes to be part of its soil, the beloved German soil?"[41] Wagner's potent iconography of ashes and soil – which ring so ominously for our post-1945 ears – when added to the moral categories mentioned earlier fuse a complex image of Germanness and national destiny that Wagner constructed around the figure and reburial of Weber.

The last part of the speech connects the dead with the living – Weber and his surviving family, Weber and the Germans. The departed are not really dead, but live forever through those who remain. In phraseology reminiscent of Grillparzer's graveside speech delivered for Beethoven's funeral, which was "both elegy and program,"[42] Wagner also creates and then exploits a nexus that requires little explanation. By constructing a bond between dead and living, he indirectly argues for a link between Weber and himself.

---

[38] "an dieses deutsche Volksherz gekettet" (*SSD* II: 47).
[39] *SSD* II: 47 (emphasis RW).
[40] Martin Luther, *Sendbrief vom Dolmetschen*, ed. Ernst Kähler (Stuttgart: Reclam, 1962), 161–2.
[41] *SSD* II: 47.
[42] Esteban Buch, *Beethoven's Ninth: A Political History*, trans. R. Miller (University of Chicago Press, 2003), 114.

What, for reasons of historical timing, Wagner had not been able to do with Beethoven – share the stage with him, as Liszt had allegedly done – he had paradoxically now been able to do with Weber, even though Weber died the year before Beethoven. Wagner capitalized on this moment. Ernest Newman describes the oration as "perhaps the best of all his efforts in this line,"[43] but Newman should also have given Wagner credit for the subsequent spin.

The spin

Both in the short and long term, Wagner did what he could to ensure that the Weber reburial – more specifically his version of it – would not be forgotten. His success was due to his increasing notoriety: people would pay attention to what Wagner had to say. But, conversely, his image was also colored by the special relationship he constructed with a Weber who was also his construct. Scholars often talk of "Wagner's ascendancy" that relegated "Weber more frequently to the role of Wagnerian precursor."[44] By doing so, they make accidental and inherently mysterious a process that was instigated by none other than Wagner. Wagner insinuated himself permanently into Weber's biography. Today, no description of Weber's life seems complete without reference to Wagner, perhaps the most striking example being John Warrack's comprehensive Weber biography. The first sentence of the book's Preface retells the story of Wagner's speech at the 1844 ceremony, culminating with a translation of the quote: "Nie hat ein *deutscherer* Musiker gelebt, als Du!"[45] The book ends with a description of that same ceremony and a long quote lifted straight from Wagner's autobiography *My Life*.[46] Warrack not only gives Wagner the first and last words, but frames Weber's life from Wagner's perspective. Warrack's Weber biography may be the most substantial example, but for fun I conducted a web search of Weber on December 14, 2006. Every site that summarized Weber's life and death attributed the translocation to "Wagner's initiative."[47]

---

[43] Newman, *Life of Wagner*, I: 393.
[44] Tusa, "Cosmopolitanism," 486.
[45] Warrack, *Weber*, 9.
[46] *Ibid.*, 364.
[47] "In 1844 Richard Wagner, one of Weber's successors as head of the Dresden Opera, arranged to have the composer's remains brought back to the city and buried in a grave of honor." www.findagrave.com/cgi-bin/fg.cgi?page=gr&GRid=6820952 (accessed December 14, 2006). "He was buried in London, but 18 years later, his remains were transferred on an initiative of Richard Wagner and re-buried in Dresden." http://en.wikipedia.org/wiki/Carl_Maria_von_Weber

How did Wagner accomplish this? His stature as one of the leading artistic personalities of the nineteenth century means that whatever he touched has become a source of enduring interest. But the "hype" he generated, both in terms of noise as well as content, is also a factor in how we choose to remember events in which he was involved, however tangentially.

After the reburial, Wagner created opportunities to restate and remind the world of his role in it. In correspondence that had nothing at all to do with Weber, Wagner would mention the event. He would also complain about insufficient reporting by the press, revealing – as if anyone had doubted – that its significance for him was not as an altruistic display of mourning for a fellow composer and important predecessor. Already on December 18 in a letter to Kietz in Paris, he writes about the fact that the translocation "was brought about and arranged by me," and that his graveside speech gave the ceremony the "proper and most poignant significance." But he is "saddened and embittered" about the "jealousy" that this and other successes of his seem to cause.[48] Even a half-year later, he still refers to the Weber reburial. A lengthy complaint-filled letter to Karl Gaillard characterizes the event as entirely his work, and yet another example of his selfless fight against bureaucracy, philistinism, and other obstacles, only to be ignored by the press.[49] And two months after that, in a letter to Franz Liszt, he again states that the return of Weber's ashes was his initiative.[50]

The formalized narrative of the Weber episode appears both in *My Life* and in volume two of Wagner's *Gesammelte Schriften und Dichtungen* where, under the collected title *Bericht über die Heimbringung der sterblichen Überreste Karl Maria von Weber's aus London nach Dresden* (Report on

---

(accessed December 14, 2006). "In 1844, on instigation of the Dresden Kapellmeister Richard Wagner, coffin was shipped back to Ger. and buried in Dresden Catholic cemetery on 15 Dec. after funeral oration by Wagner and the perf. of Wagner's Hebt an den Sang (An Webers Grabe) for unacc. male ch." www.classicalarchives.com/bios/codm/weber.html (accessed December 14, 2006). "He was buried in London, but 18 years later, his remains were transferred on an initiative of Richard Wagner and re-buried in Dresden." www.classiccat.net/weber_cm_von/biography.htm (accessed December 14, 2006).

[48] "die Rückkehr u. den Empfang der Asche *Weber's*, deren Uebersiedelung endlich durch mich aufs Neue veranlaßt u. bewerkstelligt worden ist … [D]ie Feier war schön und würdig und es gelang mir besonders durch meine *Rede* am Grabe, dieser Feier die richtige und ergreifendste Bedeutung zu geben. Wie ich bei dieser u. ähnlichen Gelegenheiten den *Neid* wider mich errege, ist wahrhaft betrübend u. verbittert mir oft sehr meine schöne Stellung" (emphasis RW), Letter to Ernst Benedikt Kietz, December 18, 1844 (*SB* II: 406).

[49] "Trotz der entscheidenen Abneigung des Hofes u. des Generaldirector's setzte ich die Uebersiedelung der Asche *Weber's* nach Dresden durch; ihre Bestattung, die würdige Weise der Feier ist *mein* Werk … Haben Sie von alle dem etwas in Dresdener Berichten gelesen?" (emphasis RW), Letter to Karl Gaillard, June 5, 1845 (*SB* II: 432).

[50] Letter to Franz Liszt, August 5, 1845 (*SB* II: 448).

the Return of the Mortal Remains of Carl Maria von Weber from London to Dresden), he also reprints the full text to his two contributions for that day: his speech and the chorus.[51] Wagner's decision to memorialize his participation in the event and, even more, the words he spoke on the occasion suggest that both the gesture and the content be scrutinized as part of what constituted his long-term investment in constructing and controlling how he would be remembered.

Wagner's version soon transcended his letters, memoirs and collected writings, taking on a life of its own in Wagner biographies and in personal recollections of others. For instance, Gustav Adolf Kietz (1824–1908) – younger brother of Wagner's Paris companion Ernst Benedict Kietz – resided in Dresden during this period and was a frequent visitor to the Wagner home. Gustav's memoirs, published in 1905, especially devoted to these years, became an eyewitness source for subsequent biographers.[52] However, Kietz often simply repeats Wagner's own assertions, raising questions about his reliability. One example is Kietz's description of the Weber episode. Kietz credits Wagner for generating public interest as well as for organizing the reburial, and inserts lengthy quotes from Wagner's speech, including of course: "Nie hat ein *deutscherer* Musiker gelebt, als Du!"[53]

There is no historical account of the Weber reburial beyond contemporary press reports and the biography written much later by his son Max Maria. Thus, Wagner's version has not only dominated the record, it has become the official record, frustrating Ernest Newman's laudable intention of "hearing the other side," of not making the mistake of earlier Wagner biographers who "accepted far too unquestioningly Wagner's account of his dealings," which has made Wagner scholarship the "equivalent of our listening to one end of a telephone conversation."[54] This is not the place to analyze every retelling of the Weber reburial, an admittedly brief moment. Every Wagner biography and of course every Weber biography mentions it, almost always as an example of Wagner's organizational skills, natural talent at public speaking and, most importantly for his image, as promoter of the German national operatic tradition.

So, while Robert Gutman devotes only one paragraph to it, and Martin Gregor-Dellin simply assumes the veracity of Wagner's account and focuses

---

[51] "Rede an Weber's letzter Ruhestätte" and "Gesang nach der Bestattung" (*SSD* II: 41–9). See also *ML* 308–12.
[52] *Richard Wagner in den Jahren 1842–1849 und 1873–1875. Erinnerungen von Gustav Adolf Kietz*, recorded by Marie Kietz (Dresden: Carl Reissner, 1905).
[53] *Ibid.*, 45.
[54] Newman, *Life of Wagner*, I: ix.

on Wagner's self-described "emotional state" (*Ergriffenheit*), the introduction to volume II of Wagner's letters asserts that this "significant event" resulted "essentially thanks to Wagner's commitment."[55]

Only Helmut Kirchmeyer offers a realistic assessment in his exhaustive study of the press reaction to Wagner:

> The translocation of Weber's remains … was a test case: for Wagner the tactician, to again persevere against all mounting obstacles … and for his devotees, to be amazed at his adroitness in obfuscating his own initiative and those of others, and to arrange historical facts themselves according to their wishful memory.[56]

Wagner seized on the opportunity of the Weber translocation to further construct and cement his media image. He engineered his role as the event's pre-eminent figure and, even more, shaped our historical memory of it.

The prodigal son, Part II

If the Weber translocation was an opportunity Wagner seized and made his own, the performance of Beethoven's Ninth Symphony on April 5, 1846, at the annual Palm Sunday concert was even more of a media "event" conceived, produced, directed, managed, executed, and reported by Richard Wagner.

As we already saw hinted in the previous chapter, the Ninth Symphony became crucial not only in the development of and justification for Wagner's aesthetics, but in the construction of his media image. At regular intervals in his life, Wagner would (re)affirm his relationship with Beethoven's last symphony on several levels: conceptual, historical, and personal. The textual strategies of these affirmations need scrutiny.

In *My Life*, Wagner stresses the "revelation" (*mit einem Schlage*) of witnessing François Antoine Habeneck's performance of Beethoven's Ninth at the "Société des Concerts" of the Paris Conservatoire sometime in late 1839 or early 1840.[57] This experience is presented within a specific narrative frame, however, which serves to add to its significance. As a teenager, Wagner writes, the Ninth became the "mystical center of attraction for all

---

[55] Gutman, *Wagner*, 124–5; Gregor-Dellin, *Richard Wagner*, 217–18; and *SB* II: 13: "Sie ist zum wesentlichen Teil dem Einsatz Wagners zu danken."

[56] Kirchmeyer, I: 678.

[57] There is disagreement in the literature about exactly when Wagner might have heard Habeneck's performance of the Ninth Symphony, or exactly which rehearsal his autobiography refers to. See Andreas Eichhorn, *Beethovens Neunte Symphonie. Die Geschichte ihrer Aufführung und Rezeption* (Kassel: Bärenreiter, 1993), 74, note 17.

my fantastical-musical musings and aspirations."[58] This originally childlike (i.e. intuitive, hence genuine) enthusiasm, was subsequently eroded by bad performances he witnesses, specifically what Wagner describes as Christian August Pohlenz's "execution" (*Hinrichtung*) of it on April 14, 1830, at the Leipzig Gewandhaus.[59] Structurally analogous to the prodigal son narrative of the "Autobiographical Sketch," Wagner's depiction of his relationship with the Ninth goes through the same triadic motion of attraction, rejection, and born-again reaffirmation. Wagner feels "shame and regret" that his "dulling" experience with the "horrible" theater had "corrupted" his taste.[60] Like his reawakened patriotism, indeed as its musical-aesthetic corollary, Paris again serves the dual function of corruptive and redemptive space, now rekindling for this prodigal son twice over a pre-existing love for Beethoven ("the newly regained old spirit").[61] The Habeneck experience makes "crystal clear" (*sonnenhell*) what, in his youth, had seemed nothing more than "mystical constellations and soundless magical figures," reuniting him with what he could only "imagine" of this "amazing work" in his "youthful enthusiasm."[62] Independent sources confirm the excellence of Habeneck's performances, so Wagner may indeed have had an epiphany, gaining new insights into the piece's possibilities. But by describing his earlier relationship with the piece as confused and uncomprehending, Wagner overdraws the moment of revelation and colors his biographical development in order to add emphasis and contour to the new turn of his artistic development.[63]

The rhetorical strategy is clear: the immature Wagner's emotional response to the work has now matured. Wagner strayed, but has now returned. But this misrepresents the case. In his first published letter, dated October 6, 1830 (two months after the Pohlenz "execution" and ten years before the "rediscovery"), the seventeen-year-old Wagner writes to the music publisher Schott about his "most intensive study" of the Ninth Symphony, expressing regret that the wider public is not yet familiar with the "great significance of the work."[64] For this reason, Wagner encloses his

---

[58] "zum mystischen Anziehungspunkt all meines phantastisch-musikalischen Sinnens und Trachtens" (*ML* 42).

[59] Eichhorn, *Beethovens Neunte*, 73. *Hinrichtung* only means "capital punishment" as opposed to "carrying out."

[60] "Scham und Reue … Verwilderung meines Geschmackes … durch meinen verflachenden Verkehr mit dem schrecklichen Theater" (*ML* 186).

[61] "der neugewonnene alte Geist" (*ML* 186).

[62] "mystische Konstellationen und klanglose Zaubergestalten" … "das in meiner Jugendschwärmerei von mir geahnte Bild von diesem wunderbaren Werke" (*ML* 185–6).

[63] "von welcher in jeder Hinsicht ich zuvor gar keine Ahnung hatte" (*ML* 185–6).

[64] Letter to B. Schott's Söhne, October 6, 1830 (*SB* I: 117).

two-handed piano transcription of the first movement of "Beethoven's last magnificent Symphony" for Schott's consideration, since the existing four-handed version has not spread sufficient awareness of the work. Clearly, Wagner's interest in marketing the Ninth Symphony as a way of marketing himself begins early and is evidently not as clouded by youthful fancy as the later Wagner would have us believe.[65]

Wagner's Ninth Symphony

The "Pilgrimage" novella of 1840, written shortly after the Habeneck performance, is a crucial moment in Wagner's appropriation of the Ninth. In the novella, Wagner transposes his personal epiphany from the concert hall to the home of the Master. Beethoven himself brings up the Ninth Symphony as a way out of the inconclusive discussion about opera and the solutions to its aesthetic shortcomings. Within the timeframe of the novella, the Ninth has been composed but not yet performed. So Beethoven's extensive ruminations grant the protagonist *R* insights not available to anyone else, and constitute the second part of the *Weihekuss* discussed in the previous chapter. A divine revelation, "the master initiates his disciple into the secrets of his art," a gesture that supports Wagner's "own self-estimation as one of the elected."[66] Stunned, *R* admits later that he can still hardly believe his luck that "Beethoven himself gave [him] a full understanding of his gigantic last symphony, which back then had just been completed, but was known to no one."[67] Beethoven rather chauvinistically ponders why vocal music of the "frivolous singing nations" (*leichtsinnige Sängervolk* i.e. French and Italians) cannot be as great and "serious" (read: German) as instrumental music.[68] He demands that vocal and instrumental music be "brought together, combined!" This union will provide a solution to the problem of the symphony Beethoven himself had caused, given his encyclopedic set of contributions

---

[65] See Christa Jost, "… mit möglichster Klarheit und Fülle. Zu Wagners Klavierauszug von Beethovens neunter Symphonie," *Wagnerliteratur – Wagnerforschung: Bericht über das Wagner-Symposium München 1983*, ed. Carl Dahlhaus and Egon Voss (Mainz: Schott, 1985), 47–58. Jost writes in passing but quite perceptively about Wagner's "excellent sense for market gaps [Marktlücken]" (49).

[66] Kropfinger, *Wagner and Beethoven*, 15, and Eichhorn, *Beethovens Neunte*, 78.

[67] "Noch heute kann ich das Glück kaum fassen, das mir dadurch zuteil ward, daß mir Beethoven selbst durch diese Andeutungen zum vollen Verständnis seiner riesenhaften letzten Symphonie verhalf, die damals höchstens eben erst vollendet, keinem aber noch bekannt war" (*SSD* I: 109).

[68] *SSD* I: 108.

to that genre. Beethoven shows the way forward in the last movement of his last symphony, thereby setting the stage for the *Gesamtkunstwerk* of the future. Taken together, the private explanation and Beethoven's public aesthetic gesture make Wagner nothing less than the executor of Beethoven's musical will.

The difficulty, Beethoven sighs, is in finding the right words to sing: "Who would be capable of capturing in words the poetry that lies at the heart of such a union of all elements?" Schiller's *Ode* is a "noble and uplifting poem, albeit very far from being able to express what, in this case, no verses in the whole world could."[69] Beethoven is forced to compromise. Read psychoanalytically, Wagner betrays his insecurity at breaking with operatic tradition to write his own texts. As a public-relations exercise, he legitimizes what will become his possibly self-important and conceited practice by making it seem as though he is simply fulfilling Beethoven's mandate.

For Wagner, the Ninth Symphony represents the solution to multiple crises, aesthetic and otherwise. While Johannes Brahms – ultimately Wagner's chief nineteenth-century rival in terms of "German" music – continued the symphonic tradition despite Beethoven, Wagner's text-based, culturally specific works were poised to sacrifice the "universal" potential of the Beethoven legacy. But this would not do. Wagner wanted to be the "most German" without foregoing the German Romantic notion of instrumental music's universal appeal and transcendental aspirations. Because he was writing in a genre not only dominated by cultural rivals, but also interpreted as representative of their national typology, Wagner was compelled to construct an alternative account for his kind of opera. Though linguistically bound and thus national – like all opera – Wagner's particular brand was to continue the German (read: universal) symphonic tradition of Mozart and Beethoven. The last movement of the Ninth Symphony – with its unprecedented incorporation of a literary text – would be the aesthetic bridge connecting the purely instrumental symphony with the Wagnerian music drama. Aesthetic considerations aside, "because of its very unprofitability, the symphony enjoyed a certain aura of aesthetic superiority," and, I would add, moral superiority also.[70] So Wagner could take the high ground by claiming the self-sufficient non-commercial symphonic tradition for his music dramas, making his brand of opera conceptually superior to the "commercial" variety of the French and Italians.

---

[69] "eine edle und erhebende Dichtung, wenn auch weit entfernt davon, das auszusprechen, was allerdings in diesem Falle keine Verse der Welt aussprechen können" (*SSD* I: 109).
[70] Bonds, *Music as Thought*, 3.

Wagner hero

In the continuum that starts with the 1830 piano transcription, continues with the 1840 novella, and ends with the 1872 gala commemoration in Bayreuth, the 1846 performance of Beethoven's Ninth Symphony is simply the next installment in Wagner's effort to link himself with this work in the public imagination. It is an effort Wagner mounts against all odds, an image he and his biographers constantly use to describe his life, perhaps to complement Beethoven's own personal heroic struggle to continue composing despite enormous obstacles.[71] Baudelaire famously defined the modern poet as a "hero." But clearly, some of these "heroes" were so by dint of successful public relations.[72]

Although the Ninth had been used prominently the year before (1845) in Bonn to crown the festival celebrating the new Beethoven statue, in Dresden the symphony was associated with entirely different memories. Wagner's senior colleague, Reissiger, had conducted what by all accounts were two disastrous performances of the work in 1838.[73] Because of the widespread prejudice, even within some musical circles, against late Beethoven's remote and esoteric works, the fiasco was attributed to the composer, not the conductor. So, from the start, there was opposition in Dresden to Wagner's programming choice for the annual Palm Sunday benefit concert. Reissiger was outraged. The orchestra, which considered the work unperformable, felt Wagner had thrown them a gauntlet. The concert organizers – the Widow and Orphan Pension Fund for the Royal Orchestra – feared it would undermine the very purpose of the benefit concert.[74] Even the press was against him. Julius Schladebach, Wagner's Dresden nemesis and surely a model for Beckmesser, wrote a lengthy preview article which appeared on February 26 in the *Wiener allgemeine Musik-Zeitung*. Schladebach documents the "resistance from all sides" and the "precarious choice given the financial goal which needs to be taken into account in this case."[75] The work's

---

[71] See, for example, Glasenapp, *Leben Richard Wagners*, II: 153.
[72] See Scott Burnham, *Beethoven Hero* (Princeton University Press, 1995). Burnham's book is devoted to an exploration of Beethoven's "heroic" style and its paradigmatic role in Western musical aesthetics. He does not pursue the iconography of the heroic as a means of public image-making.
[73] See Eichhorn, *Beethovens Neunte*, 81.
[74] Unterstützungs-Fonds für die Wittwen und Waisen der königlichen Kapelle. For Wagner's account which forms the basis of most biographies (see *ML* 341–6).
[75] "mehrseitige Widestreben" … "prekäre Wahl in Rücksicht auf das bei dieser Gelegenheit doch auch zu berücksichtigende pecuniäre Resultat," *Wiener allgemeine Musik-Zeitung* February 26, 1846 (Kirchmeyer, III: 32–3).

difficulty and "lack of popularity," Schladebach predicted (or hoped) will "doubtless detract from attendance of the concert, even if someone tries to do everything possible ahead of time to awaken public interest through tendentious journal articles and similar maneuvers."[76]

By predicting failure, Schladebach had thrown down a gauntlet of his own.

Wagner responded by using three different, though complementary, tactics, all dedicated to preparing and engineering success.[77] He rehearsed the orchestra allegedly over 200 times, devoting twelve rehearsals alone to the notoriously difficult opening recitative of the fourth movement for double basses and cellos.[78] Second, Wagner wrote explanatory notes for the concert program, which I will discuss later. Third, he publicized the event more creatively than even Schladebach had sarcastically proposed.

Wagner placed a series of four anonymous announcements in the "Besprechungen. Privatsachen" section of the local paper, the *Dresdner Anzeiger*. Similar to today's "personals" sections, its main purpose was for private often coded communication of an amorous nature, though other types of messages appeared.[79] It was an "open secret" in Dresden that the paper's popularity was due to the "Besprechungen. Privatsachen" section which people habitually read first. Some even used it to post urgent messages rather than sending the intended recipient a letter by regular mail.[80] The readership of the *Anzeiger* would have been much broader than for the *Abend-Zeitung* (where Wagner's Paris writings, including the "Pilgrimage" novella had appeared) or even for the Leipzig-based *Zeitung für die elegante Welt* (where the "Autobiographical Sketch" had appeared). So Wagner was deliberately increasing the concert's visibility and potential audience. Wagner's audacious idea of publicizing his "serious" concert in the widely read fluff section of a local newspaper indicates the tenuousness of separating "high" and "low" culture especially when it comes to marketing strategies. That such tactics would be employed by the self-styled high priest of high culture already in 1846 is remarkable.

---

[76] "Mangel an Popularität" … "wird ohne Zweifel dem Besuch des Konzertes Abbruch thun, wenn auch Jemand alles Mögliche thun möchte, durch leitende Journal-artikel und dergleichen Manöver das Interesse des Publikums vorher zu erregen" (Kirchmeyer, III: 32).

[77] See Kirchmeyer, I: 628–36, esp. 636.

[78] See Kietz, *Erinnerungen*, 49–53, for detailed descriptions of the rehearsals, including how Wagner invited orchestral players to his home for extra practice sessions.

[79] See Kirchmeyer, I: 22–32, for an extensive discussion of the *Dresdener Anzeiger* in general, the "Besprechungen. Privatsachen" section in particular, as well as a host of reprinted examples of announcements.

[80] Kirchmeyer, I: 26.

Wagner's four announcements in the *Dresdner Anzeiger* were a carefully timed and minutely staged sequence of articles, designed to build excitement and anticipation while also providing a good deal of information. They appeared with increasing frequency as the performance date – April 5 – approached. The first was published on March 24 (about one month after Schladebach's challenge), the second on March 31, then April 2, and April 4 respectively.[81] Reminiscent of Robert Schumann's device of writing music reviews using the imaginary voices of different characters, Wagner's four notes form a sort of conversation between seemingly different persons. Some appear knowledgeable, whereas others are ignorant but want to know more.

The first announcement, written as if by an enthusiastic member of the public, draws attention to the forthcoming performance of the Ninth Symphony, praising the orchestra for the programming choice. It makes no secret of the difficulty of the work, but promises a great revelation to the listener, ending with the enticing words: "Listen and be amazed [*O, höret und staunet!*]." Surely a morale booster for anxious orchestral members who read it.

The next insert, enigmatically signed "Gg" is from someone less knowledgeable. Responding to the idea of the work's difficulty mentioned in the first note, the author asks: "Wouldn't it be great if something were done – or at least tried – to increase the wider public's understanding of Beethoven's last symphony?"[82]

In what Andreas Eichhorn perceptively calls a "psychologically carefully steered popularization campaign,"[83] Wagner creates the demand, which he himself will satisfy with the next newspaper insert and, later, with his explanatory concert program notes. The second insert pleads for more information, so the third delivers an intimate human portrait of Beethoven to create a bond between audience and work.

Written by an expert (perhaps the author of the first note, but perhaps by someone yet different), the third note is the longest. Both in style and content, it is reminiscent of the "Heiligenstadt Testament," Beethoven's purported suicide note written in 1802 when he became resigned to his own irreversible deafness. Well known to Wagner, the "Testament" was

---

[81] For reprints see Kirchmeyer, III: 35–7, 45–7. For full documentation of the Palm Sunday Concert, see also Richard Wagner, *Sämtliche Werke*, vol. XX.1: *Klavierauszug von Ludwig van Beethovens Symphonie Nr. 9 mit einer Dokumentation zu Wagners Beschäftigung mit dem Werk als Bearbeiter und Dirigent*, ed. Christa Jost (Mainz: Schott, 1989).

[82] "Würde es nicht gut sein, wenn – wenigstens versuchsweise – irgend etwas geschähe, um auch dem größeren Publikum das Verständniß der letzten Symphonie Beethoven's, deren Aufführung wir in diesen Tagen entgegensehen, näher zu rücken?" (*SSD* XII: 204). Also Kirchmeyer, III: 45.

[83] Eichhorn, *Beethovens Neunte*, 76.

discovered amongst Beethoven's papers shortly after his death and published immediately thereafter in October 1827.[84]

The "Heiligenstadt Testament" is "a portrait of the artist as hero" where Beethoven "metaphorically enacted his own death in order that he might live again. He recreated himself in a new guise, self-sufficient and heroic."[85] It thus belongs to the same genre of textually staged existence and constructed identity characteristic of Wagner's writings, and is a document which anticipates Baudelaire's definition of the modern poet. The difference between Beethoven and Wagner – perhaps reflecting the difference between 1800 and 1840 – is that while Beethoven files his self-dramatization away in a drawer, Wagner repeatedly publishes his.

Wagner's third note echoes all of what Maynard Solomon considers the "Heiligenstadt Testament's" key ingredients: the "artist as hero, stricken by deafness, withdrawn from mankind, conquering impulses to suicide, struggling against fate."[86] In addition, Beethoven is once again presented as the poor German composer. Here are representative passages with Beethoven's original for comparison:

Beethoven[87]	Wagner (note three)
I had to separate myself early on, to live my life alone … I live as if in exile.	He found himself at home in a wondrous world … but alas, this world was that of loneliness.
[*Muste ich früh mich absondern, einsam mein Leben zubringen … Wie ein Verbannter muß ich leben*]	[*In welch wunderbarer Welt ward er nun heimisch … Diese Welt aber war, ach! Die Welt der Einsamkeit.*]
I was close to ending my own life – only *art* held me back.	Alas, he came close to robbing himself of the power to speak: but his good spirit held him back; he continued by speaking in tones.
[*Es fehlte wenig, und ich endiget selbst mein Leben – nur sie die* Kunst, *sie hielt mich zurück.*]	[*Ach, da kam er nahe daran, sich der Sprache selbst auch berauben zu wollen: sein guter Geist hielt ihn zurück; er fuhr fort … in Tönen auszusprechen.*]

[84] See, for example, Maynard Solomon, *Beethoven*, 2nd rev. edn (New York: Schirmer, 1998), 383.
[85] *Ibid.*, 157.
[86] *Ibid.*, 158.
[87] Beethoven an seine Brüder Kaspar Karl und Johann van Beethoven, "Heiligenstadt Testament," Heiligenstadt, October 6 and 10, 1802, in Ludwig van Beethoven, *Briefwechsel Gesamtausgabe*, vol. I (1783–1807), ed. Sieghard Brandenburg (Munich: G. Henle, 1996), 121–3.

The third note does nothing to explain the Ninth Symphony in musical terms. Instead, its creator is established as a human being whose story of personal struggle and triumph against all odds has universal resonance. Inadvertently, Wagner of course undermines the claim of "universality" by providing the musically uneducated listener extra-musical means to identify with the sounds. A similar device has become common in the television broadcast of epic events like the Olympics. Background stories of athletes are presented "up close and personal" with a "human interest" dimension in order to intensify enjoyment especially for lengthy or arcane sporting events, enabling the audience to identify with the individuals and their personal stakes.

The fourth note, printed on April 4, the day before the concert, is the shortest but most interesting in marketing terms. Signed "A friend of music, who speaks from experience," the anonymous author reminds readers of the concert and announces a public dress rehearsal that evening.[88] Wagner's strategy evidently worked because, by all accounts, the auditorium at the final dress rehearsal was packed. Opening the rehearsal to the public was brilliant. First, it seemed to respond directly to the suggestion in the second notice that "repeated hearing" is essential for "true enjoyment" of all "powerful musical creations."[89] Secondly, success at the dress rehearsal ensured that any remaining tickets for the actual concert would be snapped up.

The concert

The concert on April 5 was sold out, raising a record-breaking amount for the charity. The bold advertising campaign had made the concert into an event; Wagner had created its audience. By popular demand, Beethoven's Ninth became a staple at future Palm Sunday concerts. But this was also because, as independent sources confirm, the performance Wagner produced from the orchestra and chorus was extraordinary.[90] Clearly not only the number of rehearsals but the ways in which Wagner conducted himself

---

[88] "Ein Musikfreund, der aus Erfahrung spricht" (Kirchmeyer, III: 47).

[89] "Wer es weiß, wie nöthig für das Verständniß jeder gewaltigen Tonschöpfung und mithin für den wahren Genuß derselben ein mehrmaliges Hören ist, der lasse sich ja die hierdurch gebotene Gelegenheit nicht entgehen" (Kirchmeyer, III: 47).

[90] See, for example, the notice in the *Dresdener Anzeiger* April 9, 1846, signed "A. S. gewiß im Namen Vieler" (repr. in Kirchmeyer, III: 49): "Ist es einer hohen königlichen musikalischen Kapelle nicht möglich, an Einem der kommenden Festtage noch einmal die *Simphonie von Beethoven* aufzuführen? Die Erinnerung an den göttlichen Traum der letzten Aufführung würde sich befestigen und Früchte tragen können."

at them had everything to do with the final result. Wagner also had the stage specially constructed and the musicians innovatively arranged in order to maximize the audio-visual effect, evidently with enormous success as numerous newspapers, not least the *NZfM*, reported subsequently.[91]

The experience for lay listeners was enhanced by explanatory program notes Wagner produced specifically for the "less prepared and thus easily confused listener."[92] Chrétien Urhan, violinist and violist in Habeneck's Conservatoire orchestra, had published notes on the Ninth in 1838 using quotes from Dante's *Divine Comedy*.[93] Perhaps using Urhan as his model, Wagner also cited a monumental literary work to assist his lay readership, though – predictably – instead of an Italian, he selected the magnum opus of Germany's national poet, Goethe.

Taking each movement in turn, Wagner describes their unfolding mood as a narrative interspersed with brief citations from *Faust*, referred to by one reviewer as "our most powerful German poetic work."[94] These quotes serve lyrically to accentuate Wagner's main points, though he does concede the conceptual problem of using literature, since "the essence of higher instrumental music is to express in sounds what cannot be expressed in words."[95] While *Faust* has "no immediate connection with Beethoven's work, and in no way indicates the meaning of his purely musical creation," both works nevertheless share "a fundamental higher human spirituality."[96] Again, as in the third note, Wagner uses extra-musical cues to mediate between "absolute" music – a term he coins here for the first time – and an uncomprehending audience.[97] In a footnote, Wagner quotes Romantic author Ludwig Tieck's notion of instrumental music's verbally inexpressible (*unaussprechlich*) qualities and its unique ability to convey the deepest human emotions – a conception of music, Wagner argues, Beethoven shared.

---

[91] See *NZfM* May 17, 1846. See also Raymond Holden, *The Virtuoso Conductors: The Central European Tradition from Wagner to Karajan* (New Haven: Yale University Press, 2005), 3–4.

[92] "weniger vorbereiteten und somit leicht verwirrbaren Zuhörer" (*SSD* II: 56).

[93] Eichhorn contends that Wagner may have seen this publication: see *Beethovens Neunte*, 48, 61, and 75.

[94] "unser mächtigstes deutsches Dichtwerk," *Deutsche Allgemeine Zeitung* April 7, 1845 (repr. Kirchmeyer, III: 47–9).

[95] "daß das Wesen der höheren Instrumentalmusik namentlich darin besteht, in Tönen das auszusprechen was in Worten unaussprechbar ist" (*SSD* II: 56).

[96] "auch keineswegs mit Beethovens Werke in einem unmittelbaren Zusammenhange stehen und auf keine Weise die Bedeutung … zu bezeichnen vermögen" … "zu Grunde liegenden höheren menschlichen Seelenstimmung" (*SSD* II: 57).

[97] See the entry for "Absolute Musik" in the *Handwörterbuch der musikalischen Terminologie* by Albrecht von Massow. Massow traces earlier stages in the combination of the terms "absolute" and "music" as a "culmination of preexisting terms" (3). Wagner applies "the term as though it were already in use" (3).

Nevertheless, Beethoven himself breaks through the bonds of "absolute music." Significantly, this first breach occurs not with the insertion of sung text, but when the bass strings launch into their recitativo, giving the music "a distinctly more conversational character ... the way only human speech functions."[98]

As the Goethe quotes give way to the text from Schiller's "Ode to Joy," Wagner's strategy becomes clear. The seamless transition in the program notes suggests that instrumental music was only just waiting to be joined by words. In terms of Hegel's dialectic historiography, instrumental music was originally considered inferior to vocal music because of its inability to express ideas. The antithetical model proposed during the late eighteenth century argues that this very inability to express phenomenal specificity assures (German) instrumental music's superiority, precisely because it held the greatest potential for conveying the noumenal, transcendental.[99] Now that instrumental music – with the symphony as its most ambitious expression – has gained supremacy, Beethoven (and Wagner) creates a synthesis, adding words back to achieve an expressibility and sophistication far superior to that of French and Italian vocal music. Instead of mere accompaniment, this new form unites poetic expression with instrumental music resulting in what we should properly call linguistic-symphonic music. Wagner's interpretation of Beethoven's Ninth constitutes an Orwellian revaluation of values, once again turning aesthetics on its head.

According to Wagner's narrative, the fourth movement presents the dying cry of absolute music. Instrumental music is no longer "capable" of saying what is needed, so the "human voice counters the wild flailing of the instruments" with the "clear, assured expression of language."[100] Wagner, as Beethoven's authorized spokesperson, articulates in the program notes what the music communicates: the death of the Classical symphony and its transfiguration into music drama.

The program notes appeal to two different sets of readers. The interested but uneducated listener is offered a gentle and vividly written account of the Ninth Symphony using extracts from a familiar text. Wagner's speaks not to the reader's "critical faculties" (*kritische Beurteilung*), but "purely to their feelings" (*rein auf das Gefühl*): as if saying, to understand music, all

---

[98] *SSD* II: 60–1.
[99] See Bonds, *Music as Thought*, for a thorough discussion of this process.
[100] "Es scheint dieß wie der letzte Versuch, durch Instrumentalmusik ... freudiges Glück auszudrücken: das unbändige Element scheint aber dieser Beschränkung nicht fähig zu sein ... Da tritt eine menschliche Stimme mit dem klaren, sicheren Ausdruck der Sprache dem Toben der Instrumente entgegen" (*SSD* II: 61).

you need is a heart and everybody has got one.[101] Appealing directly to the consumer's emotions was Wagner's recurring approach. But the same program notes also offer musical sophisticates a glimpse of Wagner's revised aesthetic theory. By weaving Goethe into the fabric of the program notes to complement Schiller's role in the Ninth, Wagner marries the finest German literary tradition with its highest musical expression, a gesture which has as much to do with aiding audience comprehension as it does to prepare it for Wagner's coming attractions.

The program notes also continued to strengthen the association between Wagner and Beethoven's Ninth. They were reprinted on the occasion of future performances of the work, even when Wagner was not at the podium, for instance in Weimar and at the Ballenstedt festival (June 22–3, 1852), not to mention the full reprint of the program notes in the *NZfM* in October 1852 accompanied by Theodor Uhlig's detailed description of the 1846 concert and its circumstances, as part of a multi-installment series on Wagner and Beethoven.[102] But this aspect of Wagner's marketing will be reserved for a more detailed discussion in the next chapter.

The aftermath

Press coverage of the concert was widespread and overwhelmingly positive, despite what one reviewer conceded were the "divided expectations,"[103] and the *NZfM* more accurately described as the attempt "to create an unfavorable atmosphere."[104] With multiple calls for a repeat performance, reviewers, unrestrained in their effusiveness, described the Ninth as a "heavenly dream."[105] Wagner, "unsurpassed,"[106] conducted "masterfully"[107] and received the "roaring applause"[108] of the audience. The Danish composer and conductor, Niels Gade (1817–90), visiting from Leipzig, apparently said that he would gladly have paid admission twice, just to hear the bass and cello recitative again.[109] Particular mention was made of the program notes;

---

[101] *ML* 343.
[102] See *NZfM* 37.13 (September 24, 1852), 37.14 (October 1, 1852), and 37.16 (October 15, 1852).
[103] "geteilte Erwartungen," *Deutsche Allgemeine Zeitung*, April 7, 1846 (repr. Kirchmeyer, III: 47–9).
[104] "eine ungünstige Stimmung zu verbreiten," *NZfM*, May 17, 1846 (repr. Kirchmeyer, III: 73–5).
[105] "göttlichen Traum," *Dresdner Anzeiger*, April 9, 1846 (repr. Kirchmeyer, III: 49) (in *Besprechugen. Privatsachen*).
[106] "unübertrefflich," *Kleine Musikzeitung*, April 19, 1846 (repr. Kirchmeyer, III: 70).
[107] "meisterlich," *Allgemeine Theater-Chronik*, April 13, 1846 (repr. Kirchmeyer, III: 57).
[108] "rauschenden Beifall," *Dresdener Correspondent*, April 10, 1846 (repr. Kirchmeyer, III: 55–6).
[109] Kietz, *Erinnerungen*, 53.

one newspaper even reprinted a large section of Wagner's explanatory introduction.[110]

The press also commented on Wagner's prepublicity and marketing tactics. One lengthy article, describing Wagner as the "Kapellmeister who pushes everything through,"[111] devotes significant space to a discussion of the preparations, musical and otherwise. It describes the "several announcements" that appeared in the *Dresdner Anzeiger*, "each one different in voice to soften up the public for the upcoming concert."[112] With tongue in cheek, the critic acts as if he is the only one to have noticed "that they all originated with the same person, not to mention that his name is known."[113]

Only one lone voice stands out amongst the jubilation: Julius Schladebach. Like Beckmesser, he fumes and stamps at the success he failed to predict or undermine. His five-page harangue, which in part cost him his job at the *Abend-Zeitung*, is by far the longest review of the concert.[114] It would not be worth serious attention were it not an exemplary piece of the anti-Wagneriana that still today continues to be repeated by opponents and is thus integral to the Wagner phenomenon, its necessary companion.

Still, even Schladebach has no choice but to concede the tremendous success of the concert which, he notes, raised more money than any Palm Sunday concert before. With little opportunity for attack, he questions Wagner's methods. Coyly pretending not to know the identity of the authors – "or perhaps there was only one" – he chastises Wagner for the "puffery" of his "anonymous recommendations and encouragements" published "calculatedly" in "detestable" areas of the *Dresdner Anzeiger*.[115] Wagner is a like a "market crier," a "charlatan" who appeals to the masses, and emulates "papal infallibility" by conducting from memory.[116] Certainly this constituted "conduct unbecoming the serious artist" (*des Künstlers ... unwürdig*), and Schladebach now wonders aloud about the source of other

---

[110] *Leipziger Zeitung*, April 9, 1846 (repr. Kirchmeyer, III: 50–5).

[111] "Alles durchsetzenden Kapellmeisters," *Signale für die musikalische Welt*, April 13, 1846, signed Epslein (repr. Kirchmeyer, III: 70–3). "Epslein" was a pseudonym for the Dresden critic Julius Becker (Kirchmeyer I: 643).

[112] "Menge Annoncen" ... "deren jede einen andern Ton anschlug, um das Publikum für das bevorstehende Concert ... windelweich zu machen" (Kirchmeyer I: 643).

[113] "daß sie sämmtlich von einer einzigen Person ausgegangen, geschweige daß man deren Namen kennt" (Kirchmeyer I: 643).

[114] Kirchmeyer, I: 638.

[115] W. J. S. E. [Julius Schladebach], "Das Palmsonntagsconcert," *Abend-Zeitung* (Dresden), April 16, 1846 (repr. Kirchmeyer, III: 57–69, here 62): "marktschreierischen anonymen Empfehlungen und Aufforderungen, welche in sehr umsichtig gewälten Zwischenräumen der 'Dresdener Anzeiger' in seiner detestabeln Rubrik: 'Besprechungen, Privatsachen,' brachte."

[116] Kirchmeyer, III: 57–8.

enthusiastic utterances in the press. He despairs that the uneducated public would allow itself to be taken in by "such morsels, such coarse charlatanry, presented with all the subtlety of a carnival barker,"[117] and he implicitly attacks the program notes for "preaching or whispering an opinion, which can then be parroted." Schladebach may have been the first, though certainly not the last, to accuse Wagner of grandstanding, demagoguery and other base means of arousing popular sentiment.[118] Already in 1846, the dismissal of Wagner as nothing but smoke and mirrors (*selbsterregte Dampf und Qualm*) had made its way into print.

Looking back

From comments in the press, it is clear that Wagner's anonymity was already compromised before the concert; Wagner also mentions the notices in his autobiography. But no sources state how many notes were published. Wagner's first multi-volume biographer, Carl Friedrich Glasenapp, talks of three (he misses the last one on April 4), an oversight formalized in the posthumously added volume XII of Wagner's *Collected Works*, which also only reprints the first three.[119]

Helmut Kirchmeyer was the first to discover the fourth note.[120] Nevertheless, the omission perpetuates itself, even in landmark biographies written after the 1972 publication of Kirchmeyer's encyclopedic archival work.[121] This oversight misses both an essential element of Wagner's marketing acumen – to draw the public into the dress rehearsal – and epitomizes the ongoing problem of Wagner scholarship: its chronic imprecision, the unquestioned perpetuation of misinformation, as well as the unreliability even of purportedly source materials, like the *Sämtliche Schriften und Dichtungen*. The oversight, and the century it took to correct, also underscores the lack of interest, if not discomfort, in examining Wagner's marketing tactics.

Wagner is partly to blame, for instance explaining the anonymous notes as a way "of drawing the public's attention to the work which, up till then

---

[117] Kirchmeyer, III: 62.
[118] See Kröplin, *Richard Wagner*, 17–18. Kröplin never connects these issues with the notion of marketing.
[119] *SSD* XII: 205–7.
[120] Kirchmeyer, I: 629.
[121] For example Gregor-Dellin, *Richard Wagner*, 220. Most recently, Walter Hansen, *Richard Wagner: Biographie* (Munich: dtv, 2006), 132.

suffered from ill repute in Dresden – as I had been led to believe."[122] All in the service of Beethoven, of course. Critics have continued this line of argumentation. Eichhorn contends that Wagner "consciously" inaugurated "a performance tradition of the Ninth in opposition to the prevailing Mendelssohn school."[123] For Eichhorn, this has to do with "music politics" (*musikpolitische Tendenz*). Similarly, he is concerned only with the aesthetic merits of Wagner's program notes, which are "intimately connected to his study of the score" and "inseparable from his personal artistic preparations."[124]

Gregor-Dellin briefly concedes that Wagner proved to be a "professional advertiser" (*Werbefachmann*) who launched what "for its time was a unique campaign."[125] But only Helmut Kirchmeyer seems to appreciate sufficiently Wagner's overall strategy "to sensationalize" the Palm Sunday concert, to make it "a topic of conversation."[126] Although Kirchmeyer does not analyze the four notices individually, he recognizes Wagner's instinct "for playing on the human weakness" of needing to be part of an "event" (*Ereignis*) where "anyone who was anyone had to attend."[127] Even the "controversy served Wagner as negative publicity," ultimately making "Beethoven's success Wagner's success."[128] "Wagner transformed the question of the concert into an issue of his own personality, making the whole event more about Wagner than about Beethoven."[129] Liszt was accused of the same by his contemporaries following the 1845 Beethoven festival in Bonn.[130]

When it comes to the program notes, Kirchmeyer again sees their meta-aesthetic value as "distraction-therapy" (*Beschäftigungstherapie*) to keep the audience from boredom or, worse, vocal demonstrations of criticism.[131] The program is part of Wagner's "psychologically calculated campaign to influence the public using stimulants little known back then."[132] Kirchmeyer's

---

[122] "durch allerhand kurzbündige und enthusiastische Ergüsse das Publikum auf das ... 'verrufene' Werk anregend hinzuweisen." See "Bericht über die Aufführung der neunten Symphonie von Beethoven im Jahre 1846 in Dresden (aus meinen Lebenserinnerungen ausgezogen) nebst Programm dazu" (*SSD* II: 50–64); also *ML* 341–6, here 343.
[123] Eichhorn, *Beethovens Neunte*, 72.
[124] *Ibid.*, 75.
[125] Gregor-Dellin, *Richard Wagner*, 220.
[126] Kirchmeyer, I: 628.
[127] Kirchmeyer, I: 629.
[128] Kirchmeyer, I: 628.
[129] Kirchmeyer, I: 632–3.
[130] "Beethoven festival in support of Liszt," in Ryan Minor, "Prophet and Populace in Liszt's 'Beethoven' Cantatas," in *Franz Liszt and His World*, ed. Gibbs and Gooley, 118.
[131] Kirchmeyer, I: 631 and 633.
[132] Kirchmeyer, I: 631.

attention to Wagner's public-relations efforts in no way invalidates Eichhorn's emphasis on the aesthetics, but the rarity of observations such as his reflects a troublesome habit in scholarship to ignore the pragmatic side of Wagner's activities.

Even Wagner is less reluctant than his critics in this regard, though his conduct had changed between the 1844 Weber episode and the 1846 concert. While he had placed his person at the forefront of the Weber celebration, overstated his role in its organization, and published all the music and texts he generated for the memorial, he was now more nuanced. The four newspaper notices focus attention exclusively on Beethoven, briefly mentioning the orchestra in the first, but never the conductor. The program notes similarly focus instead on Beethoven, Goethe, and Schiller. Even the prefatory justification uses passive, modal and infinitive constructions, making Wagner linguistically all but invisible.

Later, in his collected works, Wagner would publish the program notes and a narrative description of the concert, thematizing the resistance he overcame and the personal risk he took.[133] Against all odds, just like Beethoven. But he did not publish the newspaper announcements: was he embarrassed? And yet, looking back, Wagner admits that "the performance provided me with very influential experiences for my entire subsequent development."[134] "This [Dresden] experience confirmed the comforting feeling that I had the ability and strength to push through whatever I earnestly desired with irresistible good fortune."[135] Still ahead lay the unrealized goal of turning his own works into a similar success: "This was and remained the secret question upon which my life developed long-term."[136]

We should not underrate this all but explicit admission that successful marketing was Wagner's "secret" agenda lifelong. The 1846 concert anticipates much of the theory conceived and written during Wagner's exile in Switzerland between 1849 and 1852. The next chapter will deal in detail with these theories and the ways in which Wagner began to "sell" his *Ring* project.

---

[133] "ward somit für mich in jeder erdenklichen Hinsicht zu einer Ehrensache, deren Gelingen alle meine Kräfte anspannte" (*ML* 342).

[134] "Diese Aufführung brachte mir … für meine ganze weitere Entwickelung sehr einflußreiche Erfahrungen ein" (*ML* 341).

[135] "In mir bestärkte sich bei dieser Gelegenheit das wohltuende Gefühl der Fähigkeit und Kraft, das, was ich ernstlich wollte, mit unwiderleglich glücklichem Gelingen durchzuführen" (*ML* 346).

[136] "Das war und blieb die geheime Frage, an welcher sich mein ferneres Leben entwickelte" (*ML* 346).

3 | Niche and branding

The period around 1850 marked not only a new and more aggressive phase in Wagner's own promotion of his persona and work, but was a watershed in the marketing of the Wagner phenomenon *per se*. In the space of less than three years, Wagner came to dominate the music-cultural scene of the German-speaking world and beyond in ways that perhaps no composer or cultural figure before him had. He was fortunate to have committed supporters on his side, because he could not have accomplished this alone. These included figures of stature, foremost Franz Liszt, as well as those who simply had access to what we call "the media," foremost Theodor Uhlig. If there was a single moment when the "Wagner Industry" (as we know it today) was born, it was at this time when the constellation of his own efforts, those of his advocates, and the possibilities offered by the media combined to produce an unprecedented effect.

That effect was immediate. On February 11, 1853, the *Neue Zeitschrift für Musik* published as its lead article a letter to the editor which announced that Richard Wagner "postulates an artwork which at its very foundation has no competition with any other."[1] The letter was written by Joachim Raff, Franz Liszt's assistant in Weimar, and a composer in his own right. Wagner was not impressed with Raff and found his article "disheartening."[2] Maybe Raff hit a nerve? By using a term – "competition" – also associated with the business world, Raff, perhaps inadvertently, captured something essential about Wagner's efforts during his first years in exile between 1849 and 1852.

Wagner used this time to produce his main theoretical texts. Often referred to in German as the "Zürcher Kunstschriften," these include *Art and Revolution* (1849), *The Artwork of the Future* (1850), the mammoth three-part *Opera and Drama* (1852), and his *Communication to my Friends* (1852).[3] They range in content from sweeping archeologies, to ideological

---

[1] "An die Redaction der *NZfM*," *NZfM* 37.8 (February 11, 1853): "postulirt ein Kunstwerk, welches sich von Hause aus außer Concurrenz aller übrigen stellt" (66).
[2] Letter to Franz Brendel, March 19, 1853 (*SB* V: 226).
[3] I cite the year these works were published – i.e. appeared in print for public consumption and discussion – rather than the more commonly cited date they were written.

and sociological commentary, but primarily contain an exposition and defense of Wagner's forthcoming aesthetic direction which proclaimed the death of opera and the creation of a new kind of artwork. This was also when he wrote his notorious anti-Semitic tirade: "Jewishness in Music" ("Das Judentum in der Musik" [1850]).[4] Long considered an anomaly by Wagner apologists, I suggest that it was integral to his undertaking.

These texts alone constitute a substantial body of writing but, perhaps more significantly, they generated even more text in the form of support and criticism, so that Raff's comment resonates with the aura surrounding Wagner's publications and the heated discourse they precipitated. The fact that Raff wrote to Franz Brendel, editor of the *NZfM*, was part of this effort.

From 1850 on, Brendel increasingly devoted space – often the cover story – to articles written by Wagner or about him, principally by Wagner's faithful Dresden friend, Theodor Uhlig. This represented nothing less than a drastic shift from the *NZfM*'s former relatively balanced – though still agenda-driven – focus on the classic masters, above all Beethoven, as well as a variety of contemporary composers and issues.[5] In a sequence of two New Year's editorials, January 1852 and 1853, Brendel articulates "a *new program*" (*ein neues Programm*) which merely states the obvious to anyone who had been reading his journal for the previous two years. Brendel's 1852 formulation was still rather general: "henceforth, this journal assumes the task of decisively representing to all concerned the approaching transformation of art" (*Diese Blätter haben fortan die Aufgabe, die Umgestaltung, welche der Kunst bevorsteht, nach allen Seiten hin entschieden zu vertreten*).[6] But, in 1853, he openly declares "partisanship on Wagner's behalf" (*die Parteinahme für Wagner*).[7]

The *NZfM*'s intense advocacy for Wagner is unprecedented – and quite possibly unsurpassed – in the history of music journalism. Between 1850 and 1852, there is hardly a month without a major Wagner piece. This prompted an equal and opposite reaction from other journals, perhaps foremost the *Rheinische Musikzeitung*. The noise generated around Wagner's person and works in the span of a few years saturated the music and culture media to such an extent that one dismayed critic wrote in 1853, "Wagner, always

---

[4] I prefer "Jewishness" to the standard translation "Judaism," see my "Note on translation."
[5] For a detailed discussion of the *NZfM* and its transformation between 1848 and 1850, see Sanna Pederson, "Romantic and Enlightened German Music Criticism, 1800–1850," Ph.D. diss., University of Pennsylvania, 1995.
[6] Franz Brendel, "Zum neuen Jahr," *NZfM* 36.1 (January 1, 1852), 4. (Emphasis in the original.)
[7] Franz Brendel, "Zum neuen Jahr," *NZfM* 38.1 (January 1, 1853), 2. (Emphasis in the original.)

Wagner!" (*Wagner und immer Wagner!*) sighing that there was "now no way around" what Raff later termed "The Wagner Question" anymore.[8]

Wagner seems at times to have been uncomfortable with the situation. Sensing the direction of the *NZfM* already in April 1851, Wagner wrote to Uhlig that he did not want the journal to be seen "as a party organ for me and my direction,"[9] begging Uhlig "for heaven's sake don't use the journal for any more polemics!"[10] But did Wagner really mean it? One year later, in January 1852, Wagner pleads with Uhlig: "write as much as you can about me, so that the music journals are filled and I'll at least be really famous."[11] Then, a year later, shortly after Uhlig's untimely death in January 1853, Wagner again with apparently changed heart wrote directly to Brendel to leave his person out of the discussion and focus solely on the matter (*die Sache*), and that "it's really not necessary for you to talk so much about me."[12]

But Wagner's protests ring hollow, especially considering how much he sought attention, and to what extent he fed Uhlig the lines which would later appear in print under Uhlig's name. Wagner constantly placed demands on Uhlig during the key years from 1850 to 1852, requests for professional support which continued unabated even as Uhlig lay on his deathbed, albeit unbeknownst to Wagner.[13] At the same time, Wagner was not always happy with the kind of attention he received, especially blatant declarations of partisanship, and with the lack of sophistication that characterized much of the discussion about his person and works. All manner of discursive devices were employed in the press: militaristic, political, religious and ideological analogies and metaphors were commonly used in what appeared at the time to be a total war between points of view. Even today, martial terms, such as the "War of the Romantics," and political-ideological ones like

---

[8] "Zur Würdigung Richard Wagner's," *NZfM* 38.19 (May 6, 1853), 201, "daß sich das musikalische Interesse zunächst um ihn gruppirt, daß jede allgemeinere Frage in Zusammenhang mit den von ihm angeregten gebracht werden, wie umgekehrt jede Erörterung über ihn auf die allgemeinen Voraussetzungen der Kunst zurückführen muß … Er ist also nicht zu umgehen." See also Joachim Raff, *Die Wagnerfrage* (1854). Liszt makes fun of this title in his letter to Wagner of February 21, 1854.

[9] Letter to Uhlig, April 19, 1851: "als parteiblatt für mich und meine richtung" (*SB* III: 553).

[10] Letter to Uhlig, March 10, 1851: "um Gottes willen führe in diesem blatte aber nur keine polemik mehr!" (*SB* III: 524).

[11] Letter to Uhlig, January [ ],1852: "schreibt nur wenigstens recht viel über mich, daß die musikalischen Zeitungen recht voll, und ich wenigstens recht berühmt werde" (*SB* IV: 247–8).

[12] Letters to Brendel, February 2, 1853, and February 7, 1853: "Es ist wirklich nicht nöthig, daß Sie über mich speciell so viel bringen" (*SB* V: 174).

[13] See, for example, Wagner's letter to Uhlig, December 24, 1852.

"propaganda" continue to appear in academic discourse on the subject.[14] Far less common, then as now, were analogies to business and the market, which is perhaps why Wagner was all the more perturbed by Raff's comment about "competition."

But Raff got it right when he hinted at the issue of "competing" products, because Wagner's writings from this period constitute a concerted effort to brand his compositions with a trademark concept and, in the process, to create for himself a singular niche in the world of music and theater that still today continues to exert its claims to uniqueness. It is from the perspective of "conquering" *the market* that we should, for instance, understand the martial rhetoric. Wagner, his allies, and their adversaries were not only engaged in a war of ideas but, and this is my point, a struggle to gain or hold on to ground in what was turning out to be the increasingly lucrative business of opera and its various secondary spin-offs, such as piano reductions of selected hits. In this struggle, Wagner behaved like a guerrilla, an outlaw often engaging in verbal "terrorist" tactics, a term he even uses in a letter to Liszt (*künstlerischen terrorismus*).[15] But, like a latter-day Robin Hood, he believed he was on the side of truth and righteousness and, as such, sought the sympathy, understanding and support which desperate heroes battling against the superior and entrenched forces of the status quo often desire.

Wagner: outlaw

Fleeing an arrest warrant following the failed uprising in Dresden during May 1849, Wagner escaped with little else but his life. Propelled out of his comfortable niche as Royal Kapellmeister, Wagner suddenly found himself out of work and quite literally an outlaw. To his wife Minna's dismay, he would later describe this precarious situation as a "liberation" (*Befreiung*).[16] He capitalized on this outlaw status and made disregard of rule and convention the essential principle of his ethical conduct and aesthetic practice.

Though Dresden had given him the recognition and the security he had failed to acquire in Paris, Wagner had yet to find a situation that suited his aspirations, as his writings even before the uprising already indicate. Despite the polar opposites that Paris and Dresden represented – freelance

---

[14] James Deaville, "The Controversy Surrounding Liszt's Conception of Programme Music," *Nineteenth-Century Music: Selected Proceedings of the Tenth International Conference*, ed. Jim Samson and Bennett Zon (Aldershot: Ashgate, 2002), 98–124, here 105.
[15] Letter to Liszt, June 5, 1849 (*SB* III: 74).
[16] See also letter to Röckel, August 24, 1851.

work in the international operatic metropolis versus a salaried position at a large and distinguished German court – both represented socio-economic states and relationships between art and life that Wagner rejected: Paris as the capital of the modern music industry, Dresden as an antiquated remnant of feudalism. Both stood for convention, for existing business models and music markets, however different. Wagner's attempt in 1848 to reform the Dresden theater was met with "derision" (*Hohn*)[17] by his bosses, perpetuating the pattern of disappointment, rejection, even humiliation – already the story of his Paris stay. Subtext: there was no existing place on earth for Wagner, so he would have to make one for himself. Wagner was all about not fitting in, being unconventional, new and "extraordinary."

Wagner's claim of extraordinariness – meaning simply "out of the ordinary" as well as "marvelous," but also "breaking (out of) the ordinary" – takes place on many levels. On the surface it concerns his pioneering aesthetic theories and their socio-historical justification. This is how he wanted to be read and, for the most part, how critics have read him since. More insidiously, part of this aesthetic theory is aimed at destroying and obliterating the competition: Meyerbeer above all. Beyond that, it also stakes out an entirely new terrain (or claims to), where there was quite literally no competition – as Raff suggests so perceptively. This was a solitary and heroic struggle against the behemoth of convention and ordinariness: David against Goliath. Or, in business terms, the energetic innovative "start-up" against the monopolistic mega-corporation: or, more starkly, a mom-and-pop operation against global capital.

Wagner milked the aura of desperation and danger that came with his status as political refugee and exile, and used it to frame his professional and personal existence. One example was the world premiere of his opera *Lohengrin* on August 28, 1850, in Weimar under Liszt's baton. Unable to be present at the launch of his stunning new work, the exile Wagner sat in a Luzern tavern aptly named "Zum Schwan," mentally keeping track of the performance by looking at a watch and imagining the music unfolding, a scene he describes with characteristic detail in his autobiography.[18]

The *Lohengrin* premiere of 1850 was also significant because it was the last new Wagner opera to be performed until *Tristan und Isolde* in 1865. Not that Wagner stopped composing. But his next project – ultimately titled *Der Ring des Nibelungen* – would require more than two decades to complete. It represented the musical and dramatic expression of the ideas articulated in

[17] *SSD* II: 2.
[18] *ML* 465.

his aesthetic treatises which called for nothing less than the death of opera. "With this enterprise," Wagner would "have nothing more to do with our contemporary theater."[19]

Wagner turned his back on both contemporary theater and its urban setting, foremost Paris, and on the whole notion of modernity's new center: the metropolis. Hence Wagner's irritation, dismay and derision when his friends (above all Liszt) insisted that the solution to his stalled career would be a success in Paris.[20] They failed to understand the scope of his undertaking and the radical totality of his "break." In a move both new, yet harking back to an older modus, Wagner would eventually set up his "court" – perhaps "hub" would be more apt – in the provinces. Rather than compete during the regular season, approximately September to June, Wagner chose the late summer. The theater he built would also break with convention by eliminating social stratification: no more boxes.[21] Thinking "outside the box" in every respect, Wagner not only reconceived the location, the timing, and the venue but more importantly the genre and its rationale. Even before Nietzsche's bold call for a "reevaluation of all values," Wagner's conception was to be so radical, so radically different, that he famously declared in *A Communication to my Friends* that he would no longer be writing operas[22] – at least, this is how he would market himself: Wagner the aesthetic and political outlaw.

Art and politics

This link between art and politics is reflected in the title of Wagner's first major treatise written and published after he escaped into exile: *Art and Revolution*. The theme was already central to Schiller's theoretical work between 1795 and 1796. In his *Aesthetic Letters*, written in the wake of the disastrous turn taken by the French Revolution, Schiller proposed using art rather than violence as a means of transforming the corroded political and social constitution which, in his view, characterized modernity. To restore the more harmonious order which he located in ancient Greece, Schiller advocated a "sentimental" art, not a "realistic" or "naïve" portrayal of the world as it is, but a tendentious art that would show the world as it should be. In *Art and Revolution* Wagner takes up this idea almost

---

[19] *SSD* IV: 595.
[20] See letter to Röckel, August 24, 1851.
[21] See *Das Kunstwerk der Zukunft*, *SSD* III: 160.
[22] "Ich schreibe keine Opern mehr" (*SSD* IV: 345).

verbatim.[23] But the idealism of Schiller's age had been eroded in the wake of Napoleon's defeat and the oppressive restoration of the *ancien régime*. By contrast, "Young Germans," a group of authors, thinkers, and artists to which Wagner also belonged, sought political solutions to political problems. Many of them were progressive nationalists who advocated varying combinations of parliamentary system and constitutional monarchy. Some, like Karl Marx, proposed even more radical solutions to the social and political crises triggered both by repression and by the demographic shifts caused by industrialization.

When in *Art and Revolution*, Wagner writes "thus the poet's art has become political: no one can write without politicizing,"[24] he simultaneously echoes Schiller, reflects his own "Zeitgeist," but also anticipates Walter Benjamin's often quoted, though not unproblematic, distinction in the twentieth century between the Nazi "aestheticization of politics" and the Communist "politization of aesthetics."[25] But Wagner is neither cloaking a political campaign with an art that beguiles and entices, nor is he proposing a new more politically committed form of artwork, some precursor to *agitprop*.

Instead, his political stance frames an archeological project which, like Schiller's, locates in ancient Greece the original perfected work of art. According to Wagner's account, ancient Greek drama, which he refers to as the *Gesammtkunstwerk*, was a fusion of sight, sound, and verbal text, performed for free to the entire *Volk* during a festival, and functioned as a communal event reflective of a socially and politically harmonious culture. Already in the early part of the nineteenth century, a tradition of music festivals sprang up around Germany, communal events where mainly amateur musicians performed, reminiscent of ancient Greek festivals even for contemporaries.[26] (The importance of these festivals as a conceptual model for Bayreuth has not been sufficiently explored.)

In Wagner's reading, ancient Greek principles were shattered with the arrival of the materialistic Romans and, subsequently, of the life-hating Christians. The former caused art to break up into its constituent self-serving

---

[23] Wagner reproduces this argument as follows: "Zur Zeit ihrer Blüthe war die Kunst bei den Griechen daher konservativ, weil sie dem öffentlichen Bewußtsein als ein gültiger und entsprechender Ausdruck vorhanden war: bei uns ist die echte Kunst revolutionär, weil sie nur im Gegensatze zur gültigen Allgemeinheit existirt" (*SSD* III: 28).

[24] "So ist die Kunst des Dichters zur Politik geworden: Keiner kann dichten, ohne zu politisiren" (*SSD* IV: 53).

[25] See also Philippe Lacoue-Labarthe, *Musica Ficta: (Figures of Wagner)*, trans. Felicia McCarren (Stanford University Press, 1994), 17–18.

[26] Bonds, *Music as Thought*, 92–9.

branches, while the latter killed its life-affirming spirit. Wagner describes the history of art's fragmentation as a Tower of Babel (*Thurmbau zu Babel*) to emphasize the idea of moral decline.[27] He then offers a critique of modernity common to German thought from the late eighteenth century to the present day, which bewails the impact of "progress": alienation, depersonalization, social problems, pollution. For Wagner, art follows an identical trajectory: freed from the slavery of medieval patronage it has become the whore of "industry":[28]

The decline of tragedy is exactly concurrent with the dissolution of the Athenian State. Just as the communal spirit was shattered into a thousand egocentric directions, the *Gesamtkunstwerk* of tragedy dissolved into its constituent individual artforms.[29]

As with Schiller, for Wagner, art, politics and morality form a reciprocal triadic constellation:

Behold the art that fills the civilized world of today! Its true essence is industry, its moral goal is profits, its aesthetic purport is the diversion of the bored.[30]

Now, as then, the theater captures perfectly the essence of the social constitution. Divided in modernity between spoken theater and opera, the former has lost the musical component while the latter has been robbed of drama: both serve merely to entertain and distract a public, tired after a long day of activity. Art has been prostituted as a commercial object and the artist degraded into a mere tradesman working for pay. In Wagner's combined moral, political, and aesthetic judgment, this condition epitomized in Paris exemplifies the profit-driven entertainment scene of the new bourgeois age. But he also indicts the emergent *l'art pour l'art* movement for preaching a separation between the artwork and life. The "absolute [i.e. self-contained] artwork" and the "absolute artist" – a term he coined – characterizes the isolated condition and isolationist attitude of the elitist artist in modernity.[31]

The anticipated revolution will effect a *tabula rasa*, sweeping away an entire establishment along with its representative works of art. In its place will come the "artwork of the future" (*Kunstwerk der Zukunft*).[32] Wagner's

---

[27] See *SSD* III: 76.
[28] *SSD* III: 18.
[29] *SSD* III: 12. Repeated in *SSD* III: 29.
[30] "Das ist die Kunst, wie sie jetzt die ganze civilisirte Welt erfüllt! Ihr wirkliches Wesen ist die Industrie, ihr moralischer Zweck der Gelderwerb, ihr ästhetisches Vorgeben die Unterhaltung der Gelangweilten" (*SSD* III: 19).
[31] *SSD* IV: 234 and 247; Borchmeyer, *Theater Richard Wagners*, 103.
[32] *SSD* III: 30.

term used here for the first time was a variation of an idea in circulation for a while. Nevertheless, it was Wagner's term that was taken and, in its perverted form, *Zukunftsmusik* (music of the future), became the buzzword for the warring factions.[33]

Though so little of what Wagner wrote was conceptually original, he would soon fuse ideas of aesthetic revolution, artwork of the future, and festival, combining them into a single concept and transforming them into a reality that continues to be uniquely Wagner.

Packaging (words before music)

The unsuccessful uprising and the flight into exile doubtless focused Wagner's emphasis on revolution. But, as we already saw in the case of Paris, Wagner would again characterize the act of writing as a sacrifice. Given the fear that his works might not be staged, given his status as wanted fugitive, he was now "merely … a writer" (*nur als Schriftsteller*) and he would complain that writing was a chore.[34] Again circumstances "forced" Wagner to write instead of compose.[35] I will not speculate on whether the desperation, with which Wagner characterizes the necessity to turn to explanatory prose, was genuine or contrived. As with Berlioz, complaints about "having to write" mask a need to communicate verbally and a sense of pleasure and empowerment at being able to do so, a thrill Wagner voices in a letter to Uhlig: "I am overflowing with the necessity to write again."[36] Indignation was a pose to preserve the "integrity" of the artist as creator of self-sufficient works (i.e. not requiring explanation).

Writing about the artwork before creating it was a relatively new practice. As already discussed in Chapter 1, the habit of conceptualizing

---

[33] See Deaville "Programme Music" for a valuable discussion of the journalistic fireworks on either side of this debate. Herbert Schneider discusses "Zukunftsmusik" and shows how permutations of the term, especially in French, can be found in the 1840s and without any reference to Wagner, see "Wagner, Berlioz, und die Zukunftsmusik," *Liszt und die neudeutsche Schule*, ed. Detlef Altenburg (Laaber: Laaber, 2006), 77–95.

[34] "welche Pein diese Art der Mittheilung für mich ausmacht, brauche ich Denen, die mich als Künstler kennen, wohl nicht erst zu versichern" (*SSD* IV: 572).

[35] "Das Gefühl der Nothwendigkeit meiner Empörung machte mich zunächst zum Schriftsteller" (*SSD* IV: 262). The Paris and Exile periods may have been linked in Wagner's mind (see Wagner, *Oper und Drama*, ed. Kropfinger, 430).

[36] Letter to Uhlig, December 27, 1849: "nach allen seiten hin quillt in mir die nothwendigkeit hervor, wieder zu schreiben" (*SB* III: 197). On Berlioz, see Bloom, *Life of Berlioz*, 75, and Holoman, *Berlioz*: "Berlioz enjoyed newspaper work, I think, more than he was prepared to admit" (237).

and articulating an aesthetic agenda before the corresponding artwork was created had become a hallmark of the avant-garde. The genre of the theoretical manifesto, pioneered by German Romantic authors starting around 1800, may have been imbued with the aura of pecuniary disinterestedness, but nevertheless functioned as an ideal "advertising medium" (*Werbemedium*),[37] because "the work's value is defined" by its ability to "generate discourse."[38]

As early as 1842, Wagner admits, his prose works helped him "considerably to become known and respected in Paris."[39] Already then, Wagner used the medium and the media to explain his aesthetic taste and creative process, publicize his existence, promote his compositions, and fashion himself as a public personality.

A decade later, while in Zurich, his series of theoretical and autobiographical publications "established Wagner's public image."[40] Typically, this comment by Dieter Borchmeyer does not refer to self-marketing. Instead, he is perturbed that Wagner's image was based on misunderstandings caused by the works' "titles and by the utopian concept – spread more by hearsay than by first-hand reading – of a music drama that would unify all the arts."[41] For Borchmeyer, this (false) public image of Wagner was an unintended consequence of a genuine project of aesthetic revolution. Perhaps. But Wagner overwhelmed the media with text: small wonder that it was not all read. Borchmeyer's friendly echo of Wagner's constant complaint that he was misunderstood by those who either had not read his writings at all, or with sufficient care, perpetuates Wagner's self-generated image of victimization.[42]

Even Wagner admitted that writing, a project in its own right, had "grown larger than initially anticipated."[43] Writing was evidently Wagner's way of working out ideas. His essays thrill with their conviction, illuminating insights, and compact thoughts, but they also frustrate with murky, unwieldy

---

[37] Anke Finger, *Das Gesamtkunstwerk der Moderne* (Göttingen: Vandenhoeck & Ruprecht, 2006), 51.
[38] Mann, *Theory-Death*, 23.
[39] *SSD* I: 17.
[40] Borchmeyer, in Richard Wagner, *Dichtungen und Schriften*, 10 vols., ed. Dieter Borchmeyer (Frankfurt am Main: Insel, 1983), X: 303 (hereinafter *DS*).
[41] Borchmeyer, *DS* X: 303.
[42] "Das unerträglich klare Wissen hiervon verleidete mir von Neuem mein Vorhaben; ich griff – im Gefühle davon, daß ich in meinem Streben meist doch noch so gänzlich misverstanden würde – wieder zur Schriftstellerei, und schrieb mein Buch über 'Oper und Drama'" (*SSD* IV: 337). See also Richard Wagner, *Oper und Drama*, ed. and commentary Klaus Kropfinger (Stuttgart: Reclam, 1984), 431 and 433.
[43] "Meine arbeit über das wesen der oper … dehnt sich zu größerem umfange aus, als ich anfangs vermuthete," Letter to Liszt, November 25, 1850 (*SB* III: 467).

expositions and opaque even incoherent ruminations. Rather than refine what he had written, he published and then moved on to the next work, suggesting not merely his impatience but also his concern to remain in the public eye ceaselessly. Wagner reveals this strategy to Uhlig with disarming clarity: "it's the one thing that makes sense and has a purpose right now: this is not the time to create the artwork, but rather to prepare it."[44]

By contrast, Robert Bailey argues that "Wagner made sketches for the music of *Siegfrieds Tod* before he had written *Opera and Drama*," making the treatise "to some extent the result of at least some practical experience in working out a new manner of writing musical drama, rather than purely a presentation of theoretical ideas in advance, as we have always supposed."[45] Bailey may be chronologically correct, but he misses an important point. Even if there may have been some exceptions, Wagner's publication of all manner of prose – essays, treatises, books, journal articles, occasional pieces, even originally private letters – served to promote and advertise products often not yet available to the public. In the age of cinema this technique is known as a "preview of coming attractions." There was no precedent for what Wagner did, nor has any creative artist since managed anything quite on the same scale.

This strategy caused a considerable amount of confusion at the time. In the absence of new theatrical works, readers compared Wagner's aesthetic ruminations to his existing operas. Despite the stunning musical language and vivid orchestral sounds he had begun to conceive between *The Flying Dutchman* (1843), *Tannhäuser* (1845), and *Lohengrin* (1850), it was not clear how the radical new theories related to these pieces. Of course, they were not supposed to. More than anything, Wagner was developing his forthcoming *Ring* project.

Made in Germany

If exile status provided Wagner with the reason for writing his prose works, their content was sociologically a reaction to the failure of the 1848–9 revolutions to solve the German problem, aesthetically a response to the inordinate operatic success of Meyerbeer's latest work, *Le prophète*, which also premiered in 1849. Though the conceptual seeds of Wagner's Zurich

---

[44] Letter to Uhlig, December 27, 1849: "es jetzt das einzige ist was sinn und wirklichen zweck hat: das kunstwerk kann jetzt nicht geschaffen, sondern nur vorbereitet werden" (*SB* III: 197).
[45] Robert Bailey, "Wagner's Musical Sketches for *Siegfrieds Tod*," *Studies in Music History. Essays for Oliver Strunk*, ed. Harold Powers (Princeton University Press, 1968), 459–94, here 462.

works are already evident from 1840 on, Wagner had nevertheless continued to operate within the existing market up to this point. But now, Wagner declared his break with conventional theater, mapping out his proposed alternative path. In the process, he transformed himself into a brand, filling a specially constructed niche in the opera world with his trademark works.

This transformation was a complex revolutionary process of de(con)-struction and separation on the one hand, and niche creation on the other, with Meyerbeer and Germanness serving as crucial polarizing ideas. Although an aesthetic product was at issue, Wagner used every rhetorical device: non-aesthetic terms, cultural tropes, gendered metaphors, and even biological language in order to stage his argument.

The Wagner brand was based on the claim that his persona and works were "truly" German. In his diary entry for September 11, 1865, he writes: "I am the most German of all; I am the German spirit. Just look at the unparalleled magic of *my* works; compare them with all the others: for now you can say nothing other than – it is *German*."[46] This was nothing new. As we have seen, Germanness was already central to his "Pilgrimage" essay of 1840 and, later, in his instrumentalization of Weber at the 1844 reinterment in Dresden.

For Wagner (and not only for him), Germanness had both a national and a universal dimension – more narrowly in contrast to the national culture of France, more broadly to the Jews who function as the "universal" Other.[47] In both senses, Wagner would stand for Germanness, while Meyerbeer embodied national and universal foreignness.

Crucial to his national argument was Wagner's contention that "opera" – which Meyerbeer ruled – was, from the German perspective, a foreign product.[48] The consistent academic practice of calling Wagner's aesthetic writings from this period "Reformschriften" is thus inappropriate. Wagner did not attempt to "reform" opera at all, because it is both alien to the

---

[46] Richard Wagner, *Das braune Buch: Tagebuchaufzeichnungen 1865 bis 1882*, ed. J. Bergfeld (Munich and Zurich: Piper, 1975), 86: "ich bin der deutscheste Mensch, ich bin der deutsche Geist. Fragt den unvergleichlichen Zauber *meiner* Werke, haltet sie mit allen Übrigen zusammen: Ihr könnt für jetzt nichts anderes sagen, als – es ist *deutsch*" (emphasis RW). For more on the nexus between Wagner and Germanness, see Nicholas Vazsonyi, "Marketing German Identity: Richard Wagner's Enterprise," *German Studies Review* 28.2 (2005), 327–46.

[47] Brendel talks of two strands in German music: "eine specifisch deutsche, und eine universelle" in his speech introducing the idea of the "New German School" later published in *NZfM* as: "Zur Anbahnung einer Verständigung" as well as in Pohl, *Die Tonkünstler-Versammlung*, 75–95. See also Rainer Kleinertz, "Zum Begriff 'Neudeutsche Schule,'" in *Liszt und die neudeutsche Schule*, ed. Altenburg, 23–31, here 26.

[48] "Nach Deutschland gelangte die Oper als vollkommen fertiges ausländisches Produkt, dem Charakter der Nation von Grund aus fremd" ("Zukunftsmusik," *SSD* VII: 91).

Germans and a fundamentally flawed aesthetic enterprise (the two are connected). Instead, Wagner declared opera "dead" to make space for something conceptually "brand new": in the long history of attempts at operatic "reform," this was an unprecedented gesture.

Starting in 1840, Wagner appropriates the German symphonic tradition as the musicological basis of his new path. Borrowed from late eighteenth-century discourses concerning the superiority and universality of German instrumental music, subsequently epitomized by the symphonies of Beethoven as interpreted by critics like E. T. A. Hoffmann, Wagner had already added his own dimension to the aesthetic significance of the text in the fourth movement of the Ninth Symphony, as we have seen. Wagner now treated the German language similarly. Whereas the French and Italians had lost contact with their linguistic roots through "racial mixing" (*Völkermischung*), and consequently "no longer speak their own language," the German language remained pure and thus superior.[49] The specter of German linguistic purity based on racial purity is ominous from a post-WWII perspective, but in his *Germania* (AD 98), Tacitus had already defined the Germanic peoples as being of "pure blood" because they refrained from intermarriage. The linguistic argument merely perpetuates and underscores, from an additional angle, Wagner's persistent dichotomies of decay and purity. The new artform would thus combine German, the only remaining "genuine" language,[50] with the universal reach of German symphonic music. Music drama®: made in Germany, for worldwide distribution.

Just as French culture serves as the opposite of Germanness on a national level, Jews become the foil for Germanness as universal principle. As we have seen, Wagner's earliest expressions of anti-Semitism from his days in Paris transformed German-Jewish bankers as a group into foreigners; he even called fellow countryman Rothschild a "Universaljude" (universal Jew). What back then had been a passing comment becomes a core contention in 1850 with the anonymous publication of "Jewishness in Music."

Traditional Wagner scholarship has treated "Jewishness in Music" as an anomaly,[51] separating it from the other programmatically aesthetic writings

---

[49] "von diesen drei Nationen nur die deutsche eine Sprache besitzt, die ... noch unmittelbar und kenntlich mit ihren Wurzeln zusammenhängt" (*SSD* IV: 211).

[50] "von allen modernen Opernsprachen ist nur die deutsche befähigt, in der Weise, wie wir es als erforderlich erkannten, zur Belebung des künstlerischen Ausdruckes verwandt zu werden" (*SSD* IV: 211). Also "das vollendete dramatische Kunstwerk ... könnte ... jetzt nur in deutscher Sprache geschehen" (*SSD* IV: 212).

[51] Most blatantly, Borchmeyer omits the essay from his ten-volume edition of Wagner's writings (*DS*). Weiner rightly argues against Wagner scholarship that "decontextualizes" the work and

of the 1850 period, as if it were "untimely"[52] or constitutes an "abrupt" change of heart,[53] or that Wagner wrote it primarily to work his way out of a creative impasse.[54] Although such designations surely have no exculpatory intent, to label the essay as an "offensively drastic expression of a personal idiosyncrasity,"[55] or as a result of professional frustration which required a "scapegoat"[56] nevertheless does make the sentiment personal and private, even if Wagner's gesture was public. Instead, far from being "merely" an expression of personal feelings, Wagner's essay is an act of professional sabotage, integral to the marketing initiative he undertook at this time.

Wagner's central claim in the essay is that Jews constitute a "foreign element." Foreign not only to Germans, but to all non-Jews. Moreover, this "foreignness" is a quality non-Jews react to "instinctively." This is not a culture-based argument, but rather a proto-racist assertion that Jews are biologically different. Heinrich Laube, Wagner's long-time friend and supporter, had similarly claimed already in 1847 that Jews were a "foreign element" (*ein fremdes Element*), a "totally alien people" (*wildfremde Nationalität*) against whom Germans defend themselves "instinctively" (*instinktmäßig*).[57] He talks of their "deep-seated ways of life" which disturb "us" and which are too embedded to be capable of change. Implicit is that Jews possess "by nature" specific characteristics which conversion to Christianity (i.e. cultural assimilation) cannot erase. As chance would have it, Laube's essay was also an attack on Meyerbeer, this time because he suspected the composer of conspiring to ensure that Laube's play *Struensee* would not be performed so that a play on the same topic by Meyerbeer's deceased brother Michel could be. An act of *ressentiment*, Laube rhetorically transforms his fellow countryman Meyerbeer into a "foreigner," dubbing him "a businessman with Parisian know-how," which succinctly connects Jewishness, the anti-capitalist critique of commerce, with the global capital of sin: Paris.

---

treats it as an "aberration," but he too fails to read the essay within the ongoing anti-Semitic attack on Meyerbeer (*Anti-Semitic Imagination*, 53).

[52] Jacob Katz, *Richard Wagner: Vorbote des Antisemitismus* (Königstein im Taunus: Athenäum, 1985), 40.

[53] Sieghart Döhring, "Meyerbeers Konzeption der historischen Oper und Wagners Musikdrama," *Wagnerliteratur – Wagnerforschung: Bericht über das Wagner-Symposium München 1983*, ed. Carl Dahlhaus and Egon Voss (Mainz: Schott, 2000), 95–100.

[54] Ulrich Drüner, *Schöpfer und Zerstörer: Richard Wagner als Künstler* (Cologne and Weimar: Böhlau 2003), 146–8.

[55] John Deathridge and Carl Dahlhaus, *New Grove Wagner* (New York: W. W. Norton, 1984), 80.

[56] Barry Millington, *Wagner*, rev. edn (Princeton University Press, 1992), 47.

[57] Heinrich Laube, "Einleitung des Verfassers," *Struensee, Gesammelte Werke in 50 Bdn*, ed. Heinrich Hubert Houben (Leipzig: Hesse, 1909), XXIV: 123–45.

Not unlike Laube, Wagner attacks Jews biologically by explaining that "our" objections come from an "instinctive aversion" (*instinktmäßige Abneigung*) and a "natural loathing" (*natürlichen Widerwillen*) because wherever they find themselves, Jews in the Diaspora are always a "foreign element."[58] Importantly, Wagner never refers to "Germans" in his essay, and instead uses an unspecified generic personal pronoun "us" against a Jewish "them." By doing so, Wagner unites all non-Jews (German or otherwise) in an international brotherhood. By precisely not stressing "Germanness" (a point overlooked or misunderstood by most commentators of the work, who read it as an expression of nationalism) Jews become the "universal" other.

This "otherness" is evident both in the way Jews speak the language of the host nations where they reside and in their music.[59] Cultural constructions, such as conversion and baptism cannot efface what is innate. Even the most talented among them (Felix Mendelssohn) proves this. Wagner frames the issue of "instinctive" aversion in terms of preserving art but, with inflammatory exhortations like it is "we who need to be emancipated from the Jews," Wagner is talking about preserving the race.[60]

Paul Rose is mistaken when he polemically paraphrases Wagner's position: "It is real, it is moral, and it is rational."[61] While Wagner does indeed argue that the aversion is "real," the whole point is that it is not "rational": it is biological. "Instinct" is Wagner's trump card, because while rational arguments are subject to debate, there is no way around biology, the "way we are wired." Wagner's emphasis on "instinct" is crucial, and he reinvokes this category to describe his compositional technique and the "feeling-based" response – instead of intellectual "understanding" – he sought from audiences.[62]

Wagner's arguments in "Jewishness in Music" seem counterproductive for a successful marketing campaign in a Germany where anti-Semitism was much less evident than in earlier or later periods, even if this claim of national tolerance by Jacob Katz is overstated.[63] Moreover, the essay

---

[58] "Das Judentum in der Musik," *SSD* V: 67, 69–70.

[59] "Der Jude spricht die Sprache der Nation, unter welcher er von Geschlecht zu Geschlecht lebt, aber er spricht sie immer als Ausländer" (*SSD* V: 70). Also "der Jude [redet] die modernen europäischen Sprachen nur wie erlernte, nicht als angeborene Sprachen" (*SSD* V: 70).

[60] *SSD* V: 68.

[61] Paul Lawrence Rose, *Wagner: Race and Revolution* (New Haven: Yale University Press, 1992), 79.

[62] Wagner writes: "Der Künstler wendet sich an das Gefühl, und nicht an den Verstand" (*Mittheilung, SSD* IV: 232), and talks of "die Gefühlswerdung des Verstandes" (*Oper und Drama, SSD* IV: 78).

[63] For an opposing view, see Rainer Erb and Werner Bergmann, *Die Nachtseite der Judenemanzipation: Der Widerstand gegen die Integration der Juden in Deutschland 1780–1860* (Berlin: Metropol, Veitl, 1989).

does indeed appear anomalous when placed against his contemporaneous writings on aesthetics.

However, "Jewishness in Music" is integral to this undertaking and functions together with *Opera and Drama* as a "one-two punch."[64] It is the devastating first blow, because its proto-racist defamation of Meyerbeer – which sidesteps the substantive aesthetic issues – leaves no recourse for remediation. Because of his Jewishness, Meyerbeer literally "embodies" a morally corrupt and aesthetically sterile genre (sterility caused by corruption). The essay holds little hope for Jews and offers no aesthetic resolution to the problems facing opera.

Wagner was not alone, even though he liked to portray himself as the solitary artist, and even though he has been singled out in the twentieth century's rewriting of history as a leading villain of the nineteenth. The popular success of *Le prophète* provoked a critical backlash, just as *Les Huguenots* a decade earlier. In 1837, Schumann had used his journal to attack Meyerbeer. Now, the current editor, Franz Brendel, used the *NZfM* similarly. Among his most prolific allies was Uhlig, whose friendship with Wagner intensified after his escape from Dresden in 1849.

In April 1850, six months before Wagner wrote "Jewishness," Uhlig began a series of articles for the *NZfM* titled "Zeitgemäße Betrachtungen" (Timely Meditations) declaring categorically, "we are fighting against Meyerbeer" (*Wir bekämpfen Meyerbeer*).[65] Uhlig talks about "the Jewish element in music,"[66] assails Meyerbeer's "unnaturalness,"[67] his "Hebraic taste in art,"[68] his "talent for speculation,"[69] that he composes for "effect at all cost"[70] in response to "the gravitational pull of money bags."[71] As Jens Malte Fischer perceptively notes, Wagner "draws his most important arguments from Theodor Uhlig, right down to the choice of words."[72] Uhlig's term "Hebraic

---

[64] "Doppelschlag," see Jens Malte Fischer, *Richard Wagners "Das Judentum in der Musik": Eine kritische Dokumentation als Beitrag zur Geschichte des Antisemitismus* (Frankfurt am Main: Insel, 2000), 76. Drüner also characterizes the "Judentum" essay as the "polemic" and *Opera and Drama* as the "theoretical" confrontation with the same issue (*Schöpfer*, 139).

[65] T. U. (Theodor Uhlig), "Zeitgemäße Betrachtungen: Reminiscenzen," *NZfM* 32.35 (April 30, 1850), 177.

[66] "das jüdische Element in der Musik," Theodor Uhlig, "Zeitgemäße Betrachtungen: Außerordentliches," *NZfM* 33.7 (July 23, 1850), 29.

[67] "Unnatur," Theodor Uhlig, "Zeitgemäße Betrachtungen: Dramatisch," *NZfM* 32.34 (April 26, 1850), 173.

[68] "hebräischen Kunstgeschmacks" (Uhlig, "Dramatisch," 170).

[69] "Speculations-Talent" (Uhlig, "Außerordentliches," 31).

[70] "Effect um jeden Preis" (Uhlig, "Dramatisch," 171).

[71] "die Anziehungskraft der Geldsäcke" (Uhlig, "Dramatisch," 169).

[72] Fischer, "*Judentum*," 27.

taste in art" provoked its own backlash from other music critics, putting Uhlig on the defensive. Wagner makes a direct reference to the term at the beginning of his essay indicating that he intends to join the discussion. This has prompted some scholars to view Wagner's essay simply as a reaction to and participant in that relatively isolated debate.

But Uhlig's remark was not isolated, and his series of "Timely Meditations" was as much about pushing Wagner as it was about critiquing Meyerbeer: for Uhlig, the two were inseparable. Uhlig had already reviewed *Le prophète* negatively following its Dresden premiere in January 1850,[73] so there needs to have been a reason for him to launch a renewed and more blatantly anti-Semitic attack on Meyerbeer and his opera between April and July. That impetus, I suggest, came from Wagner, who sent Uhlig two inflammatory letters, dated February 24 and March 13, while visiting Paris.[74] Both letters complain of the renewed degradations and frustrations he endured, and both mention the performance of *Le prophète* Wagner saw there. Especially the second letter drips with sarcasm about Meyerbeer's "genius" and the opera as "revelation."[75] Wagner had seen "the prophet of the new world" (*den Propheten der neuen welt*), a pun that quite possibly inspired Uhlig's own refrain for the subsequent article series: "A false prophet is traveling through the regions of a divided and unfree Germany."[76] Since we only have Wagner's side of their by all appearances intense exchange, we are forced to speculate. While Fischer is right to shift the blame and make Uhlig share in the responsibility for the reanimated anti-Semitic discourse directed against Meyerbeer, he did not consider sufficiently their correspondence as another source of mutual

---

[73] Theodor Uhlig, "Der Prophet von Meyerbeer," *NZfM* 32.11 (February 5, 1850).

[74] Stefanie Hein ignores Wagner's letters, and thus treats all of Uhlig's anti-*Prophète* essays as one unbroken sequence, despite the gap in time and the changed titles, see *Richard Wagners Kunstprogramm im nationalkulturellen Kontext: Ein Beitrag zur Kulturgeschichte des 19. Jahrhunderts* (Würzburg: Königshausen & Neumann, 2006), 99–100.

[75] Letter to Uhlig, March 13, 1850 (*SB* III: 249). Sieghart Döhring cites this passage from Wagner's letter at length, but takes it completely seriously ("Meyerbeers Konzeption," 99). Part of the problem is that he misquotes Wagner as having written "immer schwärmen" (a real verb meaning in the context "I will always gush") instead of what Wagner actually wrote, "immer schwärmer" (a non-existent comparative adjective Wagner invents and which would mean "more and more gushy"; Wagner plays with language to poke fun at his preceding effusive comments which are thus not to be taken seriously). Given Döhring's fatal misunderstanding, no wonder he interprets the "Jewishness" essay as an anomaly. But, if one reads Wagner's long letter in toto, his mischevious mood is clear. For instance, he ends his long sign off in overly obsequious French by spelling his name "Richard Vanier."

[76] "Ein falscher Prophet zieht durch die Gauen des uneinigen und unfreien Deutschlands" (Uhlig, "Dramatisch," 169).

encouragement and inspiration.[77] Rather than blame Uhlig for providing Wagner with the vocabulary for "Jewishness in Music," I think it is fairer to suggest that Wagner and Uhlig engaged in a reciprocal exchange which yielded both essays, especially given their mutual objective: the promotion of Wagner and the obliteration of the competition.

This agenda is revealed with some degree of subtlety in a later "Timely Meditation" appropriately subtitled: "Schön" (Beautiful). To contrast with Meyerbeer's tasteless dramatic stagings and musical "effects," Uhlig describes a sublimely simple setting and offers the synopsis of an unidentified opera. Without naming either the composer or the work, Uhlig finally quotes one of its most famous lines: "O! du mein holder Abendstern" (O, beautiful evening star). Then, with quiet understatement, he continues: "Now, Ladies and Gentlemen of Dresden and Weimar, you all know the Wartburg, and you know this *Lied*, so you also know what I am talking about. Is there anyone out there whose heart didn't cry out: Ah, how beautiful this is!"[78]

To the end, the article never reveals that the subject is Richard Wagner and his most recent opera, *Tannhäuser*. Instead, Uhlig declares this work the unmistakable creation of "a true artist, a German artist": all loaded terms, especially when juxtaposed with Meyerbeer whom Uhlig already earlier declared to be "not a priest of true art" and who, because he is Jewish (i.e. foreign), is not a "true" "German."[79] Only Wagner (by now, it is obvious) fulfils the requisite criteria. While Meyerbeer is a foreign import, Wagner is made in Germany.

Wagner®

In stark contrast to Laube's retrospective and rather impotent attack on Meyerbeer for an offense already suffered, Wagner's defamation of Meyerbeer is not engaged with the past. Instead, and this is where Wagner is both different from his contemporaries and new, the attack is preemptive. It functions to clear Meyerbeer and his products out of the way so that the resulting void may be filled by none other than Wagner's own artworks

---

[77] More recently, Eva Martina Hanke has relied heavily on Fischer in her discussion of Wagner's essay, and so attributes Wagner's impetus based solely on his reading of Uhlig's essays in the *NZfM*, see her *Wagner in Zürich – Individuum und Lebenswelt* (Kassel: Bärenreiter, 2007), 308–12.
[78] Theodor Uhlig, "Zeitgemäße Betrachtungen: Schön," *NZfM* 32.43 (May 28, 1850), 218.
[79] Uhlig, "Dramatisch," 170 and 173.

of the future, works which were only just being composed. I suspect that Uhlig, acting as Wagner's passionate accomplice, was only dimly aware of the strategy.

The echo of Uhlig's anti-Meyerbeer campaign at the heart of Wagner's "Jewishness in Music" is remarkable enough, but in the massive tome *Opera and Drama* which Wagner began to draft immediately thereafter, Uhlig's inflammatory terms "unnaturalness," "speculation," "effect" find not only their repetition, but their exploration and elaboration.[80]

Pleading that he does not intend to attack Meyerbeer or his operas, merely to discuss them as representative of a modern malady, Wagner sets out to assassinate and bury both.[81] Opera composers are not artists, but mere craftsmen because they "speculate on the public."[82] Their works mere "products of fashion"[83] calculated for "effect" only, a term Wagner famously defines as "producing results without cause."[84] He declares the competition *passé* in order to create as much distance between it and the "new" product he is pushing: "drama." He slanders opera as both conceptually and tangibly "unnatural," the outcome of an "unnatural" partnership between composer and librettist, what Wagner homophobically terms a "barren insanity."[85] Opera represents a form of original sin[86] given the flawed intentions and false consciousness of its beginnings as court entertainment, making it an immoral expression of "luxury and splendor."[87] (Quite an astounding charge, given Wagner's personal tastes.) "Opera has no historical [meaning: natural] origins; it did not originate from the *Volk*, but rather from artificial arbitrariness."[88] Instead of creating art "organically," opera composers construct mechanisms, an analogy that recalls Victor Frankenstein. Modern opera is a monstrosity, revealing "the whole *monstrous* development of

---

[80] This is not the place to analyze *Opera and Drama*'s aesthetics, mostly because it has been done before and more thoroughly than the focus of this book allows. My discussion limits itself to the work's relevance for Wagner's twin undertaking to establish himself as a brand and carve out a niche for his works. Consult Borchmeyer, *Das Theater Richard Wagners*; Rainer Francke, *Richard Wagners Zürcher Kunstschriften* (Hamburg: Wagner, 1983); Jean-Jacques Nattiez, *Wagner Androgyne: A Study in Interpretation*, trans. Stewart Spencer (Princeton University Press, 1993); Grey, *Wagner's Musical Prose*; see also the extensive commentary at the end of *Oper und Drama*, ed. Kropfinger.
[81] *SSD* III: 301 and 305.
[82] "Spekulanten auf das Publikum" (*SSD* III: 308).
[83] "Modeerscheinung" (*SSD* III: 308).
[84] "'Effekt' übersetzen durch 'Wirkung ohne Ursache'" (*SSD* III: 301).
[85] "unfruchtbaren Wahnsinn" (*SSD* III: 308).
[86] "verderblichen Charakter" (*SSD* III: 228).
[87] "Luxus und Pracht" (*SSD* IV: 16).
[88] "daß die Oper keinen geschichtlichen (soll heißen: natürlichen) Ursprung hat, daß sie nicht aus dem Volke, sondern aus künstlerischer Willkür entstanden ist" (*SSD* III: 228).

modern humanity."[89] Applying a Hegelian-inspired historical model of decline and decay – a negative dialectics of opera, so to speak – Wagner pronounces opera dead: "Rossini marks the historical end of opera."[90]

The personal defamation of Meyerbeer in "Jewishness" is coterminous with the charge of opera's moral turpitude. Moreover, Wagner's "moral revulsion against conventional musical taste reflects an attitude towards mass culture that has become commonplace in the modern world," at least among intellectuals.[91]

Wagner amplifies his moral-historical survey with an iconoclastic discussion of gender. Music embodies the feminine principle and poetry the masculine, so poetry inseminates music which, in turn, bears.[92] The progeny all depends on what kind of woman is being inseminated: the music of French opera is a "coquette" (*Kokette*)[93] the music of Italian opera is a "prostitute" (*Lustdirne*)[94] and German (pre-Wagnerian) opera is a "prude" (*Prüde*).[95] Each nation exemplifies some form of sexual dysfunction or "infertility" (*Zeugungsunfähigkeit*),[96] which suggests divine aesthetic retribution for the misbegotten outcome of immorality.

Gendered musical discourse was certainly not Wagner's invention. Already in the second half of the eighteenth century, German music critics asserted the "femininity" of French and Italian (vocal) music as opposed to the "masculinity" of German (instrumental) music.[97] Wagner perpetuates this discourse when he describes Beethoven's music as "männlich."[98] But the gender metaphors in Wagner's discussion of opera go beyond these established practices, even if he is not always coherent or consistent.[99] Given the infertile coupling, characteristic of the traditional relationship between

---

[89] "den ganzen ungeheuren Entwickelungsgang der modernen Menschheit!" (*SSD* III: 311) (my emphasis).
[90] *SSD* III: 255.
[91] Weber, "Wagner, Wagnerism," 36.
[92] See Grey, *Wagner's Musical Prose*, and Nattiez, *Wagner Androgyne*, for an extensive reading of Wagner's gendered discussion of opera, the inconsistencies of the argument, and its manifestation in his music dramas. See also Daniel K. L. Chua, *Absolute Music and the Construction of Meaning* (Cambridge University Press, 1999), Chapters 15 and 16, for the gendering of instrumental music in the late eighteenth century.
[93] *SSD* III: 318.
[94] *SSD* III: 317.
[95] *SSD* III: 318.
[96] *SSD* III: 267; also "Hier liegt das ganze Geheimniß der Unfruchtbarkeit der modernen Musik!" (*SSD* III: 314).
[97] See in particular, Morrow, *German Music Criticism*.
[98] *SSD* VIII: 36.
[99] "The androgynous implications of Wagner's gendered metaphors are difficult to assess, in any case, since they are generated as much by improvisatory accident as by rhetorical design" (Grey, *Wagner's Musical Prose*, 143).

librettist and composer, Wagner presents an alternative. The (masculine) poet has intimate knowledge of the land, and the (feminine) musician is at home on the oceans: they must meet to share their knowledge so that, ultimately, the poet feels as at home upon the waters as the composer is on dry land. In consequence, "they become one; because each of them knows and feels what the other knows and feels. The poet has become musician and the musician has become poet. Now both of them are complete (perfect) artists."[100]

Wagner's androgynous discourse is reminiscent of tropes developed at the close of the eighteenth century where instrumental music, formerly coded feminine, underwent a "sex-change" operation.[101] However, though certain aspects of music were coded male – modulations, harmonic density, etc. – emotional responsiveness to instrumental music remained a feminine quality. Hence, the "great artist was the feminine male."[102]

Wagner does not rule out the possibility that poet and composer can be two separate people. Indeed they can be.[103] However, modern society fosters separation, fragmentation, specialization, and undermines the spirit of community required of such a successful union. So, while a poet/composer team is theoretically viable, right now "the impossible is possible only by someone acting alone."[104] For Wagner, Beethoven was already an androgynous figure: "in order to become fully human, Beethoven had to become someone totally subject to the sexual conditions of both the masculine and the feminine."[105]

Wagner embodies the union of poet and composer, and signifies the resolution of a historical-aesthetic crisis. Again, following a Hegelian model of dialectical historical movement, an idealized antiquity (thesis) undermined by a decadent modernity (antithesis) will be resolved (synthesis) in the aptly named *Gesamtkunstwerk* of the future.[106] Anticipating a strategy used by Friedrich Engels and Georg Lukács, who habitually rescued pre-Marxist authors they favored, Wagner modifies his dialectical historiography to

---

[100] "Sie sind Eins; denn Jeder weiß und fühlt, was der Andere weiß und fühlt. Der Dichter ist Musiker geworden, der Musiker Dichter. Jetzt sind sie Beide vollkommener künstlerischer Mensch" (*SSD* IV: 159).

[101] Chua, *Absolute Music*, 126.

[102] *Ibid.*, 139–40.

[103] *SSD* IV: 208.

[104] "Nur der Einsame vermag … das Unmögliche zu ermöglichen" (*SSD* IV: 209).

[105] "Um Mensch zu werden, mußte Beethoven ein ganzer, d.h. gemeinsamer, den geschlechtlichen Bedingungen des Männlichen und Weiblichen unterworfener Mensch werden" (*SSD* III: 312).

[106] See his Hegelian utterance which anticipates Darwin: "Nicht aber eine Rückkehr zu dem Alten ist der Gang der Entwickelung alles Menschlichen, sondern der Fortschritt: alle Rückkehr zeigt sich uns überall als keine natürliche, sondern als eine künstliche" (*SSD* IV: 150).

include precursors who, albeit with "false consciousness," nevertheless pave his way. Importantly, all such composers are now dead (Gluck, Mozart, above all Beethoven).[107] Wagner is honest about "only being able to speak well of the dead, but hounding the living with unsparing acrimony!"[108]

Wagner was not the first to find fault with opera, or even to search for a musically and dramatically satisfying solution to its aesthetic flaws. Opera has been the butt of jokes from the start and there have been recurrent attempts to reform the genre. Even Wagner's invocation of an ancient Greek model was not original. Music historian Emil Naumann's response to the first Bayreuth Festival of 1876 argues that Wagner's "music of the future" merely repeated claims of originality and innovation already propagated by the Florentine Camerata, specifically Giulio Caccini in his *Nuove Musiche* (New Music – 1602).[109] Guido Adler argued similarly that Wagner's program had been fully anticipated by another member of the "Camerata," Marco da Gagliano (1582–1643).[110] In contrast to polyphonic music or *prima prattica*, seventeenth-century Florentine composers advanced a *seconda prattica* which they dubbed *stile rappresentativo*: a monodic recitativo style to ease comprehension of the sung text and, hence, the dramatic impact of the newly developed operatic genre. Wagner's emphasis on the aristocratic beginnings of opera obscures the fact that the "new music" of the Florentine school and the rationale for opera was aesthetically similar to some of the basic principles of Wagnerian music drama.[111]

This is not to deny the novelty of Wagner's approach. As close as Wagner's theories may have been to those of the "Camerata," his music dramas resulted in a product radically different from anything the Florentines might have conceived, even if Philippe Lacoue-Labarthe announces that "the *stile rappresentativo* culminates in Wagner."[112] Moreover, neither in form nor content can the earlier "reform" debates be compared with the polemics generated by and around Wagner in the years following 1850, especially given the drastically increased capabilities and reach of the media. More importantly, Wagner critiques opera from the outside, as if he were not an

---

[107] Georg Lukács rescued selected pre-Marxist "bourgeois" authors (for example Goethe, Balzac, Tolstoy) who, though with false consciousness, nevertheless and "inspite of themselves" wrote "correctly." See Nicholas Vazsonyi, *Lukács Reads Goethe: From Aestheticism to Stalinism* (Columbia: Camden House, 1997).
[108] *SSD* III: 295–6.
[109] Emil Naumann, *Musikdrama oder Oper? Eine Beleuchtung der Bayreuther Bühnenfestspiele* (Berlin, 1876).
[110] See Kropfinger, ed., "Anhang," *Oper und Drama*, 404–5.
[111] *SSD* III: 231. Wagner never mentions issues surrounding the Florentine Camerata.
[112] Lacoue-Labarthe, *Musica Ficta*, 31.

opera composer. Earlier attempts at reform only resulted in a perpetuation of the "mistaken" and unsalvageable premise of the genre:[113]

> The means of expression (music) became the goal, while the goal of expression (drama) became the means.[114]

Wagner uses bold typeface and block indent to make this statement, like "a newly painted legend ... to hang above the critical workshop of *Opera and Drama*" (to use Tom Grey's colorful and apt description).[115] But then, just as suddenly, Wagner seems to take it all back, claiming he does not suffer from "the vain delusion of having found something new."[116] He wants it both ways, apparently. On the one hand, he "didn't set out, as some self-conscious form-changer, fundamentally to destroy the basic structure of opera ... instead, the omission of arias, duets, etc happened on its own from the nature of the material."[117] Wagner essentially denies any personal responsibility; he is only a conduit for nature. Two rather convoluted sentences reveal his attempt to both affirm and deny the radicality of his aesthetics:

> The novelty that I'm talking about is nothing other than the unknown nature of the thing which has become known to me, of which I have become conscious as a thinking artist, of which I have grasped in its totality what till now artists have only perceived in its parts. So I have not invented anything new, just found the totality.[118]

According to Wagner, the answer to the problem of opera has been there all along. But this is hardly the case. Wagner had developed a concept, a complete package that comes "with batteries included."[119] When Tom Grey uses this wonderful metaphor – a merchandizing ploy common to toy and

---

[113] Wagner escapes the "collusion" Bourdieu refers to, that is inherent in all seemingly acrimonious debates within a field of production, but which do not pose "the forbidden question," about the assumptions of the field itself (*Rules of Art*, 166–7).

[114] "der Irrthum in dem Kunstgenre der Oper bestand darin, daß ein Mittel des Ausdruckes [die Musik] zum Zwecke, der Zweck des Ausdruckes [das Drama] aber zum Mittel gemacht war" (*SSD* III: 231).

[115] Grey, *Wagner's Musical Prose*, 14.

[116] "so geschieht dieß keinesweges in dem eitlen Wahne, etwas Neues gefunden zu haben, sondern in der Absicht, den in dieser Formel aufgedeckten Irrthum handgreiflich deutlich hinzustellen" (*SSD* III: 231).

[117] *SSD* IV: 321.

[118] "Das Neue, das ich etwa sagte, ist nichts Anderes als das mir bewußt gewordene Unbewußte in der Natur der Sache, das mir als denkendem Künstler bewußt ward, da ich Das nach seinem Zusammenhange erfaßte, was von Künstlern bisher nur getrennt gefaßt worden ist. Ich habe somit nichts Neues *er*funden, sondern nur jenen Zusammenhang *ge*funden" (*SSD* IV: 205 [emphasis RW]).

[119] Grey, *Wagner's Musical Prose*, 318.

gadget manufacturers – he refers only to the aesthetics. However, aesthetic innovation is only one component. The concept extends beyond the work itself, to encompass an experience (a "sensation") over which Wagner exerts total control. Wagner's "batteries" also power an explanatory narrative which contributes to the unique features of his "brand." Like textual packaging, the narrative conveys the rationale, conditions, and prescribed circumstances for performance and consumption. Integral to the new idea is a distinctive infrastructure and organizational plan inseparable from the practicalities of performance. As a condition of participation, the concept is to be digested and accepted in its entirety by the prospective consumer. A quarter-century before its realization in Bayreuth in 1876, Wagner first sets forth these basic ideas privately in the famous 1850 letter to Kietz:

I am toying with the boldest of plans, which would require no less a sum than 10,000 *thalers* to realize. According to this plan of mine, I would have a theatre erected here on the spot, made of planks, and have the most suitable singers join me, and arrange everything necessary for this one special occasion, so that I could be certain of an outstanding performance of the opera. I would then send out invitations far and wide to all who were interested in my works, ensure that the auditorium was decently filled, and give three performances – free, of course – one after the other in the space of a week, after which the theatre would then be demolished and the whole affair would be over and done.[120]

One year later, in 1851, at the conclusion of *A Communication to my Friends*, Wagner makes his first public announcement of the *Ring* cycle:

I intend to present my myth in three complete dramas with a large prelude. With these dramas I do not mean theater "repertory pieces" in the modern sense, although each one should constitute a self-contained entity, but rather have the following plan for their performance in mind:

In the course of three days with a preceding evening, I intend to present these three dramas with the prelude at a festival planned specifically for this purpose: I consider the goal of this performance to be fully achieved, if I and my artistic comrades succeed on these four evenings to convey artistically an emotional (not critical) understanding of our intentions to the audience – who have gathered in order to become acquainted with my intentions. A further result is as irrelevant to me as it is superfluous …

With this enterprise, I have nothing more to do with our contemporary theater.[121]

---

[120] Letter to Kietz, September 14, 1850, in *Selected Letters of Richard Wagner*, trans. and ed. Stewart Spencer and Barry Millington (New York: W. W. Norton, 1987), 216–17 (slightly modified by the present author).
[121] *SSD* IV: 595.

Wagner, a founding figure of anti-market aesthetic modernism, nevertheless anticipates the totalizing strategies of contemporary consumer culture. As with Disney, the full Wagnerian experience is a package deal: the *total work of art*.[122]

Like the hidden orchestra, Wagner conceals the marketing entailed in his venture by overlaying his strategies with a veneer of the esoteric, which explains why both he and his many adherents bristle at comparisons of his project with consumer culture, comparisons made already in his lifetime. But Wagner was self-confessedly preoccupied with the business of art. His *Entwurf zur Organisation eines deutschen National-Theaters für das Königreich Sachsen* (1849) (Plan for the Organization of a German National Theater for the Kingdom of Saxony), the first of many and increasingly iconoclastic attempts to articulate theatrical reform, includes an itemized budget. He even republished the "Entwurf" in the second volume of his *Gesammelte Schriften*, apologizing in the introduction for the rather tedious (*lästig*) cost analysis he includes. Its presence, he explains, functions "to counter the conventional prejudices of unimaginative people who like to assume that imaginative, creative artists – the so-called "Genius" – are impractical and incapable of coldly assessing reality."[123] Wagner was well aware of what business people call the "bottom line." There is no way out of the money economy.

Buying (into) Wagner's idea is as significant an aspect of consuming the Wagnerian product as is the "purely aesthetic" enjoyment of the works. Being a Wagnerian means to study both the works and the conceptual assumptions which lie at their core. It is a category of commitment entirely different in range, scope, and intensity from the kind demanded by any other composer of the modern Western or any other tradition. Wagnerism has been likened to a cult, but the religious simile – which points to an essentially timeless phenomenon – fails to encompass the modern characteristic of investment in a product and the personality who created it.

It is precisely this dimension which Wagner both demands and retracts. He simultaneously hones his public persona and then disavows the notion of the personality. A lengthy footnote Wagner adds to *Opera and Drama* does just this. He denies the suggestion that he has actually written the kind of work he is describing. The time is not yet here, because the creation of this

---

[122] "Opera in this place is a total experience from the moment of arriving to the moment of leaving," Frederic Spotts, *Bayreuth: A History of the Wagner Festival* (New Haven: Yale University Press, 1994), 26.

[123] *SSD* II: 2.

work will require the kind of community and cooperation which does not yet exist. On the other hand, the works he is writing – as "humble" as their success may be – are the only ones at least pointing in the right direction.[124] But his humility rings hollow when considered against his bold declarations about his own work, and the devastation he wreaks on Meyerbeer.

Wagner was certainly not the only musician to write. But the exhausting quantity of it all separates Wagner from the rest. He even comments on his commentary to the point of redundancy. The music historian August Wilhelm Ambros, for one, was dismayed at Wagner's efforts "to comment, and to reflect on" his works, and to twist "every perhaps accidental formality into a new theory. But it is not good," Ambros adds, "when a Homer carries a whole pack of critics and commentators along with him."[125] What Christian Thorau describes as the "hermeneutic model"[126] Wagner supplied with his works also applies to his entire undertaking. A contemporary of Wagner's suggested as much when he mocked the composer for providing his own "instruction manual" (*Gebrauchsanweisungen*) adding: "the public is supposed to know exactly what it should think at every one of his words, what it must feel at every bar of his music: and they must think and feel exactly as he has prescribed it."[127] Like Raff's comment which opened this chapter, the observation links Wagner's enterprise with the domain of commercial products. Nietzsche is more sinister: "not every music so far has required a literature … Is it that Wagner's music is too difficult to understand? Or is he afraid of the opposite, that it might be understood too easily – that one will *not* find it *difficult enough* to understand?"[128]

Leitmotif™

One constitutive aesthetic element more identifiable with Wagner's new brand than any other is the so-called "leitmotif," even though he neither used nor authorized the term in connection with his works. The concept of recurring and recognizable musical ideas which suggest meaning is also not

---

[124] *SSD* IV: 229.
[125] August Wilhelm Ambros, *Culturhistorische Bilder aus dem Musikleben der Gegenwart* (Leipzig: Heinrich Matthes, 1860), 142.
[126] "hermeneutisches Modell," Christian Thorau, *Semantisierte Sinnlichkeit: Studien zu Rezeption und Zeichenstruktur der Leitmotivtechnik Richard Wagners* (Stuttgart: Franz Steiner, 2003), 38.
[127] Theodor Goering, *Der Messias von Bayreuth: Feuilletonistische Briefe an einen Freund in der Provinz* (Stuttgart: Richter & Kappler, 1881), 126.
[128] Nietzsche, *Case of Wagner*, §10.

Wagner's invention.[129] Nevertheless, in a series of statements on the subject, Wagner proposes to replace the former structuring principle of opera – isolated musical units interspersed with some efficient method for advancing the plot – with a more free-flowing and fully integrated drama. Holding together what he eventually called "endless melody"[130] would be a device he initially terms "melodische Momente" (melodic moments) but also refers to as "Grundmotive" (basic motifs). These "melodic moments" imprint themselves on our hearing through repetition.[131] Functioning like a musical "rhyme" these "main motifs of the drama" shape both smaller scenes as well as "stretching out over the whole drama as a connecting sinew."[132] Wagner invests the method with a powerful psychological and hermeneutic potential: the "melodic moments" transmit what Wagner terms "motifs of feeling or appearance" (*Gefühls- oder Erscheinungsmotive*) which appeal directly to the emotions of the audience, offer insight into the "deepest secrets of the poetic intent" and function to unify both form and content.[133]

The leitmotif is mediated by the orchestra which, under Wagner, now assumes a new, improved role, transformed from being a "monstrous guitar"[134] (i.e. providing chordal accompaniment to a vocal melody line) into an agent integral to the unfolding of the drama. Wagner compares his use of the orchestra to the function reserved in ancient Greek drama for the chorus[135] but, in contemporary terms, he effects the Germanization of an Italianate body. By means of the leitmotif, the orchestra can communicate what is not conveyed linguistically on stage. It comments on the action, adds layers of meaning, and provides a primary level of interpretation. Wagner originally planned to limit the number of musical motifs in an effort to

---

[129] The terms starts to be used in connection with Wagner in the 1860s, see Ambros, *Culturhistorische Bilder*, 142: "Beide [Liszt und Wagner] suchen die höhere Einheit des Ganzen mittelst durchgehender Leitmotive zu wahren." In his essay on *Meistersinger*, Eduard Hanslick refers to "die sogenannten Gedächtniß- oder Leitmotive" (*Moderne Oper*, 304) and "Erinnerungs- oder Leitmotive" (ibid., 305). For a discussion of the term and its early use, see Thomas S. Grey "… *wie ein roter Faden*: On the Origins of the 'Leitmotif' as Critical Construct and Musical Practice," *Music Theory in the Age of Romanticism*, ed. Ian Bent (Cambridge University Press, 1996), 187–210. For simplicity, I use "leitmotif."

[130] "Unendliche Melodie" ("Zukunftsmusik," *SSD* VII: 130).

[131] *SSD* IV: 114.

[132] "Hauptmotive der dramatischen Handlung" … "über das ganze Drama selbst als ein bindender Zusammenhang erstreckt" (*SSD* IV: 202).

[133] "tiefsten Geheimnisses der dichterischen Absicht" (*SSD* IV: 202). See also "wird die Absicht des Dichters, als eine durch das Gefühlsempfängniß verwirklichte, am verständlichsten" (*SSD* IV: 201).

[134] "Monströse Guitarre" (*SSD* VII: 130).

[135] "Der Chor der griechischen Tragödie hat seine gefühlsnothwendige Bedeutung für das Drama im modernen Orchester allein zurückgelassen" (*SSD* IV: 190–1).

simplify and clarify.[136] As "emotional guideposts" (*Gefühlswegweisern*),[137] their meaning evolves associatively in relation to textual and visual cues. The haunting effect of their repetition – through infinite musical variation and transformation – is one of the most studied aspects of Wagnerian music drama, yet it remains resistant to satisfactory description, "a practice in search of a theory."[138]

As his compositional tool of choice, the leitmotif evokes a feeling of always already having existed, merging a sense of familiarity (*Erinnerung*) with presentiment (*Ahnung*).[139] The application of leitmotifs across time sublates the time-bound element of music; past and future enjoy a union in which time is transformed. Memory becomes presentiment, while presentiment takes on the feel of memory.[140] Time in Wagner's music is malleable, destabilized as an ordering principle. The absence of pulse during the beginnings of both *Rheingold* and *Tristan*, at once liberating and unsettling, establishes a "timelessness" whose dramatic corollary is found in the realm of "myth" as Wagner defines it: "the incomparable quality of myth is that it is always true, and its content in concentrated form is forever inexhaustible."[141]

The conceptual complexity of this technique is undercut by Wagner's claim that understanding (*Verstand*) of his works is achieved through feeling (*Gefühl*) – what he calls "the transformation of understanding into feeling."[142] True to Romanticism, Wagner privileges emotion over reason, a gesture of anti-intellectualism that rhetorically returns art to the people (*das Volk*) and preempts sophisticated dissections of his works by trained critics, since educated responses to his artwork represent a misunderstanding:

The artist addresses the heart, and not the mind; if a response comes from the mind, that is as much as to say that he has not been understood. Our critics do nothing but admit to their non-comprehension of the artwork, which can only be understood through feeling.[143]

Critics – arbiters of taste and fashion in the media age – are dismissed by Wagner, who instead appeals directly to his audience, encouraging them to

---

[136] *SSD* IV: 201.
[137] *SSD* IV: 200.
[138] Grey, "*roter Faden*," 187.
[139] Wagner refers to leitmotifs as "diese ahnungs- oder erinnerungsvollen melodischen Momente" (*SSD* IV: 200).
[140] "Diese melodischen Momente, in denen wir uns der Ahnung erinnern, während sie uns die Erinnerung zur Ahnung machen" (*SSD* IV: 201).
[141] *SSD* IV: 64.
[142] "die Gefühlswerdung des Verstandes" (*SSD* IV: 78).
[143] "Der Künstler wendet sich an das Gefühl, und nicht an den Verstand: wird ihm mit dem Verstande geantwortet, so wird hiermit gesagt, daß er eben nicht verstanden worden ist, und

rely on their (natural/instinctive) feelings and emotions as opposed to what they read in the papers the morning after.[144] It is a curious move by someone who relied on the media as much as Wagner did.

But there is no contradiction. Wagner is the historical link between the early nineteenth-century Romantic emphasis on feeling, and the commercial instrumentalization of feeling in the twentieth, which targets consumer impulse rather than reason to sell products. Wagner's hegemonic treatment of time and subliminal manipulation of consciousness induce moments of narcosis: "I fell asleep during the Wagner opera" may be a comment causing general merriment at the dinner table, but that is surely when Wagner exerts the greatest control.[145] Writing to the Intendant of the Weimar Theater, Wagner reveals the extent to which he was conscious of the technique he was developing and the results he sought – subliminal absorption of sound stimuli by means of recurring musical ideas that are powerfully suggestive, yet not always graspable:

It is a huge mistake to think that the public in the theater must especially understand music in order to get the right idea of a music drama ... quite the opposite, the music needs to help make the drama clear and understandable at every instant, so that when one experiences a good (i.e. a reasonable) opera, one doesn't even think about the music anymore, but only senses it involuntarily.[146]

Wagner's description of music which does not draw attention to itself and yet is integral to establishing mood and meaning lies at the conceptual heart of film music. In its "degenerated" form, the leitmotif technique "leads directly to cinema music where the sole function of the leitmotif is to announce heroes or situations so as to help the audience to orientate itself more easily."[147] Wagner's calculated use of sound to manipulate audiences is a technique we now understand as crucial to successful advertising, a point Adorno makes: "Among the functions of the leitmotif can be found, alongside the aesthetic one, a commodity-function, rather like that of an

---

unsere Kritik ist in Wahrheit nichts Anderes als das Geständniß des Unverständnisses des Kunstwerkes, das nur mit dem Gefühle verstanden werden kann" (*SSD* IV: 232).
[144] See *SSD* IV: 78.
[145] For a different take on this point, see Thorau, *Semantisierte Sinnlichkeit*, 32–3.
[146] "ein großer Irrthum ist es nun, wenn wir glauben, ein Publikum müsse im Theater speziell Musik verstehen, um den Eindruck eines musikalischen Drama's richtig empfangen zu können ... Umgekehrt soll die Musik nur in höchster Fülle dazu beitragen, das Drama jeden Augenblick auf das Sprechendste klar und schnell verständlich zu machen, so daß beim Anhören einer guten (d.h. einer vernünftigen) Oper gewissermaßen an die Musik garnicht mehr gedacht, sondern sie nur noch unwillkürlich empfunden werden," Letter to Freiherr von Zigesar, September 9, 1850 (*SB* III: 397–8).
[147] Adorno, *In Search of Wagner*, 46.

advertisement: anticipating the universal practice of mass culture later on, the music is designed to be remembered, it is intended for the forgetful."[148]

That the leitmotif's modernity lies in its anticipation of the so-called "sound bite" finds early articulation in the critique of Wagner's "atomistic agitation."[149] Despite their immensity, Wagner's works are composed "of infinite tiny particles."[150] The "leitmotif" offers the appearance of predigested simplicity to facilitate consumption and comprehension, conceptually the crux of the "sound bite."

The egalitarian intent and demagogic gesture – *music speaks to the heart, and everyone has got one* – would suggest a contrast between Wagner's product and the historically elitist and aesthetically inaccessible grand opera. However, Wagner's application of the technique resulted in what Kropfinger calls a "fundamental break"[151] between theory and practice. Especially in the *Ring*, interlocking and interwoven musical ideas are subjected to sophisticated variation and development which overwhelm. While it is tempting to assign each motif a simple and constant identifying tag, this ignores how their meaning changes as they are modified and transformed, and overlooks too how their musical kinship to other motifs also colors their meaning. In ways that tie him to the modernists a half-century later, Wagner's fluid technique of leitmotifs displays the permanent instability of meaning rather than establishing permanent markers, as some of his critics and even some supporters mistakenly asserted. Wagner's operas offer a richness of interpretative possibility which explode previous (and, arguably, subsequent) attempts at the genre. In this respect, Wagner legitimately wanted to call his creations something other than "opera." It is telling that Wagner never really found a satisfactory descriptor for his mature works: he would refer to them as "stage festival play" (*Bühnenfestspiel*) as a "nameless artistic deed" (*namenlose künstlerische That*), famously as "musical deeds made visible" (*ersichtlich gewordene Thaten der Musik*) but more properly asserted that they "lacked any name" (*ohne alle Benennung*).[152] Making his works nameless and un-nameable only added to their mystique. Posterity has conferred the term "Gesamtkunstwerk," even though Wagner used the word five times and only to describe ancient Greek drama, never his own.

---

[148] *Ibid.*, 31.
[149] "atomistische Unruhe," Louis Ehlert, "Das Bühnenfestspiel in Bayreuth," I-IV, *Deutsche Rundschau* (October–December 1876), quoted in Susanna Großmann-Vendrey, *Bayreuth in der deutschen Presse: Beiträge zur Rezeptionsgeschichte Richard Wagners und seiner Festspiele* (Regensburg: Bosse, 1977), I: 190.
[150] *Ibid.*, 185.
[151] *Oper und Drama*, ed. Kropfinger, 493 (note 6).
[152] All from "Über die Benennung 'Musikdrama'" (1871), *SSD* IX: 306–8.

Critics also refer to Wagner's works as "music dramas," a term Wagner ridicules in his 1871 essay, "Über die Benennung 'Musikdrama.'" Elsewhere, though, he describes his works alternately as "musikalisch-dramatisch" and "dramatisch-musikalisch" underscoring the equal significance of both elements.[153] So much about Wagner's works becomes a point of discussion, controversy, disagreement: even how we are to call them.

Publicity agents

The leitmotif masterfully functions both to make Wagner's works consumable and more complex. It accounts in part for his success as a popular icon while also being the icon of the elitist French *l'art pour l'art* movement of the second half of the nineteenth century.

Discussions concerning Wagner's technique of recurring motifs feature prominently already between 1850 and 1860, two decades before Hans von Wolzogen would popularize the concept and its exegesis.[154] This is significant because, while Wolzogen's books participate in the emergent "Wagner industry" (in the form of "how-to" handbooks),[155] the recognition and instrumentalization of what Liszt called Wagner's "new method" as a means of promoting (and attacking) the composer and his works, and distinguishing them from the competition, began much earlier. Yet another reason why 1850 marks the beginning of the crucial decade. It was the moment when Wagner's still rather general self-image as "German" composer and Beethoven's chosen successor – formulated in the 1840s – was merged with Wagner's specific articulation of a unique concept. It was also the decade when the composer's solitary efforts at self-promotion were joined and supported by others: disciples (Theodor Uhlig), "friends" (Franz Liszt), early Wagnerites (Charles Baudelaire) not to mention the institutional support of the *NZfM* under the editorship of Franz Brendel and, ultimately, its allied organization the *Allgemeiner deutscher Musikverein*, founded in 1859 at the close of the decade.[156]

Without diminishing the significance of Wagner's own self-marketing efforts that were without precedent, the degree of public visibility Wagner

---

[153] See, for example, his essay "Zukunftsmusik" (1860).
[154] See also Grey, "roter Faden," 187–210.
[155] Thorau refers to it as a "Deutungsindustrie" (interpretation industry) (*Semantisierte Sinnlichkeit*, 17).
[156] On the Allgemeine deutsche Musikverein, see Pohl, *Tonkünstler-Versammlung* (1859) including Brendel's opening speech: "Zur Anbahnung einer Verständigung" (75–95). See also Weber, "Wagner, Wagnerism," 63–5.

achieved at this early stage in his career could not have been managed alone. Two passionate advocates, who began to write about him simultaneously, stand out: Theodor Uhlig – previously unknown but indefatigable – and Franz Liszt, a star who shared the limelight with Wagner: an act both generous and self-serving.

Referred to in the Wagner literature primarily as an "apologist" or a "disciple,"[157] Uhlig could also be called Wagner's first publicity agent, a function Wagner himself noted with evident discomfort in a letter to Uhlig from December 1850: "what sort of unholy promotion of me are you undertaking! If you were a Jew, one would think you were getting a percentage."[158] Wagner's revelatory two sentences simultaneously concede the "value" of Uhlig's effort but critique it using religious terms twice over, coupling Christian "sacrilege" (*heilloses*) with an attack on Jewish mercantilism which places earthly profit over the transcendental. Of course, Uhlig is no Jew getting a percentage: he is doing it for art's sake, hence he is a "disciple" and precisely not an "unholy" publicity agent. Our hesitancy or even refusal to call him so merely perpetuates Wagner's own duplicitous discourse.

Though anachronistic, the term "publicity agent" is justified, because there was much to be gained on earth, for Wagner in the first place, and perhaps also for Uhlig (had he lived longer). Moreover, encouraged if not pushed by Wagner and facilitated by Brendel, Uhlig's *coordinated* and *concerted* effort anticipates aspects of professional PR campaigns of later centuries. "Coordinated" because there is often a close correlation between letters Wagner wrote to Uhlig and articles he published subsequently. In the case of the *Le prophète* series, discussed earlier, two letters from Wagner plausibly functioned as a catalyst for Uhlig's assault. "Concerted," because Brendel actively enlisted Uhlig for the specific purpose of pushing Wagner. In the two-part obituary that marked Uhlig's death in 1853, Brendel confessed that he had encouraged Uhlig to start writing about Wagner in 1849, because Uhlig "seemed so conversant with Wagner's entire direction."[159] Between 1850 and 1852, the *NZfM* published an uninterrupted stream of articles by Uhlig. These can be sorted into three groups: general musicology

---

[157] For "apologist," see James Deaville, "Die neudeutsche Musikkritik: Der Weimarer Kreis." For "disciple," see, for example, Gerhard J. Winkler, "Der 'bestimmte Ausdruck': Zur Musikästhetik der Neudeutschen Schule," both in Altenburg, ed., *Liszt und die neudeutsche Schule*, 55–76, here 59; and 39–53, here 49. Winkler also refers to Uhlig as a "Trabant."

[158] "Was machst Du für ein heilloses aufheben's von mir! Wenn Du ein jude wärest, sollte man glauben, Du hättest procente davon," Letter to Uhlig, [December 1850] (*SB* III: 476).

[159] "Nun forderte ich U. auf die Sache in die Hand zu nehmen, da ich schon bemerkt hatte, wie vertraut er mit Wagner's Richtung war," *NZfM* 38.4 (January 21, 1853), 33–7, here 36.

and music history, (book) reviews of Wagner's recent theoretical works, and music criticism of contemporary works (by Wagner and others). In every case, even if Uhlig purports to be writing about something or someone else, he is actually supporting the Wagnerian cause. Some of this can be attributed to Uhlig's own convictions, but Wagner was always close at hand, pushing, prodding, even supplying the basic text.

This pattern first appears with a letter Wagner writes to Uhlig, dated October 26, 1849. In it, Wagner expresses the hope "that the interest [my writings] spread, will not just be a passing fad, but rather be substantial and sustained."[160] We can only surmise that the intervening reply from Uhlig mentioned his willingness to support the effort with his own writings because, on November 21 or 22, Wagner sent Uhlig the manuscript for *Artwork of the Future*. In the accompanying letter, Wagner talks of his hope that his writings will be widely read[161] and, without putting undue pressure on Uhlig, reminds Uhlig of his own intention to publish "favorable reviews" of his prose writings.[162] Uhlig apparently never replied to the reminder so, in December, Wagner writes quite impatiently: "Are you publishing your writings soon? Hurry up."[163] Uhlig may have been a willing devotee, but Wagner also pushed him aggressively.

Wagner need not have worried; Uhlig had already written. The opening volume of 1850 contained an article by Uhlig titled: "The Natural Basis of Instrumental Music with Regard to Beethoven's Symphonies." A central argument of this article is that the "natural basis of instrumental music is dance." Beethoven's symphonies represent the perfection of dance rhythms and dance melody: not dance in the contemporary (common) sense, but the higher idea of dance.[164] Starting January 22, Uhlig continued with a series of articles titled "Beethoven's Symphonies in Context" ("Beethovens Symphonien im Zusammenhange betrachtet") which pursued the notion of dance as the analytical key to Beethoven's symphonies.

Is it a coincidence that Uhlig's articles reproduce and expand on Wagner's own exploration of Beethoven's symphonies in the "Tonkunst" section from the as yet unpublished *Artwork of the Future* where Wagner writes: "Harmonized dance is the basis of the richest works of the modern

---

[160] "daß das interesse, welches sie verbreiten wird, nicht ein nur vorübergehendes tagesinteresse, sondern ein stoffreiches u. stoffgebendes anhaltenderes hervorrufen soll" (*SB* III: 141).

[161] "Wichtig ist mir nur Eines, – daß sie möglichst viel gelesen werden" (*SB* III: 166).

[162] "günstige besprechungen meiner schriftstellerischen arbeiten" (*SB* III: 165–6). Wagner seems to refer back to an intent expressed in an earlier letter from Uhlig, which is sadly lost.

[163] "Kommen Sie nun bald einmal mit ihren schriften heraus? Eilen Sie" (*SB* III: 198).

[164] Theodor Uhlig, "Die natürliche Grundlage der Instrumentalmusik im Hinblick auf Beethoven's Symphonien," *NZfM* 32.1 (January 1, 1850), 2–4, here 4.

symphony," a line of argumentation that climaxes with Wagner's famous line about Beethoven's Seventh Symphony being "the apotheosis of dance."[165]

Uhlig would eventually write a book review of *Artwork of the Future*,[166] but in the January 1850 articles he (re)produces Wagner's argument *avant la lettre* and without attribution. Does this constitute plagiarism, or an inspired tactic to fulfill Wagner's desire that his writings spark a sustained conversation to (re)shape musicological discourse along the lines he envisioned? Already at the end of the eighteenth century and with increasing emphasis in the early nineteenth, German critics had appropriated the originally Italian "sinfonia" as the quintessential German form.[167] Wagner participates in this process of Germanization, but by introducing the element of dance as an "organic" precursor to the symphony, increases the slippage by further obscuring its cultural historical origins as an Italian form of instrumental music that accompanied operatic works. If the symphony was meant to be the highest expression of German instrumental music (of which Wagnerian opera was the continuation), it would clearly never do for the genre to originate with Italian opera.[168]

It is almost certain that Wagner did not see Uhlig's essays when they came out in January 1850, because he first mentions them in a July 27 letter, confirming receipt of the last half year of *NZfM* issues. "For starters, I just read your essays: they pleased me beyond all measure and, what's more, I *learned* from them."[169] He goes on: "your two essays on the Beethoven symphonies are of utmost importance."[170] Far from accusing him of plagiarism (which he had no problem with in any case), Wagner implies that Uhlig has come to original conclusions independently. Wagner was not possessive of his musicological ideas because he had a bigger goal. By shifting musicological discourse, Uhlig was generating support for Wagner's "direction." To have cited Wagner would not have been as effective as if others were seen coming to the same conclusions as Wagner "on their own." Wagner may even have given Uhlig the idea when he wrote, immediately before Uhlig's

---

[165] "Der harmonisirte Tanz ist die Basis des reichsten Kunstwerkes der modernen Symphonie" (*SSD* III: 90 and 94).

[166] Uhlig's review appeared almost a full year later in the *NZfM* 33.45 (December 3, 1850) and 33.48 (December 13, 1850) respectively.

[167] See Bonds, *Music as Thought*, 88–91.

[168] Grey does not make this national argument, but similarly describes Wagner's emphasis on dance as "polemical" (*Wagner's Musical Prose*, 272).

[169] "Zuerst las ich nur Deine aufsätze: sie haben mich über alle begriffe erfreut, und mehr als das, sie haben mich oft auch *belehrt*" (emphasis RW). Letter to Uhlig, July 27, 1850 (*SB* III: 365–6).

[170] "Deine zwei aufsätze über die beethovenschen symphonieen sind von der entscheidendsten wichtigkeit" (*SB* III: 366).

articles came out: "whoever helps me personally only wants to help my art and the holy cause [*der heiligen sache*] I am fighting for."[171]

It is unlikely that Uhlig had come to his reading of the Beethoven symphonies independently. He had evidently read *Artwork of the Future* with great care, because on January 12, 1850, Wagner received a letter from him which – judging from Wagner's reply written the same day – discussed in detail his reactions to Wagner's manuscript. Uhlig's letter must also have given Wagner some inkling of the degree of support he was offering, even though it would be several months before Wagner would get his own copies of the *NZfM*, because Wagner's reply took the immense step of addressing Uhlig by the informal and intimate "Du"-form, a significant gesture for grown-up unrelated males in nineteenth-century Germany.

From this point on, there is a synchronicity between Wagner's letters and Uhlig's writings warranting its own careful analysis that space considerations prohibit here.[172] After the Beethoven essays came the Meyerbeer assault, which culminated with Wagner's "Jewishness in Music," part I of which appeared as the lead in the September 3, 1850, issue of the *NZfM*.

In that same September 3rd issue, Uhlig began his own multi-part series titled "Three Days in Weimar: The Herder Festival. Richard Wagner's Opera *Lohengrin*."[173] Again, the timing is significant. The sustained six-month attack on Meyerbeer – begun by Uhlig and capped by Wagner – climaxes precisely with the premiere of *Lohengrin* on August 28, which is now followed by a substantial set of articles on Wagner's new opera. Uhlig's series is much more than a review. He offers a full-scale analysis to readers who would likely not have a chance to experience the work for some time to come. Initially, more people would read about *Lohengrin* than would come into contact with the work itself: "to talk about art becomes equivalent to making it."[174] Technological advances in digital reproduction and the internet no longer constrain the distribution network of large-scale audio-visual artworks, but in the mid-nineteenth century, the media were far more equipped to disseminate and promote a discourse about the artwork, than

---

[171] Letter to Uhlig, December 27, 1849 (*SB* III: 199).
[172] Though mention of Uhlig is ubiquitous in the Wagner literature, only Kropfinger has so far devoted considerable space to an analysis of his essays, albeit from the perspective of music aesthetics and not the promotion of Wagner; see his *Wagner and Beethoven*, 12, 70–5, and 86–91.
[173] "Drei Tage in Weimar: Das Herderfest. Richard Wagner's Oper *Lohengrin*," *NZfM* 33.19 (September 3, 1850), 33.21 (September 10, 1850), 33.22 (September 13, 1850), 33.25 (September 24, 1850), 33.28 (October 4, 1850), and 33.30 (October 11, 1850).
[174] Perloff, *Futurist Moment*, 90.

the artwork itself, especially the artwork of as politically and aesthetically suspect a figure as Richard Wagner.

Declaring it to be "the most significant work of the most significant contemporary German opera composer," Uhlig offers a detailed synopsis of *Lohengrin* and asserts that "the poetic text can stand proudly aside the very best that modern German literature has to offer … and whoever thinks this is an exaggeration should purchase the libretto handsomely published in Weimar for five silver Groschen."[175] Uhlig's emphasis on the literary qualities of the text not only complements Wagner's effort to justify writing his own libretti, but raises the market value of those texts as literature *per se*, hence the call for people to go out and buy the text itself.[176]

Just as his discussions of Wagner's prose works are more like reader's digest versions of the original, Uhlig's *Lohengrin* series is not merely the work of a reviewer. Writing from the inside, Uhlig serves the Wagner agenda by becoming one of the architects of nineteenth-century Wagnerian discourse, perhaps even influencing Wagner's own subsequent formulations in *Opera and Drama*.

Uhlig proclaims *Lohengrin* to be "the exact opposite" from the rest of opera, to offer "deliverance" (*Erlösung*, also "salvation") from the status quo.[177] It is a "musikalische[s] Drama" (Uhlig uses the term twice) providing audiences "a more tangible and psychological interest" so that they may "peer into the depths of the souls of the persons who speak and act."[178]

Uhlig emphasizes Wagner's compositional technique, already evident in earlier works, here "raised to a coherent system … applied in *Lohengrin* with consistency and mastery."[179] In place of the usual set pieces, Wagner uses "principal motifs … i.e. the most characteristic musical ideas lead like a red thread through the whole opera thus creating a much higher sense of musical unity."[180] For the first time in the history of Wagner-interpretation, Uhlig isolates five of these motifs with music examples and explains their significance. His gesture underscores Wagner's innovativeness and sophistication

---

[175] *NZfM* 33.19, 107, and 33.22, 120.

[176] On this point, Wagner writes to Liszt: "Solches textbuch – bei wohlfeilem preise – ist übrigens gar kein schlechtes geschäft," Letter to Liszt July 2, 1850 (*SB* III: 346).

[177] "das vollkommenste Gegenteil," *NZfM* 33.25, 137.

[178] "ein mehr plastisches und psychologisches Interesse bieten" … "in die tieffste Seele der redenden und handelnden Personen blicken zu lassen" (*NZfM* 33.25, 136–7).

[179] "zum planvollen System erhoben … im *Lohengrin* aber mit einer Consequenz und Meisterschaft zur Anwendung gebracht" (*NZfM* 33.28, 152).

[180] "Hauptmotiv … d.h. die bezeichnendsten musikalischen Gedanken ziehen sich bei ihm wie ein rother Faden durch die ganze Oper und dadurch wird derselben eine musikalische Einheit in viel höherem Sinne verliehen" (*NZfM* 33.28, 151).

as well as his consumability. Although Uhlig mocks the petit-bourgeois listener who frequents outdoor gathering places and "who sits behind his beer stein and puffs on his cigar,"[181] his reassurance that *Lohengrin* also has extracts that one can hear "outside of the theater" (i.e. Preludes to Acts I and III; Bridal Chorus; March at the end of Act II) suggests his aspiration to increase Wagner's popularity.

At the same time, Uhlig preaches the exclusivity of *Lohengrin* by pondering whether applause is even appropriate for Wagner operas. In a remarkable anticipation of the much later practice in Bayreuth of not applauding until the very end of *Parsifal*, Uhlig makes the ultimate connection between art and religion. "When hearing an opera like this, one feels transported into a religious feeling." Just as one does not clap in church, such a "childish gesture" (*kindischen Zeichen*) is also not appropriate for a Wagner work.[182] Uhlig's elevation of Wagner to religious experience doubtless contributed to the opposing vilification of Wagner as a cult.[183]

As Wagner would also do in *Opera and Drama*, Uhlig seems to be marketing Wagner both exclusively and inclusively.

While Uhlig was writing about *Lohengrin*, so too was Liszt. The surviving correspondence even confirms that, during the time of the premiere, both men discussed and coordinated their articulations destined for publication. Liszt first informs Wagner of this and of his own intention to draft an essay in his letter of September 2, 1850, just a few days after the premiere.[184] While Liszt will write in French for the *Journal des Débats*, he reports that both Raff and Uhlig will write for German papers. These men certainly discussed both strategy and content, so that similarities between their writings are unlikely to have been coincidental.

For several reasons, Liszt's essay stands out.[185] It is exceptionally long and it inaugurates the special role Wagner would play in French cultural politics that came to a head with the 1861 *Tannhäuser* debacle, a watershed event that actually transformed Wagner into an iconic figure, idolized in French artistic circles for the remainder of the century. With *Lohengrin*, and

---

[181] *NZfM* 33.28, 152.
[182] *NZfM* 33.30, 163.
[183] For the journalistic counter-current, see also Deaville, "Programme Music," 98–124.
[184] See also *Correspondence of Wagner and Liszt*, 2 vols., trans. F. Hueffer, 2nd edn W. Ashton Ellis (New York: Vienna House, 1973), I: 87–8.
[185] Franz Liszt, "*Lohengrin* und *Tannhäuser* von Richard Wagner," also "*Lohengrin*, Grand Opéra romantique de R. Wagner, et sa première représentation à Weimar aux Fêtes de Herder et Goethe 1850," in Franz Liszt, *Sämtliche Schriften*, IV: 2–91. The volume contains the original French with parallel German translation, as well as the article "Richard Wagner's *Lohengrin*, mitgeteilt von Dr. Fr. Lißt," translated with modifications and published separately in

especially with Liszt's promotion of the work, Wagner entered the international arena for good.

Though the essay originally seems to have been Liszt's idea, Wagner was anxious that he write it. Complaining about reviews that had so far appeared in the press, Wagner's letter of October 2, 1850, to Liszt continues: "if you have not given up the idea of helping me in yet wider circles, I would almost be so immodest as to implore you to arrange for another and more favorable review of my work for publication in the *A.A.Z.* [*Augsburger Allgemeine Zeitung*] – as I mentioned before, it is the paper with the widest distribution."[186] What Wagner did not know when he wrote this letter was that, on September 25, Liszt had already written to let him know that the essay would be on its way "in about a week." In this letter, Liszt asks Wagner if he would be willing to translate his essay – or have it translated under his supervision – into German for publication in none other than the *Augsburger Allgemeine Zeitung*. The letters had crossed, but the two men were thinking identically. Wagner was embarrassed at his impatience. Upon receipt of Liszt's letter, Wagner replied: "You make me blush!"[187]

The massive essay starts with a description of the Herder festival, but quickly moves to a discussion of *Lohengrin*.[188] Beyond an almost excruciatingly detailed synopsis (with extended quotes, some of which Wagner added to the German version),[189] Liszt emphasizes the novelty of the work and the ways in which it departs from "conventional opera." The kind of language Liszt uses to distinguish this "new" work from everything that has come before betrays a flair for promotion and publicity that had served Liszt so well in his own career. Echoing Wagner, Liszt even disparages the competition when he expresses the hope "that the worst products of the imagination, for so long considered good enough, will some day be banished."[190] It is also in harmony with Wagner's own recently published *Artwork of the Future*. While it cannot be ascertained whether Liszt had

---

Germany. I quote from this latter German version. A short time later, in May 1851, another major and positive article on *Lohengrin* written by Adolf Stahr appeared in the *National-Zeitung* (Berlin).

[186] "Giebst Du die hoffnung noch nicht auf, mir noch in weiteren kreisen nützlich zu sein, so wäre ich fast so unbescheiden, Dich zu ersuchen, eine nochmalige und geeignetere besprechung meines *Lohengrin* in der *A.A.Z.* zu veranlassen, – denn, wie gesagt, es ist die verbreiteste Zeitung" (*SB* III: 434).

[187] "Du machst mich erröthen!" Letter to Liszt, October 8, 1850 (*SB* III: 438).

[188] The Herder section is structurally interesting, because it prepares several issues Liszt then thematizes in the case of Wagner.

[189] See Wagner's explanatory letter to Liszt, December 24, 1850.

[190] Liszt, "*Lohengrin*," *Sämtliche Schriften*, IV: 169.

read Wagner's essay before writing this piece, it is fairly certain that, around the time of the *Lohengrin* premiere, he would have been involved in conversational exchanges on the subject with Raff, Uhlig, and Hans von Bülow, all of whom were present.

Wagner is an "extraordinary genius" who "introduces a totally new system" into an opera world where one formerly had to "make do" with "impoverished music" and "mediocre plot."[191] Gone are those practices that "seemed good enough" – "separate set pieces … arias … customary procedures, arbitrary relationships" as well as "unbearable impossibilities," "ridiculous rhymes," and the "incoherent succession of numbers."[192] Instead, Wagner has written a "drama in which all the arts that the theater encompasses work perfectly together" to produce an aesthetic that "must topple the method used till now."[193]

Liszt stresses three aspects of the work that make it special: the quality of the libretto and dramatic conceptualization, the use of the orchestra, and the technique of recurring musical motifs which make it "more than hard to extract some arbitrary section from the perfect and tightly woven unity which constitutes his operas."[194] Uhlig's review, though not as lengthy, had emphasized the identical issues. Some of this even seeps into *Opera and Drama*, which Wagner was writing at the time, suggesting reciprocality in the development of this purpose-constructed discourse.

Like Uhlig and Wagner before him, Liszt insists on the self-sufficient literary qualities of the text using aggressive promotional language: *Lohengrin* is a "top-notch" literary work and its author a "true poet … on the same level" with other great authors.[195] In opera, you have "singers." With Wagner, there are only "roles," a distinction that elaborates on the charge of "melody only" Italianate versus the "demandingly complex" German music. Here the contentlessness (singing) of opera is played against the dramatic depth (roles) of Wagner's products which come to embody German opera *per se*.

Matching the dramatic experience, Wagner's orchestra "reflects the soul, the passions, the feelings, the slightest movements of the characters on stage,

---

[191] "außergewöhnliches Genie," … "ganz neues System," … "So begnügte man sich" (Liszt, "*Lohengrin*," 25).

[192] "Unterteilung der Gesangstücke, herkömmliche Verteilung der Arien … Hergebrachte Verfahren, willkürlichen Verhältnisse" (Liszt, "*Lohengrin*," 27) … unerträgliche Unwahrscheinlichkeiten … lächerlichen Reimereien … zusammenhanglose Folge von Nummern" (*ibid.*, 35).

[193] "Drama … in welchem alle Künste, die das Theater umfaßt, zusammen in gleicher Vollendung mitwirken" … "die bisher befolgte Methode stürzen müsse" (Liszt, "*Lohengrin*," 25).

[194] Liszt, "*Lohengrin*," 27.

[195] *Ibid.*, "ersten Ranges" (29), "wahrer Dichter" (29) … "auf gleiche Stufe" (83).

thus revealing them to us completely."[196] The music of the *Lohengrin* Act I prelude imparts the "indescribable power" and the "inexpressible beauty" of the Grail and initiates us into its secrets.[197] From the syntax, it is unclear whether Liszt is talking about the Grail or Wagner's music.

The leitmotif technique is the crucial element of the Wagnerian experience. Liszt uses it to construct a chronology of Wagner's development. He diminishes the value of early works and canonizes later ones. *Rienzi* is still an old-style opera (*huldigt noch dem alten Brauch*), but with the *Flying Dutchman*, Wagner's "new system" is evident. With each work, he comes "one step closer to the objective he is pursuing."[198] Liszt assists Wagner in jettisoning his "early" works to emphasize the new brand based on distinctive thematic content (Germanic myth) and a distinctive structure (recurring motifs).

Liszt (now resident in Weimar) also stresses the national dimension of Wagner's "thoroughly systematic structuring" that betrays a "rigor" and a "German premeditation."[199] *Lohengrin* is a "thoroughly considered, amazingly adroit" work in which Wagner "has tied the melodic knot using several themes."[200] Not only does Liszt replay the distinction between Franco-Italian superficiality versus German complexity, he also demonstrates how Wagner had found the suitable formal method for developing a German art form that no longer bears any relationship to the Italianate genre. Unwittingly, however, he also supplies the opposition – including German critics and musicians – with one of the most durable critiques of Wagner's compositional method: that it reflected a calculated ("premeditated") artificiality as opposed to the natural-organic model considered the ideal at the time.[201]

Like Uhlig, Liszt seems caught between competing claims of complexity and accessibility. On the one hand, Wagner requires "long and serious study, in order to grasp it in its full significance," just as with other "great poets."[202] On the other, the music conveys "psychological, poetic and philosophical thoughts" that "offer unparalleled pleasure even to those for whom eighth and sixteenth notes are like dead letters or hieroglyphics."[203]

---

[196] *Ibid.*, 27.
[197] "unbeschreibliche Macht" and "unaussprechliche Schönheit" (*ibid.*, 31).
[198] "einen Schritt näher dem Ziele, das er verfolgt" (*ibid.*, 27).
[199] "Systematische Strenge" … "deutsche Prämeditation" (*ibid.*, 85).
[200] "tief durchdachten, staunenswert geschickten" … "vermittelst mehrerer Themen den melodischen Knoten … geschürzt hat" (*ibid.*, 35).
[201] Further on this, see Deaville, "Programme Music," 103.
[202] Liszt, "*Lohengrin*," 35.
[203] "Diese systematische Durchgestaltung," and "psychologischen, poetischen und philosophischen Gedanken selbst denjenigen, welchen Achtel- und Sechzehntelnoten tote Buchstaben und reine Hieroglyphen sind, einen seltenen Genuß bieten müßte" (*ibid.*).

The leitmotif lies at the heart of both claims, and Liszt provides significant insight into the technique, long before Wagner had accomplished some of what Liszt describes. Starting with a static definition, Liszt explains that "all more significant situations or persons are expressed musically by a melody which becomes their permanent symbol."[204] But it is more complex, because these "melodies are the personification of ideas," and "their return expresses the feelings of the characters who can at the most hint at them with words, thus revealing to all the secrets buried within their hearts."[205] According to Liszt's explanation, the leitmotif is more than a simple permanent semantic label hanging around the neck of its corresponding figure. Instead, it opens up layers of meaning and undercurrents of thought and emotion that cannot be expressed linguistically. The significance and hermeneutic power Liszt attributes to the leitmotifs seem to anticipate their sophisticated role in the *Ring*, as opposed to their, by comparison, still rather crude application in *Lohengrin*.

Did Liszt really see all this in *Lohengrin*? Or was he just imagining their potential not unlike Wagner himself in his theoretical writings (most of which were not yet published)?

Like Uhlig, Liszt identifies five themes (Grail, Divine judgment, Lohengrin, Elsa's oath, Ortrud) which he discusses in detail. There "is not one single melodic passage which can be understood in separation from the totality. Everything develops interconnectedly and together; everything is sewn tightly together and cannot be separated."[206] Wagner belongs to the tradition of Gluck (in terms of dramatic expressivity) and Weber (in terms of expressive instrumentation) but outdoes both while also bringing the two elements together as never before.[207]

The significance and value of Liszt's hyperbolic efforts did not escape Wagner, who thanked him for his "unflagging efforts to promote" his works.[208] But, perhaps out of embarrassment, Wagner's letters to Uhlig on the subject never fail to belittle Liszt's efforts or express bemusement. On July 27, 1850, he wrote rather condescendingly: "remarkable, that a friend,

---

[204] "Alle wichtigeren Situationen oder Personen sind durch eine Melodie, welche ihr beständiges Symbol wird, musikalisch zum Ausdruck gebracht" (*ibid.*, 35–7).
[205] "Melodien sind ... Personifikationen von Ideen," "ihre Wiederkehr drückt die der Gefühle aus, welche die Worte höchstens andeuten," ... "uns alle Geheimnisse des Herzens zu enthüllen" (*ibid.*, 35).
[206] *Ibid.*, 83.
[207] *Ibid.*, 89.
[208] Letter to Liszt, November 20, 1851: "Deine [...] Broschüre über meine beiden Opern ... Dein rastloser Eifer diese Werke zu propagiren" (*SB* IV: 183).

who is quite distant from me in many important aspects of life and thinking, nevertheless with unshakable loyalty and attentiveness takes such an unusual interest in my entire existence … and seems to have dedicated his entire being to one thing only: to help me and to publicize my works."[209] He notes Liszt's "enthusiastic propaganda" (*eifrige propaganda*) which aims "to pave my way to the public at large," and he adds: "it's really touching to see Liszt's tireless efforts with diabolical energy to fan the flames of my fame."[210]

Liszt's work and its impact paved the way for Wagner "in one fell swoop," as Ambros noted already in 1860.[211] Ambros was clear about the unprecedented nature of the PR effort on Wagner's behalf: "neither Händel nor Gluck, nor Mozart, nor Beethoven, nor even Liszt, nor any other musician or artist has received such an endorsement, at least not while they were alive."[212] Moreover, Ambros is sensitive to the rhetorical specificities of what I will in this case already refer to as the Wagner industry: a kind of vehemence, "partisanship" and "intolerance" more common to the political and religious spheres but "unheard of in the history of art."[213]

The impact was lasting, and even left its rhetorical mark on Wagner, whose short program note on the Prelude to *Lohengrin*, written for the May 1853 Wagner festival in Zurich, echoes Liszt's description.[214] Liszt uses expressions like: "out of the undulating blueness" and describes sounds of "calm waters, a scented ether."[215] The listener is left with a feeling of the

---

[209] "Sonderbar, daß ein freund, der in vielem wichtigen durch leben und denken mir doch ziemlich fern steht, durch unerschütterliche treue und thätige fürsorge doch so ungemeinen antheil an meinem ganzen wesen nimmt … und scheint sich mit ganzer seele nur Einem noch zu widmen, mir zu nützen und meine werke zu verbreiten" (*SB* III: 361).

[210] "mir den weg zum größeren publikum bahnen zu können," … "Mir kommt diese rastlose bemühung Liszt's, das feuer meiner berühmtheit mit teufel's gewalt anzublasen, recht rührend," Letter to Uhlig, October 22, 1850 (*SB* III: 452).

[211] "Jedenfalls hat Liszt das Verdienst, durch sein brilliantes Buch und durch sein Auftreten in Weimar den Werken Wagners wie mit einem Zauberschlage die Bahn gebrochen zu haben" (Ambros, *Culturhistorische Bilder*, 139).

[212] "solch' ein Zeugniß weder Händel noch Gluck, noch Mozart, noch Beethoven, noch Liszt selbst oder sonst je ein Musiker und überhaupt kaum je ein Künstler erhalten, wenigstens bei Lebzeiten" (Ambros, *Culturhistorische Bilder*, 139).

[213] "durch seine heftige Vordringlichkeit, durch den gereizten Ton seiner Polemik, durch enthusiastische Hingabe an die ergriffene Parteirichtung und verbitterte Intoleranz gegen jede abweichende Meinung an Aehnliches mahnte, wovon die Geschichte auf politischem und religiösem Gebiete zu erzählen weiß, wie es aber in der Kunstgeschichte unerhört gewesen!" (Ambros, *Culturhistorische Bilder*, 131).

[214] Wagner, "Vorspiel zu *Lohengrin*," *SSD* V: 179–81.

[215] "aus dem Blau der Wellen," "ruhiger Wasserspiegel von Wohlklang, ein duftiger Äther" (Liszt, "*Lohengrin*," 33).

"highest rapture, that our hearts can bear" … "a divine breath."[216] I list selected quotes from the two versions side-by-side for comparison:

LISZT	WAGNER
Out of the blue of the waves, a scented aether	Clearest blue aether of the heavens
(aus dem Blau der Wellen … ein duftiger Äther)	(klarste blaue Himmelsäther)
Highest rapture	rapturous scents
(höchsten Entzücken)	(entzückende Dufte)
That our hearts are capable of	as no human heart has yet sensed it
(dessen unser Herz fähig ist)	(wie noch nie menschliche Herzen sie empfanden)
A divine breath	like a breath
(einem göttlichen Atem)	(Wie ein Atemhauch)

Like Liszt, Wagner syntactically connects the experience of the Grail with that of the music depicting it. Is it the Grail or Wagner's music that "seizes with irresistible power the senses of the astonished right into the deepest depths of their palpitating heart"?[217] To adapt a 1970s English Heineken commercial starring Victor Borge: "Wagner refreshes the parts other music cannot even reach."

The far-reaching effect of Liszt's essay is difficult to assess, but it did become a reference point for the Wagner camp for some time to come. Echoing Uhlig's "Three Days in Weimar," Franz Brendel published his own "Ein Ausflug nach Weimar" (An Excursion to Weimar) in which Brendel reports on his experience of a *Lohengrin* performance.[218] Brendel "greets the new genius of dramatic music," the composer of "musical drama" (*musikalisches Drama*),[219] and directs readers to Liszt's "masterful" review of the work – which eliminates the need for Brendel to do so again. Comparing the unique sensation of experiencing *Lohengrin* to nothing less than the Ninth Symphony, Brendel declares "Wagner's path is now the only correct one to take."[220]

[216] "höchsten Entzücken, dessen unser Herz fähig ist," … "einem göttlichen Atem" (Liszt, "Lohengrin," 33).
[217] "nehmen die Sinne des Erstaunten bis in die innigste Tiefe des bebenden Herzens … mit unwiderstehlicher Macht" (*SSD* V: 180).
[218] Franz Brendel, "Ein Ausflug nach Weimar," *NZfM* 36.4 (January 23, 1852), 37–40.
[219] "den neuen Genius der dramatischen Musik zu begrüßen" (Brendel, "Ausflug," 37).
[220] "daß der Wagner'sche Weg als der einzig richtige jetzt zu betreten ist" (Brendel, "Ausflug," 39, see also 38).

Whether Wagner borrowed from, or was influenced by, Liszt's essay is a matter of speculation. But, ten years later, Charles Baudelaire copied entire passages from it in his eloquent and passionate advocacy of Wagner, as a palpable exercise in canon formation.

It would be tempting to call Baudelaire Wagner's first publicity agent in France, to say that his essay has "the exaggerated enthusiasm of an advertisement."[221] Historically, it would be more sober to think of him as a "friend" in the way Wagner used the term. Baudelaire's passion for Wagner came to a head with the 1860 concert of orchestral extracts at the Théâtre-Italien, prompting the famous letter he sent to Wagner on February 17, 1860. The subsequent essay "Richard Wagner and *Tannhäuser* in Paris" makes public the spirit of that letter in response to the March 13, 1861, *Tannhäuser* fiasco. Completed March 18, it was published on April 1 in the *Revue Européenne* and then as a separate brochure a month later, "adroitly timed to profit … from the scandals of the musical season."[222] A work therefore also of (self-)promotion, the essay is anomalous for Baudelaire, but also a continuation of his own long-standing aesthetic fight where, this time, he merges his own struggles with those of the ongoing Wagner discourse.

A self-confessed musical dilettante (in the best sense),[223] Baudelaire studied every word published by and about Wagner available to French readers. He even names Wagner's theoretical works not yet available in French translation and reveals that he read *Opera and Drama* in English translation.

Baudelaire had consumed and was consumed by the total Wagnerian media package and, in turn, becomes a medium of his own: a conduit funneling Wagner, sometimes unmediated, to a French readership.[224] Baudelaire becomes the embodiment of the Wagnerian experience: responding to his music which (like the Grail) descends "with irresistible power," he is "immediately carried away and subjugated," "conquered at once," "powerless" to resist.

He quotes entire sections from Wagner's program notes on *Lohengrin*, italicizing portions of Wagner's text which suggest a narrative structure or

---

[221] Margaret Miner, *Resonant Gaps: Between Baudelaire and Wagner* (Athens, GA: University of Georgia Press, 1995), 3.
[222] *Ibid.*, 5.
[223] "Someone who, like me, *does not know music*," Letter to Wagner, in Charles Baudelaire, *Baudelaire as a Literary Critic*, trans. L. B. and F. E. Hyslop (University Park: Pennsylvania State University Press, 1964), 192.
[224] Baudelaire even makes his own reference to "consumption" by describing how he "masticated the indigestible" work on Wagner by Fétis (*Baudelaire as Critic*, 201).

semantic meaning for the instrumental music. Next, he quotes even more extensively from Liszt's article, again italicizing almost identical semantic descriptions of the Prelude. We have already speculated about the possible influence of Liszt's essay on Wagner's. But, by placing Wagner's text sequentially before Liszt's, Baudelaire reverses the historical chronology, privileging Wagner as the authoritative source. The new chronology now suggests that Wagner describes his work as he "intended it," and Liszt – the professional musician – "gets it right" by using almost identical images. Baudelaire then adds another layer, offering his own thoughts and reactions to the music "to show that true music suggests analogous ideas to different minds."[225]

Given his interest in the narrative signification of instrumental music, it comes as no surprise that Baudelaire's essay emphasizes what he calls Wagner's "mnemonic system" (*système mnémonique*).[226] To discuss this technique, Baudelaire reverses his previous sequence of allowing Wagner and Liszt to speak first. He now writes from his "disadvantaged" position as untrained musician in order to demonstrate that Wagner's operas are "completely intelligible, even to a person who does not know the libretto."[227] The new system presents characters who are "heraldically emblazoned by the melody."[228] But more than just tagging the character, the melodic idea "represents his moral character." Just as Wagner and Liszt (actually the other way around) had preached, Baudelaire argues that the orchestra reveals a linguistically unachievable depth of psychological perspective and insight. Only after presenting his own thoughts does Baudelaire repeat Liszt's claim that the music is intelligible "even for those for whom eighth notes and sixteenth notes are meaningless hieroglyphics."[229] Baudelaire is just such a person, and yet has come to understand Wagner, and passionately so. Speaking for everyman, he takes the discourse previously reserved for the cognoscenti and mediates it to a wider, though admittedly still elite, circle. The ensuing conversation amongst Wagner dilettantes will eventually form the basis for the formation and sustenance of the Wagner societies.

The reviews and essays by Uhlig, Liszt, and Baudelaire that frame the decade between 1850 and 1860 constitute a small though significant sampling of the journalistic effort to push Wagner, countered by an equal and opposite effort to retard the Wagnerian steamroller. Franz Brendel's New

---

[225] *Ibid.*, 199.
[226] Baudelaire's essay is reprinted in the appendix of Miner's book, from which I quote the French: *Richard Wagner et "Tannhäuser" à Paris*, 167–96, here 185.
[227] Baudelaire, *Baudelaire as Critic*, 212.
[228] My translation of "blasonné par la mélodie" (Miner, *Resonant Gaps*, 185).
[229] Baudelaire, *Baudelaire as Critic*, 218.

Year essay of 1852 thematizes the music world's "division into two camps," one conservative, the other moving boldly into the future.[230] But the *NZfM* was not just a positive force supporting Wagner; it also attacked the anti-Wagner camp, like Carl Gollmick's four-part review essay condemning the French critic Fétis.[231] Given its length, the article could have been printed in one or two issues, but spreading it out over four served to keep the attack active in the minds of the readership. Its appearance coincided with Uhlig's three-part and substantial discussion of *Opera and Drama*: anti- and pro- appeared side-by-side. The constant public visibility Wagner received as a result of the journalistic warfare, the controversy, has ultimately been beneficial to the Wagner industry, and to those who continue to make their livelihood from the scandals it perennially generates. All this began in the 1850s. But the promotional efforts by and on behalf of Wagner during this decade were not limited to journalism.

Still in the realm of print culture, and despite his own claim that extracting moments and hits from Wagner's works was impossible, between 1848 and 1882, Liszt arranged and published a series of fifteen piano transcriptions that brought Wagner into living rooms in ways that would be matched only later with the advent of sound reproduction technology.[232] Writing piano transcriptions was not new. But transcriptions of Wagner operas supported the claim that his music was for everyone, and precisely not some indigestible avant-garde "music of the future."

Wagner: up close and personal

Liszt's campaign to bring Wagner into everyone's living-room was accompanied textually by Wagner, who enlisted the genre of autobiography for the purpose. Originally a retrospective form written towards the end of a life, in

---

[230] "Mehr und mehr scheiden sich jetzt zwei bestimmte Parteien," "energischen Drängens nach Fortschritt," Brendel, "Im neuen Jahr," *NZfM* 36.1 (1852), 2.

[231] Carl Gollmick, "Herr Fétis, als Mensch, Kritiker, Theoretiker und Componist," *NZfM* 36.2–5 (January 9–30, 1852), 16–17, 31–2, 44–5, and 51–3. In turn, Fétis published his own extensive series on Wagner in the *Revue et Gazette musicale de Paris* starting June 6 and ending August 8, 1852.

[232] Fantasy on Themes from *Rienzi*; Spinning Chorus from *The Flying Dutchman*; Ballad from *The Flying Dutchman*; Overture to *Tannhäuser*; Recitative and Romance "Evening Star" from *Tannhäuser*; Two pieces from *Tannhäuser* and *Lohengrin*: I. Entry of the Guests from *Tannhäuser* and II. Elsa's Bridal Procession from *Lohengrin*; From *Lohengrin*: I. Festival and Bridal Song, II. Elsa's Dream, III. Lohengrin's Admonition; Pilgrims' Chorus from *Tannhäuser*; Isolde's Liebestod from *Tristan and Isolde*; "Am Stillen Herd" from *Die Meistersinger*; Valhalla from *Der Ring des Nibelungen*; Solemn March to the Holy Grail from *Parsifal*.

Wagner's hands autobiography becomes a means to craft and refine a current image and a means to claim the future. Wagner wrote and rewrote his autobiography approximately every ten years ("Autobiographical Sketch" 1842, *Communication to my Friends* 1851, "Music of the Future" 1860, *My Life* 1865–). These works are designed to elicit sympathy and understanding, to offer "the official story," reveal special insights into Wagner's intellectual and emotional development. They bring us "up close and personal," a technique developed by Roone Arledge of ABC-Sports as an approach to introducing and popularizing unknown athletes. Short bio-spots were broadcast before the sporting event, because if people cared about the athletes they were watching, the event would be more meaningful.[233] Arledge understood that being, or at least feeling, more knowledgeable was critical to the experience. Not unlike the Arledge spots and their descendants, Wagner often seeks an emotional connection by focusing on hardship overcome and perseverance against all odds. He seems to grant the reader the most intimate access to his inner self: "My true nature, which recoiled from modernity and yearned for the more and most noble … etc."[234] Wagner fashions himself as the living embodiment of the Romantic artist: "I became aware of my extreme loneliness as an artistic person."[235] He writes with apparently disarming honesty about his lack of success: "I wrote my death sentence with this work: I could no longer hope to survive in the modern art world."[236] Invariably, Wagner's language becomes intense, direct, completely shedding the obtuseness of the aesthetic works. The reader becomes an engaged participant, a moral supporter – a friend – and it is to them, "*to Friends who love me*" (emphasis in original), that he dedicates his work.[237] The division of the Wagnerian world into friend and foe is a mentality still evident in Bayreuth. For Wagner, to be loved and to be understood become identical. If you do not love, it is because you do not understand. For Wagner, everything is personal.[238]

These autobiographies serve as an interface between the composer, the work, and the audience: a means of translating the mysterious incomprehensibility of creativity. Hartmut Zelinsky correctly accuses Wagner of "mythifying the artistic creative process," but he should have added that

---

[233] Lisa Pike Masteralexis, Carol Barr, and Mary Hums, *Principles and Practice of Sport Management* (Sudbury, MA: Jones & Bartlett, 2008), 391.
[234] *SSD* IV: 485.
[235] Ibid., 510.
[236] Ibid., 485.
[237] Ibid., 407–8.
[238] "[E]in Künstler meines Strebens geliebt und seine Kunst somit verstanden werden, wenn dieses Verständniß und jene ermöglichende Liebe nicht vor Allem auch in der Sympathie, d.h. dem Mitleiden und Mitfühlen mit seinem allermenschlichsten Leben begründet ist" (*SSD* IV: 402).

Wagner's method is highly rationalized.[239] While literary scholars nowadays are at pains to avoid identifying fictional characters and their stories too closely with the autobiographical details of their creators, Wagner frustrates that separation. As the example of the Paris novellas show, his fictional works function as a blueprint for his life.[240] The opposite is also the case. His purportedly non-fictional autobiographies fictionalize his life and creative process. For instance, the rough sea passage he survived in 1839 becomes the inspiration for *The Flying Dutchman*. Wagner relates something we have all experienced or can imagine – a rough sea voyage – to something we cannot: creating a complex and compelling piece of music where there was nothing but a blank sheet of paper before. By relating the one to the other, Wagner invites the reader into the creative process, makes it seem more ordinary. Zelinsky may call it mystification, but the pretence actually appears to reduce the mystery. So too with Wagner's "vision" in La Spezia, where the opening E-flat triads of *Rheingold* allegedly came to him in a half-sleep.[241] So powerful is Wagner's description of that moment, that even those scholars who have disproved its veracity are nevertheless compelled to repeat it.[242]

Eckart Kröplin attributes Wagner's "total need for spiritual communication" reflected in the unending stream of correspondence, essays, and autobiographies to a "deep-seated psychological urge," an inborn "pseudo-theatricality" that made him want to be the center of attention at all times.[243] That may be true, but Kröplin's explanation overlooks the enormous publicity benefit Wagner derived from this apparent psychological abnormality. During the 1850s, Wagner not only conceived the *Ring* project and the special circumstances of its ideal performance, but also began to prepare the world for the event. It was not enough for the work itself to be an unprecendented accomplishment; it also needed to be marketed as such.

The next chapter looks at some of the more subtle ways in which Wagner prepares and conditions his audience. While at work on the massive *Ring*

---

[239] Hartmut Zelinsky, *Richard Wagner – ein deutsches Thema: Eine Dokumentation zur Wirkungsgeschichte Richard Wagners 1876–1976*, 3rd edn (Berlin: Medusa, 1983), 16.
[240] "Hierin stellte ich, in erdichteten Zügen und mit ziemlichem Humor, meine eigenen Schicksale, namentlich in Paris, bis zum wirklichen Hungertode, dem ich glücklicherweise allerdings entgangen war, dar" (*SSD* IV: 456).
[241] *ML* 512.
[242] See, for example, Gregor-Dellin, *Richard Wagner*, 185–8. Also Reinhard Wiesend, "Die Entstehung des *Rheingold*-Vorspiels und ihr Mythos," *Archiv für Musikwissenschaft* 49 (1992), 122–45.
[243] Kröplin, *Richard Wagner*, 72–6.

project, Wagner composed *Tristan und Isolde* and *Die Meistersinger von Nürnberg*. Both present and explore the new Wagnerian aesthetic, using the characters on stage as model consumers. The works function as consumer guides, demonstrating ideal responses to the Wagner brand in anticipation of the full Wagnerian experience of the future: *Der Ring des Nibelungen* – location and time to be announced.

4 | Consumers and consumption

Wagner operas are also about Wagnerian opera. Wagner weaves the principles of his aesthetic theories into the dramatic fiber of the works themselves, so that they both thematize and perform his aesthetics. This suggestion is not new. Already during the first run of the *Ring* cycle in 1876, the critic Wilhelm Mohr answered Wagner's opponents by explaining that, "the old forms have not been shattered … but rather, just as Siegfried does with the sword Nothung, filed, smelted, recast and newly forged."[1] Nothung – forged from the fragments of the old sword – is a metaphor for Wagner's *Gesamtkunstwerk* which unifies modernity's fragmented arts, so misused in opera. In such a reading, Mime stands for Meyerbeer, while Wagner is Siegfried.

Such an approach also applies to Wagner's earlier works. In *Tannhäuser*, for instance, Venus and Wartburg can function as allegories of voluptuous Parisian Grand Opera versus the aesthetically impoverished German opera of Dresden. The Shepherd in the third scene of Act I occupies a distinct, utopian space reserved for the music drama of the future.[2] Wagner's own analysis of the *Lohengrin* Prelude suggests that the Holy Grail is nothing other than Wagner's music itself. The *Ring* has been read as replaying Wagner's version of opera history,[3] a thesis David Levin recently embellished by proposing that Siegmund is guilty of "breaking and entering" into Hunding's (opera) house: an act both figuratively and aesthetically representative of Wagner's project.[4] Admittedly, Siegmund – like Wagner – is the outsider in a hostile world, the fugitive seeking shelter and companionship (this is also how Wagner described himself). However, it is far-fetched to suggest that Hunding's abode represents the conventional opera house.

---

[1] Wilhelm Mohr, "Brief eines baireuther Patronatsherrn," VIII, *Kölnische Zeitung*, August 23, 1876 (quoted in Großmann-Vendrey, *Bayreuth*, I: 110).
[2] David J. Levin, "Randerlösung. Zur Dramaturgie der Figuration in Wagners *Tannhäuser*," *Figur und Figuration*, ed. Gottfried Boehm *et al.* (Munich: Fink, 2007), 263–71.
[3] See Nattiez, *Wagner Androgyne*, and Grey, *Wagner's Musical Prose*.
[4] David Levin, "What Does Wagner Want? Thoughts on an Aesthetic (and Ideological) Vocabulary," *University of Toronto Quarterly* 74.2 (2005), 693–702, here 693.

Still, Levin follows an established practice that considers Wagner's works as artful demonstrations his socio-aesthetic project.

Perhaps none of his theatrical works does this more blatantly than *Die Meistersinger von Nürnberg*. Like *Tannhäuser*, *Die Meistersinger* presents a song competition. But, unlike its predecessor, *Die Meistersinger* makes aesthetics – Wagner's as well as those of his opponents – its central concern. The work also presents the people of Nuremberg as a test audience to demonstrate for the theater audience how Wagner is ideally to be experienced. In *Die Meistersinger*, the theater audience sees itself – albeit idealized – mirrored on stage.[5]

Though *Tristan und Isolde* seems to be the opposite of *Die Meistersinger* – tragedy versus comedy, intimate drama versus mass spectacle, musically chromatic and progressive versus diatonic and conservative – it, like *Die Meistersinger*, stages Wagner's aesthetics, though metaphorically rather than expressly. It leads us through the creative process and the ideal mode of experiencing, this time modeled by the solitary individual rather than the cheering crowd. Together, the two works explain and demonstrate Wagner's "new" aesthetics. They are, in effect, marketing vehicles that seek to win an audience, one by one at first, but ultimately a nation.

Audience of the future

What is this audience Wagner seeks to attract? Raymond Williams's observation that there are no masses, only ways of organizing people as masses,[6] seems borne out by Wagner's division of audiences into three groups: his "friends," "the public," and "das Volk" (a loaded and untranslatable word meaning "the people").

Wagner's "friends" begin as a circle of supporters and admirers he knew personally, who agreed with his aesthetic direction and, more importantly, were often able and willing to support him financially. By the early 1850s, these "friends" had grown in number to form what Benedict Anderson in a different context has called an "imagined community": anonymous fans whom Wagner nevertheless addresses directly, as if to distinguish them from the impersonal mass audience of his competitors. His "Communication to my Friends" is already such a gesture, apparently and "modestly" directed

---

[5] I disagree with the 2007 Bayreuth staging by Katharina Wagner, who presents a Nuremberg audience which mirrors the theater audience as a mindless, bored, mass-consuming public.
[6] Raymond Williams, *Culture and Society: 1780–1950* (Harmondsworth: Penguin, 1963), 289.

to the few who would have any interest in what he had to say, thereby giving his artwork a boutique value: those who read it are the select.

Wagner's "friends" are literally that, but also his way of being "intimate" with and projecting personal, individualized qualities onto otherwise nameless listeners, a technique that recreates the personal relationship of aristocratic patronage, but also reconstitutes the aura of an authentic community. This community exists today, even larger, assembled in Wagner societies, some founded during his lifetime, the base of popular and financial support (patronage) which perpetuates the Wagner industry, a network spanning the globe and guaranteeing an audience for Wagner's works wherever and whenever they are performed.

The concept of "friends" of the arts – meaning enthusiasts and financiers – was not Wagner's invention. In Vienna, for example, the *Gesellschaft der Musikfreunde* was founded already in 1812. But Wagner starts using the term "my friends" (*meine Freunde*) to mean *his* artistic supporters – as opposed to "merely" friends – in 1842, immediately after the successful premiere of *Rienzi*. By 1847, one paper sarcastically dubbed those loyal to Wagner as "Wagnerianer," as if to anticipate – and ridicule – the branding activities he was only on the threshold of beginning.[7] By the 1870s, "Wagnerianer" (as well as equivalents in French and English) is ubiquitous, used even by Cosima and Richard, and thus no longer exclusively a derisive suggestion of mindless idolatry.

Wagner makes no reference to the term "Wagnerianer" when it first appears, so it is not certain whether he was aware of it. However, shortly thereafter, Wagner modifies "my friends" to "friends of my art" (*Freunde meiner Kunst*), which is surely a different way of saying "Wagnerianer."[8] The timing of this shift corresponds to the articulation of his special aesthetic path. Wagner was being consistent. If his claim of an artwork different in kind and quality from anyone else's was to be valid, that uniqueness also distinguishes the audience, individually and collectively, which chooses to experience the work. Wagner describes these people as independent-minded men and women who display an aristocracy of taste that separates them from the mainstream.

---

[7] *Signale für die musikalische Welt*, May 19, 1847 (repr. in Kirchmeyer, III: 260). In a January 25, 1855, letter to Wagner, Liszt describes Karl Klindworth as a "Wagnerianer." Over time, Wagner adds adjectives to further describe both the special qualities of his friends and of his art: "besonders energischer Freunde meiner Kunst" (*SSD* XVI: 135), or "Freunde meiner besonderen Kunst" (*SSD* IX: 329).

[8] See, for example, his letters to Ferdinand Heine, November 19, 1849, and December 4, 1849.

This mainstream is the faceless body that comprises contemporary audiences. Wagner refers to them as "Publikum," sometimes as a "rabble" (*Pöbel*), and categorizes them as "philistines" and as "educated philistines,"[9] the literate middle classes who seek distraction after a day's work. While they possess the education and the means to attend opera, and the social urge to see and be seen, they have no independent taste. Wagner understands that this public is a product of modernity and is sensitive to the new dynamics of the public sphere, dominated by print media, and the developing phenomenon of popular consumer culture whose origins have been traced back to the late eighteenth century in England.[10] Racked with cultural insecurity, this new bourgeois audience was "losing faith in its own capacity to judge" (did it ever have one?) and "wanted to be told about what they were going to feel or what they ought to feel."[11] Wagner rails against the opinion-makers, art connoisseurs, and critics – whom he dubs "smart asses" (*Klugscheißer*) – who inundate the public: "ever since there have been connoisseurs, art has gone to hell. We only make the public completely stupid by drilling them with art information."[12] But Wagner also recognizes that this bourgeoisie, though reliant on the direction of the trendsetters, has the actual power in the form of disposable income.[13]

While it is perhaps historically too early to use the term "consumerism," Wagner was critiquing a behavior we refer to as consumption, meaning the acquisition and use of commodities and services that are considered luxuries, rather than necessities, with the goal of satisfying human wants and desires, rather than needs. While consumption of luxuries has always characterized the rich, the radical shift in social behavior and economic practice that occurred during the late eighteenth and early nineteenth centuries in Britain and Western Europe brought consumption of commodities increasingly into middle-class households which, in turn, created the conditions for what we call the mass market.

---

[9] "Bildungsphilister" ("Publikum und Popularität," *SSD* X: 85).

[10] "Pöbel keinesweges ein normales Produkt der wirklichen menschlichen Natur ist, sondern vielmehr das künstliche Erzeugniß Eurer unnatürlichen Kultur" (*SSD* III: 173). See also Neil McKendrick, John Brewer, and J. H. Plumb, *The Birth of a Consumer Society: The Commercialization of Eighteenth-Century England* (London: Europa, 1982).

[11] Richard Sennett, *The Fall of Public Man* (New York: Knopf, 1977), 209.

[12] Letter to Franz Liszt, October 2, 1850 (*SB* III: 431), also Letter to Ferdinand Heine (undated) presumably late September 1849 (*SB* III: 131).

[13] "Die vornehmen, feingebildeten und muthig fühlenden glauben oben zu stehen, – und wie irren sie sich! In unsrer heutigen weltordnung herrscht ganz unbedingt der Philister … Er ist die stütze des bestehenden, niemand anders – und gegen ihn kämpfen wir mit noch so adlichem muthe alle vergebens" (*SB* III: 432).

The artwork was part of this process, beginning with the explosion of the book trade. As a term, "consumption" is even more apt to describe the enjoyment of opera theater, the art form that addresses several senses, the emotions and the intellect, all directed to internalized experience. Like gourmet food, opera is consumed, giving pleasure (as opposed to mere nutrition) to body and mind. Goethe already uses the culinary analogy in the Prolog to *Faust*, when the Theater Director recommends that the poet create a "ragout" that will have something for everyone to enjoy. For the modern consumer, as Bertolt Brecht would argue when he used the term "culinary art," going to the opera has become no different than purchasing a certain kind of porcelain, or the choice of school to send the children. Like fine china and education, art becomes a commodity to be purchased and consumed; possession projects status and, to use Bourdieu's term, social distinction.[14]

Wagner's art was to have no part in this turn towards consumption. And yet, as if making literal use of Ludwig Feuerbach's pun "you are what you eat" (*Der Mensch ist, was er ißt*), Wagner worked assiduously to form and direct "taste." By separating the friends of "his" art from all others, Wagner paradoxically conferred on them an exclusivity associated more recently with higher-end "designer" commodities, purchased often to make a statement about individuality, taste, wealth, etc. Wagner may have opposed the Parisian fashion industry. But, like producers who sell goods similar to others already on the market, he separated his product and its consumers from the ordinary, labeling them for their consumption preferences: "Wagnerianer."

Even though Wagner may have reviled the contemporary "masses," he did imagine the possibility of a large audience that he once calls: "my audience of the future."[15] These were to be neither his discriminating "friends," nor the "bored smart asses of today's privileged art world ... but rather all the healthy, uncrippled people with a brave heart."[16] Instead of being pumped with predigested opinion, this audience would rely on its own – innate – artistic sensibility. Ever the idealist, Wagner wanted to eliminate the separation between creator, performers, and audience, even suggesting

---

[14] Pierre Bourdieu, *Distinction: A Social Critique of the Judgement of Taste*, trans. Richard Nice (Cambridge, MA: Harvard University Press, 1984).

[15] "mein publikum der zukunft," Letter to Ferdinand Heine, undated, presumably late September 1849 (see *SB* III: 133, note 1).

[16] "klugscheißen wollenden gelangweilten unsrer heutigen privilegirten kunstwelt ... sondern alle gesunde, unverkrüppelte menschen, die ein eben so wackeres herz im leibe haben (*SB* III: 133). He wanted to bring his audience "zu wirklichen Gefühls- (nicht kritischem) Verständnisse" (*SSD* IV: 343).

once that actors be replaced by members of the community.[17] The "artwork of the future" is a communal project – precisely not a commodity – and audiences must participate in its creation. "Who will be the artist of the future?" he asks, "to put it bluntly: the people" (*das Volk*).[18]

"Das Volk," translated as "folk" or "the people," has no adequate equivalent in English because in German it has become a historically loaded term. In its modern usage, *Volk* was introduced in the eighteenth century by Johann Gottfried Herder, the pioneer of cultural anthropology, ethnography, and what today has developed into cultural studies. For Herder, *Volk* denotes a pre-modern, preliterate, indeed prehistoric, people: the original bearers of an oral culture and a murky concept Herder calls *Volksgeist* (spirit of the people). Perhaps most importantly in our context, this *Volk* were not "consumers." According to Herder's definition, in modern times, the original *Volk* can best be compared to today's "uncorrupted children, woman, people with good common sense – educated more through activity than contemplation."[19] Coded as a feminine body,[20] the *Volk* is irrational in a positive way, meaning that it relies on instinct and common sense rather than educated reason (coded male). It is striking that advertisers have historically targeted women for consumer products, and female readers were the prime audience for the emerging book industry.

Herder's cultural archeology, primarily concerned with Germanic peoples, proved crucial to the construction of an "authentic" German national identity. Subsequent nationalist revivals throughout Central and Eastern Europe are also indebted to his project. Originally aimed at political liberation from feudalism and imperialism, nationalism mutated in the late nineteenth century into the xenophobic variety based on racial-cultural purity that became the scourge of the twentieth century, especially in Germany.[21] Hence the problem now associated with *Volk*.

---

[17] "Ein Theater in Zürich," *SSD* IV: 324. The same idea appears more abstractly in *Communication to my Friends*: "die Absonderung des Künstlers vom Menschen [ist] ... wie die Scheidung der Seele vom Leibe" (*SSD* IV: 401).

[18] *SSD* III: 169. See also "Das Kunstwerk der Zukunft ist ein gemeinsames" (*SSD* III: 162).

[19] Johann Gottfried Herder, "Auszug aus einem Briefwechsel über Ossian und die Lieder alter Völker," *Sämtliche Werke*, 33 vols., ed. Bernhard Suphan (Hildesheim: Olms, 1994), V: 182 (hereinafter *SW*).

[20] Wagner does this too. See, for example, *Communication* where Elsa in *Lohengrin* is "das Weib ... diese nothwendigste Wesensäußerung der reinsten sinnlichen Unwillkür ... Sie war der Geist des Volkes" (*SSD* IV: 302).

[21] The National Socialists used Herder as an intellectual precursor and legitimizer of its cultural-racist policies, and much was also made of his intellectual proximity to Wagner. See Arne Stollberg, *Ohr und Auge – Klang und Form: Facetten einer musikästhetischen Dichotomie bei Johann Gottfried Herder, Richard Wagner und Franz Schrecker* (Munich: Franz Steiner, 2006), esp. 110–15.

Wagner was born into and later participated in the major groundswell of the German national movement, from the victorious wars against Napoleonic occupation to the liberal-nationalist student opposition movements of the second and third decades of the nineteenth century, that resisted the re-establishment of the *ancien régime* and its repressive policies. However, it is wrong to project the more recent twentieth-century coloring of *Volk* back onto Wagner, who combined Herder's term with his own vision of ancient Greek public festivals (*Volksfest*). At least rhetorically, Wagner's notions of *Volk* and *Volksfest* suggest a communal theatrical experience which produces a deep, primarily emotional, connection between artist and audience, unmediated by the commodified artwork. Thus his ideal audience, inspired by the poet, becomes a spontaneous "necessary co-creator."[22]

Years later, Wagner offers a glimpse of what he meant. To crown the celebration for the laying of the cornerstone of the Festival Theater in May 1872, a gala performance of Beethoven's Ninth Symphony was scheduled for the ornate Margrave's Opera House in Bayreuth. Its stage was too small to accommodate the large orchestra and even larger chorus Wagner had assembled, so he proposed placing some of the chorus in the auditorium, explaining: "this will actually satisfy my most ideal requirements in quite a splendid way, whereby the audience will *sing along* (like the congregation in the church)."[23]

Both of Wagner's imagined audiences – the "friends" and the *Volk* – are devices that circumvent or negate the notion of "consumers." *Tristan* and *Meistersinger* are elaborate attempts to demonstrate exactly this point, where Isolde embodies the quintessential "friend" and the people of Nuremberg represent the ideal *Volk*. At the same time, Wagner's music becomes nothing less than a commodity for consumption, moreover one that unabashedly claims to offer the greatest consumer satisfaction of all.

Tristan und Isolde

Though set in an indistinctly mythologized Middle Ages, replete with its feudal conventions and medieval assumptions, *Tristan* is nevertheless all about the experience of the modern subject, starting with its famous

---

[22] "zum nothwendigen *Mitschöpfer* des Kunstwerkes" ("Theater in Zürich," *SSD* IV: 324) (emphasis RW).

[23] "mit singen," two letters April 7, 1872, and April [ ], 1872, to Friedrich Feustel and Theodor Muncker (emphasis RW) in Richard Wagner, *Bayreuther Briefe (1871–1883),* 2nd edn (Leipzig: Breitkopf & Härtel, 1912), 71 and 76–7.

prelude. Lacking a definitive pulse and tonality, the music of the prelude is decoupled from time and space, those coordinates on which we rely for orientation.[24] A series of extended rests, which are "alive in the silence," fragment, disorient and alienate further.[25] These opening measures are the most-analyzed in the history of music, a "magnificent obsession," as Tom Grey calls it.[26] But this is the "wrong" reaction, reflecting not only our insecurity and uncertainty, but also our inquisitiveness and inability to "let go." Each in their different ways, both the Enlightenment and consumer society unleash obsessive behaviors and desires that cannot be satisfied, or only temporarily so.

Like the listener, Isolde and Tristan, disoriented, wracked with insecurity, both ask the identical question:

Act I, scene 1:

ISOLDE: *Brangäne, du? –*   Brangäne – you?
Sag', wo sind wir?   Tell me, where are we?

Act III, scene 1:

TRISTAN: *Kurwenal – du?*   Kurwenal – you?
Wo – war ich? –   Where – was I? –
Wo – bin ich?   Where – am I?

The opera, like the Enlightenment, delivers rational answers that work in the short term. These answers are set to diatonic music, that signifier for "rationality" and "convention." Kurwenal's response, accompanied by the so-called "Kareol" motif (Ex. 1), is even thematically related to the ultimate Wagnerian marker for conventionality – the "Mastersinger" theme (Ex. 2) – with its characteristic dotted rhythm and drop of a fourth.

But only when Tristan and Isolde learn to stop asking questions, when they overcome the desire to understand and control their environment, and instead to "let go," does the drama end.

Wagner's opera presents a hellish world of insatiable desire that threatens to "drive people mad."[27] But then, at the end, offers the solution to modern

---

[24] "Prelude" is a misnomer; Wagner uses the term "Einleitung" (Introduction) instead. On the significance of the distinction, see Alfred Lorenz, "The Prelude," reprinted in Richard Wagner, *Prelude and Transfiguration from* Tristan and Isolde, ed. Robert Bailey (New York: W. W. Norton, 1985), 204–23.

[25] *Ibid.*, 206.

[26] See Thomas S. Grey, "Magnificent Obsession: *Tristan und Isolde* as the Object of Musical Analysis," *Music, Theatre and Politics in Germany: 1848 to the Third Reich*, ed. Nicholas Bacht (Aldershot: Ashgate, 2006), 51–78.

[27] Letter to Mathilde Wesendonck, April 1859, "*gute* [Aufführungen] müssen die Leute verrückt machen" (*SB* XI: 58) (emphasis RW).

Ex. 1. *Tristan und Isolde*, Act III, "Kareol" motif

Ex. 2. *Die Meistersinger von Nürnberg*, "Mastersinger" motif

maladies. He even hints at this in an often-quoted, but insufficiently noted, passage from a letter to Mathilde Wesendonck shortly after completing the opera. There, in a single sentence that is packed with meaning, he describes his music as composed of "fine mysteriously fluid juices" (*feinen, geheimnissvoll-flüssigen Säften*) which penetrate one's pores, striking at one's very core (*bis auf das Mark des Lebens eindringt*) overpowering, sweeping away everything that constitutes one's personality, leaving only "the wondrously sublime sigh of unconsciousness" (*wunderbar erhabenen Seufzer des Ohnmachtsbekenntnisses*).[28]

Wagner's description of his music as a fluid that overpowers and forces one to "let go" is particularly striking in the context of *Tristan*. It also adds an important element to the long-standing idea of music as a fluid element – particularly water.

Music as (sound)waves

Like others before him, Wagner used aquatic metaphors in his aesthetic writings to make palpable, to give conceptual substance, to the ineffable qualities of music.[29] Especially outside of musicological discourse, such

---

[28] Letter to Mathilde Wesendonck, August 24, 1859 (*SB* XI: 197).
[29] Heinrich Besseler, *Das musikalische Hören der Neuzeit* (Berlin: Akademie, 1959), 68–75, and Heike Stumpf, "… *wollet mir jetzt durch die phantastisch verschlungenen Kreuzgänge folgen!*" *Metaphorisches Sprechen in der Musikkritik der ersten Hälfte des 19. Jahrhunderts* (Frankfurt am Main: Lang, 1996), 91–104, esp. 93.

metaphors have been common. Schiller begins *William Tell* with a song that pairs music with water, and its consumption with the danger of drowning (i.e. being unable to breathe).[30] For Herder, too, music is a watery element in which one can lose one's self, though in a good way.[31] Given how Wagner often credited his sources as a way of legitimizing his own ideas, it is significant that he never mentions Herder.[32] So his influence on Wagner is difficult to assess though, after the Herder festivals of 1844 and 1850, his impact on German culture increased markedly.[33] Nevertheless, it is hard not to think of Wagner, when Herder talks of music as the "melodic ocean of voluptuousness in which the cosmos undulates," and of "voices and sounds that collect and surge, swelling, lifting and carrying us … ever higher." He even seems to describe music's effect on Isolde, who "sinks, perishes in the ocean of my art."[34]

Herder uncannily writes about a kind of overpowering music that anticipates an idiom not yet in existence. Being overpowered was appealing for some, like Baudelaire,[35] and threatening, decadent, even immoral for others.[36] When Eduard Hanslick complains of being carried away by an "ocean," he means that Wagner's compositional technique – from the perspective of Classical aesthetics – was unstructured.[37] Other contemporary critics

---

[30] Schiller, *Wilhelm Tell*, Act I: "Es lächelt der See, er ladet zum Bade, / Der Knabe schlief ein am grünen Gestade."

[31] Herder, *Ob Malerei oder Tonkunst eine größere Wirkung gewähre? Ein Göttergespräch* (*SW* XV: 233).

[32] Stollberg talks of "aesthetic meeting points" putting Herder and Wagner in the same "tradition" (*Ohr und Auge*, 175).

[33] See *Ohr und Auge*, esp. 88–9. The Herder volume Wagner possessed did not contain any works which address music. See also Bernhard Becker, "'Anonymität' der Wirkungsgeschichte, Phasen der Herder-Rezeption 1871–1945," *Johann Gottfried Herder: 1744–1803*, ed. G. Sauder (Hamburg: Meiner, 1987), 423–36, here 424.

[34] Herder, *Die Tonkunst. Eine Rhapsodie*, *SW* XVI: 268–72: "melodischen Wohllustmeer / In dem das Weltall wallt" (269). Also "Stimmen und Töne wie Wogen des Meers *sammeln* und *steigen* und schwellen hinauf, uns hebend und tragend über der Fluth des Gesangs; neue Wellen des Stroms strömen hinan und brechen jene, uns höher und höher zu tragen" (*Kalligone*, *SW* XXII: 271). "[V]ersinken, sie gehn im Ocean meiner Kunst unter" (*SW* XV: 227). See also Stollberg, *Ohr und Auge*, 183–5. John Deathridge points out the similar imagery and even identical vocabulary between Nikolaus Lenau's 1841 poem "Beethovens Büste" and the *Liebestod* (*Wagner Beyond Good and Evil* [Berkeley: University of California Press, 2008], 138–9). While I agree about the similarities, Lenau's poem describes Beethoven's music, whereas the *Liebestod* is about the effect of Wagner's music on the listener.

[35] Baudelaire felt "overwhelmed, a truly sensual pleasure, like that of rising in the air or being tossed at sea" (Letter to Wagner, February 17, 1860 in *Baudelaire as a Literary Critic*, 192).

[36] Thorau, *Semantisierte Sinnlichkeit*, 69.

[37] Eduard Hanslick, "*Die Meistersinger* von Richard Wagner," *Die moderne Oper: Kritiken und Studien* (Berlin: A. Hoffmann, 1875), 292–305, here 297, and "Ocean der melodischen Unendlichkeit" (304). See also Thorau, *Semantisierte Sinnlichkeit*, Chapter 2.

welcomed the more free-flowing style and called for listeners who would "abandon themselves"[38] describing the ideal act of listening as: "a perfect plunging into the ideas of the work … an unconditional surrender,"[39] that merges the irrational experience of music with that of religion.[40]

Wagner modified this established system of signification when describing his music, making innovative metaphorical use of "water" and "breath" in their varied states.[41] The first sentence in the "Music" (*Tonkunst*) section of *Artwork of the Future* says, "The seas separate and connect the lands just as music separates and connects the two extremes of human art: dance and poetry."[42] Music is the medium through which dance and poetry become intelligible to each other. These three sister arts (dance, poetry, music) are to be (re-)united in Wagner's artwork of the future, the *Gesamtkunstwerk*.[43] Music itself is a union of rhythm and melody where sound (*Ton*) is the "original watery element" (*flüssiges ureigenes Element*) whose infinite extension becomes the "ocean of harmony" embodied by the orchestra.[44] Sound is not yet music, because it lacks motion. Music requires movement. The agent that sets it in motion (rhythm) is the "breath of air" (*Lufthauch*) which stirs the ocean of sound and so creates the "waves of melody" (*Wellen der Melodie*).[45] When we listen to music, we immerse ourselves in this ocean of wind-swept waves (*in dieses Meer taucht sich der Mensch*) like the poet, as male principle, who must sink himself into the oceanic depths to complete the act of generation.[46]

As we saw in the previous chapter, Wagner engenders and sexualizes music: "Music is a woman."[47] Not a specific woman, but the idea of woman, the feminine principle or, to use Goethe's memorable term which concludes

---

[38] *Musikalisches Wochenblatt* 1 (1870), 168.
[39] *Signale für die Musikalische Welt* 27 (1869), 770.
[40] See James H. Johnson, *Listening in Paris: A Cultural History* (Berkeley: University of California Press, 1995), esp. the later chapters on the "Social Roots of Silence" and "The Musical Experience of Romanticism."
[41] The abundance of aquatic metaphors has been noted by many with little or no comment. For an exception, see the careful discussion of water allusions in Grey, *Wagner's Musical Prose*, esp. 154.
[42] "Das Meer trennt und verbindet die Länder: so trennt und verbindet die Tonkunst die zwei äußersten Gegensätze menschlicher Kunst, die Tanz- und Dichtkunst" (*SSD* III: 81).
[43] It is these three sisters who, according to Nattiez's provocative reading of the *Ring*, are allegorized on stage, embodied by the three Rhinemaidens at the outset of the *Ring* cycle.
[44] "Tiefe des Meeres der Harmonie" (*SSD* IV: 142), also *SSD* III: 157.
[45] *SSD* III: 83. Also "Dieser Athem aber ist – die Musik" (*SSD* IV: 127).
[46] "denn auch dem Athem des Windes gebietet nun der Dichter, – denn dieser Athem ist nichts Anderes, als der Hauch unendlicher Liebe, der Liebe, in deren Wonne der Dichter erlöst ist, in deren Macht er zum Walter der Natur wird" (*SSD* IV: 146–7).
[47] "Die Musik ist ein Weib" (*SSD* III: 316). See also Chua, *Absolute Music*, Chapters 15 and 16.

Faust, Part II: "das Ewig-Weibliche" (the eternal feminine). Music is fluid; it addresses feeling. Poetry is solid – land – the male principle, the "fertilizing seed," and it addresses the intellect, logic.[48] The biology may be flawed, the comparisons disturbingly simplified, but the imagery is clear. Music, fertilized by poetry, resembles the amniotic fluid out of which drama emerges. "Melody" – that most "visible" element of music to which the poet responds – is like the surface of the water, the perfected union of heart and mind, "the conscious unconscious," the "most urgent desire for love."[49]

Wagner's metaphors continue the Romantic idea of music which – like water and air – is unfathomable and ungraspable. In addition, the water metaphor suggests that music, pure music – Wagner's music – is not a commodity, because it is essential. Of course, both water and air were being commodified even in Wagner's day, and no one knew this better than Wagner himself who spent not inconsiderable time at water cures in the pristine air of the Swiss Alps. His first wife, Minna, even dubbed the doctor who ran the facility in Albisbrunn as a "Wasserjude" (Water Jew). Wagner was most amused and thought the idea "excellent" (*vortrefflich*),[50] the implication being that only a Jew would find a way to make money off water.

From the *Flying Dutchman* to *Lohengrin*, water is ubiquitous in Wagner's dramas, even the early ones, and its dramatic significance warrants a separate study. The grandest aquatic example is the opening to *Rheingold*, which almost biblically suggests: "In the beginning was the Sound." This sound – an E-flat in the basses and cellos – is void and without form: "an acoustic thought,"[51] not yet music. A "divine breath"[52] sweeps over the surface of the waters in the form of horns that blow a rhythmic pattern that traces an E-flat-major triad and, after a while, induces the strings to form musical

---

[48] "Denn es ist dieß das gebärende Element, das die dichterische Absicht nur als zeugenden Samen aufnimmt" (*SSD* IV: 155), and "dieser zeugende Samen ist die dichterische Absicht, die dem herrlich liebenden Weibe Musik den Stoff zur Gebärung zuführt" (*SSD* IV: 103).

[49] "der Wasserspiegel ... Jenes wogende Spiegelbild ist die Melodie" (*SSD* IV: 142). "[D]as bewußte und deutlich verkündete Unbewußte" (*SSD* IV: 142); "es ist die Liebe selbst, und nur als höchstes Liebesverlangen ist das Weibliche zu fassen" (*SSD* IV: 146).

[50] See letter to Uhlig, October 30, 1851 (*SB* IV: 151).

[51] Thomas Mann, "Es war zuviel verlangt, den Es-Dur-Dreiklang ... bereits Musik nennen zu sollen. Es war auch keine. Es war ein akustischer Gedanke: der Gedanke des Anfanges aller Dinge," *Leiden und Größe Richard Wagners*, 3 vols., ed. H. Kurzke (Frankfurt am Main: Fischer, 1978), III: 78.

[52] *The New English Bible, Oxford Study Edition* (New York: Oxford University Press, 1976). The note accompanying Genesis 1:2: "in non-Hebrew epics, the wind-god was the creator. Here, however, the sea and wind are portrayed as creations, subject to God." While the Luther and King James translations refer to "Geist" and "Spirit," the more literal translation of the *New English Bible* seems preferable in this context.

ripples.[53] Breath has turned sound into sound waves, conveying a sense of time and form; sound becomes music.[54]

But this is a new music, because the traced outline of the E-flat-major triad replaces Classical harmony with the physical overtone series making the opening "sound like a historical transition from intervals to frequencies, from a logic to a physics of sound."[55] The composer of the future will be an audio technician: instead of traditional notes, scores of the future will contain the duration and decibel levels of numerically identified sound frequencies. A century before this future was realized, *Rheingold*'s opening is already dedicated to sound as such. There, music replaces the "logos" and stages the historical "transformation of literature into sound."[56] Music drama "defeats all literature"; makes it "obsolete." It is "the first mass-medium in the modern sense," a "monomaniacal anticipation of modern media technologies" – the "revolutionary darkness" of the Bayreuth Festspielhaus a presentiment of the cinema.[57]

Friedrich Kittler transposes the water-wave metaphor from its nineteenth-century, late Romantic connotations of the unfathomable and the ungraspable to the twentieth-century concept of the wave as the basic unit of communication. Wagner's persistent invocation of waves anticipates the conceptual and fundamentally anti-intellectual foundation of the media revolution which, around 1900, would begin to replace the centuries-old culture dominated by print-technology – that made "literature" possible – with one almost solely reliant on waves of sound, light, and electric "current."

Tristan und Isolde – the medium is the message

The curtain of Act I rises on a seascape. The setting, a ship – an extension of "dry land," a piece of technology that prevents us from sinking into

---

[53] For Carl Dahlhaus this "musical image of the elemental … consists of simple sound waves derived from the broken chord of E flat major," in *Richard Wagner's Music Dramas*, trans. Mary Whittall (Cambridge University Press, 1979), 117.
[54] "die Athemkraft des allbelebenden Windhauches" (*SSD* III: 82).
[55] Friedrich Kittler, *Gramophone, Film, Typewriter*, trans. with intro by Geoffrey Winthrop-Young and Michael Wutz (Stanford University Press, 1999), 24. See also Grey, *Wagner's Musical Prose*: "In a matter of measures, music has (re-)evolved from its primitive origins into the music of the future" (266). Also Hanke, *Wagner in Zürich*, 363–8: "als wollte Wagner die Musik … nochmals gänzlich neu erfinden" (366).
[56] Kittler, *Gramophone*, 59.
[57] Kittler, *Gramophone*, 23; and Friedrich Kittler, "World-Breath: On Wagner's Media Technology," *Opera Through Other Eyes*, ed. David J. Levin (Stanford University Press, 1993), 215–35, here 215–16.

the deep – becomes a metaphor for our estrangement and separation from music. A sailor sings an "aria" about separation. Separated also from view, a disembodied voice, his lonely "air" is pure melody without accompaniment, a breath that blows as he inhales and exhales, merging with his duty as a sailor assigned atop the mast where he must be attuned to the blowing wind, the main theme of his song: "Frisch weht der Wind / Der Heimat zu."[58] The sailor gazes nostalgically and lustfully back to Ireland (*Westwärts schweift der Blick*), while the ship sails undaunted eastwards towards the future (*ostwärts streicht das Schiff*). An extended wordplay merges the wind's blowing with bulging sails, while seemingly mocking the sighs (*Wehen*) of an Irish maiden. The wind is commanded to blow (*wehe*), and the Irish maid to beware (*wehe*).[59]

In the tent below the mast, Isolde, an Irish maiden separated from her home, is enraged. She wants to destroy the ship and plunge its contents into the seas, and calls upon the winds to stir the waters. But her powers fail: she is "degenerate," has lost the skill, is "not worthy of her ancestors." The old powers replaced by the "tame art" of brewing potions.

Consuming one of these potions will set the drama in motion. Until that moment, both Tristan and Isolde, though seething with unexplored emotions, suppress – as convention demands – their deepest feelings. Tristan tends to his duty as captain of the ship. Isolde retains her composure in public. Only in the privacy of her chambers – and to her alter-ego, Brangäne – does she give full vent to her thoughts. The potion changes everything. Even before he drinks, Tristan refers to it as the "benevolent potion of forgetfulness" (*Vergessens güt'ger Trank*). He anticipates death, but the effect is like drinking from Lethe: both he and Isolde will forget all the codes that root them in their world, that make social interaction work. Released from the sphere of established modes and predictable forms, they are thrust into a new world of permanent instability, cast adrift, morally rudderless with no guide except for desire and the need to satisfy it: a solipsistic realm of unquenchable wants, a new form of slavery that consumes them until their final release. It is a delusional existence in which they believe they are the

---

[58] Some of the following is also in Kittler's "World-Breath," see esp. 225–7. Kittler even notes: "Human Voices and winds, winds as human voices" (227), but he does not take this analogy to its conclusion, rather focusing on the notion of "breath" and the physiology of acoustics.

[59] Kittler notes the wordplay as does Jeremy Tambling who points to the "pun with suggestions of sighing, woe, pain, and drifting, and seem to anticipate Isolde's death, even as they also imply that the woman's breath may destroy the male. The pains include labour pains: no wonder Isolde feels mocked," see Jeremy Tambling, *Opera and the Culture of Fascism* (Oxford: Clarendon, 1996), 61.

world, as they both exclaim during their love duet: "Selbst dann bin ich die Welt."

In the oft-quoted letter to Liszt, where Wagner first exclaims his newly found passion for the philosopher Arthur Schopenhauer, he also makes brief reference to his developing *Tristan* project, which he declares will be a "monument to the most beautiful of all dreams: love."[60] Wagner never repeated this description. Nevertheless, its ubiquitous use in the Wagner literature reflects a misconception of the completed drama. Neither Schopenhauer nor *Tristan* deal with "love" as such. Schopenhauer is concerned with "will" as the motor of nature: in living organisms, the will to live and procreate. In *Tristan*, this "will" manifests itself as desire and, at its most extreme, as passion. To be sure, there are moments in *Tristan* where both feelings and gestures of the deepest love are manifest. However, it is desire that drives the characters and propels the drama.[61]

Modernity, where insatiable desire rules in place of the old Gods, has – according to its critics – bequeathed rootlessness and instability. This is perfectly expressed by Wagner's new music, whose chromatic fluidity, freed of stricture, yet condemned to search without rest, manifests the inability to find resolution or to recover the lost harmonies of spirit, body, and nature.[62] *Tristan* offers but one solution: release to a different world. In the Wagner literature, this is alternately described as the noumenal[63] or the realm of night. Whatever name we give it, access to it is mediated exclusively by music: Wagner's music.

Tristan und Isolde is thus ultimately about Wagner's music, about the extraordinary effort required to create it in a world hostile to nature and "true" art, but also about Wagner's music as a media revolution: a demonstration of its immense power to transport and transfigure those who "use it as directed." Inextricably entwined with the very modernity it proposes to counteract, *Tristan* resembles the proverbial vaccine that contains the disease it seeks to thwart.

The transitional moment in Act I when Tristan and Isolde drink the potion represents a shift of world-historical proportions, and it is marked with a series of silences that fracture the musical flow, making Tristan's and

---

[60] Letter to Liszt, December 16[?], 1854 (*SB* VI: 299).
[61] Eric Chafe remarks that "*Tristan* is about the meaning of desire" (*The Tragic and the Ecstatic* [Oxford University Press, 2006], 86).
[62] See Wagner's own description of this new kind of music: "eine endlose, nie beruhigte, ewig ungestillt zu sich selbst zurückkehrende, ewig wiederverlangend von Neuem sich erregende [Bewegung]" (*SSD* III: 83).
[63] Barry Millington, *The New Grove Guide to Wagner and His Operas* (Oxford University Press, 2006), 83.

Isolde's disorientation palpable and clarifying the meaning of the Prelude's beginning. Guided now by a different set of principles, their perception and interpretation of the world will henceforth be different from that of those around them. As the curtain falls on Act I, Tristan and Isolde – surrounded by a cheering crew, King Marke, and his courtiers – are only aware of each other, much to the consternation of those present.

This difference in perception is even clearer at the beginning of the second act. Rather than an invisible sailor, disembodied breath now takes the form of hunting horns, again off stage, again signifying separation. As long as the horns are audible, it is not safe for Isolde and Tristan to meet.[64] Isolde impatiently wants to give the signal for Tristan to approach, but Brangäne continues to hear the horns. Isolde retorts:

Sorgende Furcht beirrt dein Ohr;	Anxious fear misleads your ear;
dich täuscht des Laubes säuselnd Getön',	The leaves' rustling sounds delude you
das lachend schüttelt der Wind	which the laughing wind stirs

Isolde confuses a wind instrument with the natural wind. This difference in perception between Brangäne and Isolde[65] is depicted by shimmering strings which replace the off-stage horns to suggest the breeze Isolde senses. Then, once again, the horns play, and so Brangäne sings: "Ich höre der Hörner Schall" (I hear the sound of the horns). Isolde disagrees again, and in one of Wagner's most spellbinding musical transitions – a technique he calls his "art of transition"[66] – there follows a cross-fade (I deliberately use a term from film editing) during which the horns are imperceptibly replaced by oscillating violins and clarinets to represent the gently flowing water.[67] Isolde sings:

Nicht Hörnerschall tönt so hold;	Horn sounds don't sound so sweet;
des Quelles sanft rieselnde Welle	it's the gently rippling waves of the stream
rauscht so wonnig daher.	That rustle so delightfully hence

---

[64] Michael Tanner notes the structural similarities between the openings of all three acts, though does not see the significance I am suggesting; *Wagner* (Princeton University Press, 1996), 142.
[65] On this, see also Chafe, *Tragic*, 176.
[66] "Kunst des Ueberganges," Letter to Mathilde Wesendonck, October 29, 1859 (*SB* XI: 329).
[67] On this moment, see Kittler, "World-Breath," 225–6. See also Anthony Newcomb, "Ritornello Ritornato: A Variety of Wagnerian Refrain Form," *Analyzing Opera: Verdi and Wagner*, ed. Carolyn Abbate and Roger Parker (Berkeley: University of California Press, 1989), 202–21, here 210.

The listener "hears" both sets of perceptions: whose is correct?

More to the point, Brangäne and Isolde can no longer communicate with each other. Brangäne blames herself for substituting the love potion for the death potion. But Isolde explains that it is irrelevant which potion it was. Either way, they are now under the power of "Frau Minne." *Minne*, a medieval term meaning "courtly love," was replaced in modern parlance by *Liebe* (love). Wagner's use of *Minne* is consistent with the drama's medieval setting, but the musical context again suggests that he is not in the first place concerned with "love." When Isolde describes *Frau Minne's* magic powers (*ihres Zaubers Macht*), the "desire" motif sounds, this time not in its previous incarnation as a sparse fragment interrupted by silence (Ex. 3), but instead lusciously orchestrated with an irresistible harmonic extension that overwhelms, and even hints at the "Liebestod" to come (Ex. 4 – "desire" motif indicated in box).

Frau Minne, understood as desire, is the Schopenhauerian element of the drama. But it is also where Wagner parts with Schopenhauer's concern with a universal and timeless force that exists within. In Wagner's thoroughly modern conception, desire may be omnipresent, but it is unleashed through and reinforced by consumption which creates a never-ending cycle of wants. Even if Tristan and Isolde consummate their desire sexually, the satisfaction will only be temporary: the interrupted sexual encounter in Act II is a drastic demonstration of the limited satisfaction hedonism offers. In a world bereft of a higher purpose which calls on us to sublate our profane feelings, desire – like will – knows no end other than death.

King Marke represents the old world which demands that individuals conduct themselves according to societal expectations and religious codes originating outside their bodies. Hence his bewilderment at Tristan's behavior. As if to underscore the impossibility of communication between two paradigms, Tristan responds to Marke's request for an explanation:

O König, das –	O King –
Kann ich dir nicht sagen;	I cannot tell you that;
und was du fräg'st,	And what you would ask
das kannst du nie erfahren. –	You can never know …

Pre-modernity and modernity are incommensurable. However, the freedom to act that modernity delivers brings neither joy nor contentment, but rather estrangement, separation, and misery.

Ex. 3. *Tristan und Isolde*, Prelude to Act I, "desire" motif (basic version)

Ex. 4. *Tristan und Isolde*, Act II, "desire" motif (in box) with extension

Ex. 5. *Tristan und Isolde*, Act III, variant of the "desire" motif

Act III begins with a bleak representation of this state, music Heinrich Porges somewhat redundantly described as "black melancholy."[68] Melancholia, that psychological response symptomatic of the modern condition, is presented in sound as a dark and somber transformation of the "desire" motif in the low strings (Ex. 5).

For Wagner – the "greatest melancholic of music"[69] – desire is the agent of modern maladies. This mood continues as a cor anglais plays off stage, feigning the sound of a shepherd's reed pipe. The unaccompanied eerie melody sounds like Julia Kristeva's description of the melancholic's speech pattern: "a repetitive rhythm, a monotonous melody … dominate the broken logical sequences, changing them into recurring, obsessive litanies."[70] Breath, still disembodied, still instrumentalized, opens yet another act, again to signify separation. Isolde is not there; the seas are barren and empty (*Öd' und leer*). The shepherd's *alte Weise* – meaning "old song" but also "the old way of doing things" – awakens Tristan from his semi-coma. Act III can be considered the structural complement to Act I where, this time, instead of Isolde and Brangäne, Tristan confides in Kurwenal. But Tristan's feverish delirium – only superficially explained by the wound he suffers from Melot's sword – comes from his death struggle between two modes of consciousness. "As Tristan tries to forget the past, he is compelled to remember it."[71] The "old way of doing things" compels him to ask "where am I?" but this consciousness only separates him from Isolde, so he willfully plunges

---

[68] "schwarze Melancholie," Heinrich Porges, *Tristan und Isolde*, intro. by H. von Wolzogen (Leipzig: Breitkopf & Härtel, 1906), 50.
[69] "grösste[r] Melancholiker der Musik," Nietzsche, *Fall Wagner*, §7.
[70] Julia Kristeva, *Black Sun: Depression and Melancholia*, trans. Leon S. Roudiez (New York: Columbia University Press, 1989), 33. Kristeva constantly uses musical terms to describe melancholia: "rhythms," "harmonize," "vocalizations," "musicality," "intonations," "tonal modulations," see, for example, 22, 26, 33, 34, 38, 44, and 55.
[71] Deathridge, *Wagner*, 219–20.

himself back into the semi-coma where he can at least fantasize his union with her.

Transfigurations and consumer satisfaction

Tristan und Isolde is not a tragedy, which is why Wagner calls it a "Handlung," a literal translation of the ancient Greek "Drama." Consumption of the potion unleashes the tragic element which holds sway until the drama's heroes are released from its grip – what Huyssen elsewhere has called a "vortex." There is no way to go backwards in history; the modern subject cannot be unmade. But there is a way out: total immersion in the aesthetic experience. Not just any aesthetic experience, but the specifically Wagnerian one. This is what the concluding moments of *Tristan und Isolde* offer.

"Liebestod" is a misnomer, and for good reason not the name Wagner gave Isolde's final aria. Despite the overwhelming consensus of critics to the contrary, the whole point is that she does not die; or, at least, her "death" is something essentially different from the fate suffered by Tristan, Melot and Kurwenal, all of whom literally "die" (*sterben*) according to the stage directions. Nietzsche tellingly refers to it as "a state of death in a living body"; Wagner uses a different word to describe Isolde's end: "transfiguration" (*Verklärung*).[72] The closing text offers crucial clues as to what is happening in these final moments, so I reproduce it here in its entirety with my literal translation:[73]

1	*Mild und leise*	Mildly and softly
	wie er lächelt,	how he smiles,
	wie das Auge	how the eye
	hold er öffnet:	sweetly he opens:
	Seht ihr's, Freunde,	do you see it, friends,
	säh't ihr's nicht?	Don't you see it?
	Immer lichter	Ever lighter
	wie er leuchtet,	how he radiates,
	Stern-umstrahlet	bathed in stars

[72] "Tot-sein bei lebendigem Leibe" (Nietzsche, *Richard Wagner in Bayreuth* §8 [in *Der Fall Wagner*, 63]). On the misnomer "Liebestod," see Wagner, *Prelude and Transfiguration*, 41–2. Deathridge describes the *Liebestod* as a "well-nigh perfect allegory of absolute music" (*Wagner*, 148).
[73] Discussions in English of the *Liebestod* often use Andrew Porter's translation (repr. in Wagner, *Prelude and Transfiguration*, 96–7). Though beautifully written, it is conceived to be sung. Kittler/Levin provide an excellent literal translation of portions of Isolde's aria which I consulted and borrowed ("World-Breath," 230).

10	*hoch sich hebt?*	Lifts himself up?
	Seht ihr's nicht?	Don't you see?
	Wie das Herz	How his heart
	ihm mutig schwillt,	proudly swells,
	voll und hehr	full and lofty
	im Busen ihm quillt?	in his breast it flows?
	Wie den Lippen,	How from his lips,
	wonnig mild,	wondrously mild,
	süsser Atem	sweet breath
	sanft entweht: –	gently blows: –
20	*Freunde? Seht!*	Friends? Behold!
	Fühlt und seht ihr's nicht?	Don't you feel and see it?
	Höre ich nur diese Weise,	Is it only I who hears this music,
	die so wundervoll und leise,	which so wonderful and soft,
	Wonne klagend,	lamenting bliss,
	alles sagend,	saying all,
	mild versöhnend,	mildly reconciling,
	aus ihm tönend,	sounding from him,
	in mich dringet,	penetrating into me,
	auf sich schwinget,	rising upward,
30	*hold erhallend*	sweetly resounding
	um mich klinget?	Ringing around me?
	Heller schallend,	Sounding brighter,
	mich umwallend,	Surrounding me,
	sind es Wellen	are they waves
	sanfter Lüfte?	of gentle airs?
	Sind es Wolken	Are they clouds
	wonniger Düfte?	of wondrous aromas?
	Wie sie schwellen,	How they swell,
	mich umrauschen,[74]	rush about me,
40	*Soll ich atmen,*	should I breathe them,
	Soll ich lauschen?	should I listen?
	Soll ich schlürfen,	Should I drink,
	untertauchen,	immerse myself
	süss in Düften	sweetly in airs
	mich verhauchen?	Turn myself into breath?

[74] Rauschen (*v/i*) is a term used for both wind and water to mean "rush" and, as a noun, it is a term for radio to mean "rustle" or "static noise," for music to mean "swelling." Rausch (*n*) is also the word for intoxication, and figuratively used to convey the sense of a drug-induced state.

	In dem wogenden Schwall	In the churning surge
	in dem tönenden Schall	in the resounding reverberation
	in des Welt-Atems	in the blowing all
	wehendem All	of the world's breath
50	*ertrinken*	drown
	versinken	go under
	unbewusst	unconscious
	höchste Lust	ecstasy

The aria contains two sections. The first ends with "Don't you feel and see it?" (line 21). The stage directions read: "Isolde, aware of nothing around her, fixes her eye with mounting rapture upon Tristan's corpse." What does she see? A sustained chord in the horns and bass clarinet seems to breathe life into Tristan. Isolde in turn describes a breath which emanates from him; the strings vibrate with a sustained tremolo. The long-delayed reunion of air and water, the male and the female, commences. But, in an astonishing gender reversal, Tristan (the male) produces the music while Isolde (the female) poetically describes the experience.[75] Tristan, reborn as music itself, his body a mere vessel for transmission (*aus ihm tönend*). Isolde, the receiver (*in mich dringet*), the vibrating membrane with the switch turned on.[76] The sexual suggestion confirmed by Isolde's musical reprise of the Act II love duet.[77] But this alternative version represents a possibility far more satisfying than sex.

So powerful are the sound waves emitted by the orchestral surge, that Isolde's commentary, her vocal line, becomes increasingly unintelligible, secondary – a comment made even by Wagner.[78] Again quoting Kristeva, it is like "depressive speech, *repetitive*, monotonous … *empty of meaning, inaudible* even for the speaker before he or she *sinks* into mutism" (my

---

[75] Lawrence Kramer discusses this moment sensitively but misses some of its subtlety: "This fictitious Tristan is then dissolved into a fluid element, explicitly identified with the music we are hearing, that pours from Tristan to Isolde and finally envelops her, its origin forgotten," *Music as Cultural Practice, 1800–1900* (Berkeley: University of California Press, 1990), 163.

[76] For Nattiez, Tristan is the "poet and creator" while Isolde is the "spirit of music," but even within the frame of his semiotic-psychoanalytic study, this metaphor does not really work (*Wagner Androgyne*, 153–4). Deathridge, for whom Isolde is "transformed into an innocent shell serving only to *receive* the sounds of Tristan's music," also suggests that Nattiez has things exactly the wrong way around (*Wagner*, 141).

[77] On the sexuality of this sequence, Kramer writes: "Libido, in short, is preeminently *fluid*, and indeed Freud's favorite metaphors for it are figures of fluidity, of currents that flow within and between persons" (*Music as Cultural Practice*, 141) (Kramer's emphasis).

[78] See Deathridge, *Wagner*, Chapter 12, esp. 148 and note 53, which discusses this point in greater detail.

emphasis).[79] The others on stage see nothing but Tristan's lifeless body and an incoherent Isolde. But we, the acoustically privileged, understand what is happening.

The second section – Isolde's "transfiguration" – conveys her growing desire to become one with the music pouring out of Tristan. But what is this wonderful medium she senses, and how does one consume it, she asks in a series of questions?[80] Are they waves of air (lines 34–5)? Or sweetly smelling clouds (lines 36–7)? How does one consume a cloud that is both water turned into air, and air as water? Does one breathe it (*atmen*)? Drink it (*schlürfen*)? Plunge into it (*untertauchen*)? Does one transform oneself into its breath-like state (*verhauchen*)? Isolde's growing urgency is matched by a similar development of musical tension.

Enveloped by sound (*um mich klinget*) which no one else senses, Isolde moves permanently into her alternate consciousness. She finally stops asking questions and submits to total sensory satiation in a life-breathing universe: *Welt-Atems wehendem All*.[81] The orgasmic release, denied in the second act, now achieved, is not sexual. Body is replaced by spirit. Isolde delivers herself whole, awash in waves of sound, unconscious, ecstatic. The desire motif is finally resolved, and the offending instrument that represented it – the cor anglais – no longer sounds. Isolde: the totally satisfied consumer.

Wagner's *Tristan und Isolde* is a work about "letting go" of critical faculties, about total release where music becomes a sensual, spiritual, religious experience: the opposite of a commodity. It resists the Enlightenment and depicts Isolde's liberation from a culture whose "core social practices and cultural values, ideas, aspirations and identities are defined and oriented in relation to consumption."[82] But by modeling instead the consumption of music, Wagner's claimed antidote to and escape from modernity ironically becomes not only a metaphorical extension but a tangible expression of the commodity culture it feigns to defy, and anticipates strategies used by advertisers of highly processed products. Consumer culture promises exactly what Romanticism accuses modernity of having lost: authenticity. *This butter was hand-churned by a farmer's wife; your SUV will get you closer to raw nature; this shampoo makes you feel as though you were under a waterfall on an unspoiled tropical island; this chocolate will give you an orgasm.*

---

[79] Kristeva, *Black Sun*, 43, again talking about the melancholic's speech pattern.
[80] Gutman misses the point, or gives up too easily, when he writes that "the text really tells little, its words having more effect than sense" (*Wagner*, 252).
[81] See Kittler, "World-Breath," esp. 231.
[82] Don Slater, *Consumer Culture and Modernity* (Cambridge: Polity, 1997), 24.

Tristan promises and delivers an authenticity of experience (orgasmic ecstasy) by artifice and, as such, anticipates the development of a consumer culture which increasingly takes the form "not of material goods at all but of signs and representations … of services and experience."[83] *Tristan und Isolde* is not just another opera about love and death, but rather claims to deliver for the audience exactly what is being modeled on stage: the satiation of desire that, in the final moments, is sublimated from the sexual to the aesthetic sphere, as if, only there, such satisfaction is possible, as if going to *Tristan* will make you feel like the best sex you never had.

Who needs sex when you have Wagner's music? – The ultimate commodity, with Isolde as blonde, blue-eyed spokesperson to demonstrate its ideal mode of consumption.[84] Wagner's music, the antidote to the melancholia of modernity – an illusory cure maybe, but no less desirable. Almost exactly one hundred years before Marshall McLuhan's memorable formulation of 1964 – in *Tristan und Isolde*, "the medium is the message."

Die Meistersinger von Nürnberg – infomercial in three acts

While *Tristan und Isolde* conceals its advocacy of the Wagnerian brand beneath layers of metaphor and allegory, *Die Meistersinger von Nürnberg* is a bold and emphatic endorsement. To draw a provocative comparison with more recent advertising techniques, *Tristan und Isolde* uses product placement ("I want what that woman is having"), while *Die Meistersinger* is structured like an infomercial, which is a more prosaic way of saying that "Wagner conceptualized *Die Meistersinger* … as an accompaniment to the composition of his other works, partially … to serve as their justification."[85] But "justification" seems too defensive a word for a work whose triumphant tone so overwhelms from start to finish. *Die Meistersinger* quite aggressively and proactively promotes Wagner's aesthetic direction by also disparaging, distorting, and ultimately silencing the competition. At its conclusion, the Wagnerian brand emerges as the only choice.

Die Meistersinger is – among other things – an exposition of aesthetic difference and choice, where Walther von Stolzing represents unbridled inspiration and talent with no awareness of formal structures, Sixtus

---

[83] *Ibid.*, 32.
[84] "the producer must create an image of use value in which potential buyers can recognize themselves" (*ibid.*, 31).
[85] Lydia Goehr, *The Quest for Voice: On Music, Politics, and the Limits of Philosophy*, The 1997 Ernest Bloch Lectures (Oxford: Clarendon, 1998), 50.

Beckmesser stands for closed-minded, rule-bound pedantry, and Hans Sachs mediates between the two, giving talent and creativity its due, though tempered by established, time-honored principles of poetic convention. Lydia Goehr has argued recently, that the opera is a calculated aesthetic failure, that Wagner demonstrates the dangers of a "too-easy satisfaction," wanting audiences to reject the pleasures of the Prize Song, in order to prepare the way for his aesthetically more difficult but ultimately more "Wagnerian" works, especially *Tristan*.[86] But her argument is as counterintuitive (one should reject or at least be suspicious of an artwork that one enjoys) as it is elitist (an aesthetically challenging work is more worthwhile than one that is easily digestible).

The mistake is to think of *Tristan* and *Die Meistersinger* as opposites. Rather, they draw from the same set of principles, mirroring each other. The unconscious realm into which Isolde sinks, never again to be seen, is the same dream world from which Walther draws his inspiration, but which he brings forth to share with the rest of us.[87] *Tristan* is innovative; *Meistersinger* thematizes the issue of innovation. *Die Meistersinger* models and elicits a calculated satisfaction identical to the experience at the conclusion of *Tristan*, which audiences in those early years found difficult to accept. The public euphoria on the festival meadow of Nuremberg echoes the intensely private feelings of the *Liebestod*: we surely have permission to enjoy both!

The aesthetic gateway to Wagner's mature operas, *Die Meistersinger* serves as a marketing vehicle constructed in a manner similar to the so-called "infomercial," a television advertisement that runs the length of a normal program while employing devices to conceal its promotional agenda. Infomercials sometimes use a talk-show format where an actor plays the moderator (salesperson) who "interviews" the product's designer. A pseudo-technical conversation imparts important "information" about the product and how it differs from previous designs or the competition. A guest star plays the "ideal" consumer, or a paid studio audience (representing the "average" consumer) samples the product at the conclusion of the program.

It would be wrong to overdraw the parallels between the normally thirty- or sixty-minute disposable infomercial on the one hand and, on the other,

---

[86] See Lydia Goehr, "The Dangers of Satisfaction: On Songs, Rehearsals, and Repetition in *Die Meistersinger*," *Wagner's* Meistersinger: *Performance, History, Representation*, ed. Nicholas Vazsonyi (Rochester, NY: University of Rochester Press, 2003), 56–70.

[87] See also Chafe, *Tragic and Ecstatic*, 35.

Wagner's five-hour masterpiece – certainly among the greatest operas ever written – that continues to provide deep aesthetic nourishment to audiences around the world. Nevertheless, it is intriguing how Wagner incorporates promotional techniques that have more recently become so familiar.

Obsolete vs. brand new?

Given Wagner's progressive agenda, it may seem ironic that the stage work blatantly espousing it would be his formally most conservative. With the possible exception of *Tannhäuser* – which opens with a rising and descending fourth – no opera by the mature Wagner begins with as marked a gesture of conventionality as the Prelude to *Die Meistersinger*, with its characteristic descending fourth (C–G) and rather basic exploration of the C-major scale. Into this conventional diatonic world, bursts a mercurial chromatic theme in E major, that suggests contrasting reference points – old and new – to be pitted against one another as the work unfolds.

This polarity is repeated musically and enacted dramatically when the curtain rises at the beginning of Act I: a traditional chorale sung by solid church-going folk begins with a descending fourth (C–G) and a rising C-major scale, reminiscent of the Prelude. Between the fermatas which normally mark the division between the chorale's phrases, the chromatic theme again interrupts as musical explanation for the audacious and desirous glances exchanged on stage between Walther and Eva, who attend to their feelings and each other, rather than to God and the religious service. As if to steal space, Wagner extends these "traditional" gaps to the limit. For a while, the two worlds coexist, occupying separate musical spheres. As the chorale ends, however, tradition and resistance mix, with the chromatic theme providing counterpoint to the chorale melody: the two worlds are, it seems, not mutually exclusive. After all, both are about devotion. This opening scene functions structurally as a metaphor of the whole.

The binary opposition finds its next variation in the figure of David, who is both a stage character as well as a historical referent in the opera. The confusion between character and image is thematized when Eva exuberantly remarks to Magdalene that Walther looks just like David. "Are you mad, like David?" (*Bist du toll? Wie David?*) asks Magdalene, thinking of her boyfriend David, Sachs's apprentice. "No, like David in the picture" (*wie David im Bild*) responds Eva. But this only causes another misunderstanding. Magdalene now thinks Eva means the image of the old King David, with long beard, playing the harp, the symbol for the mastersinger guild. No, Eva is thinking of the dashing young David who felled Goliath with the sling-shot, so handsomely painted by Albrecht Dürer.[88] Of course, these two Davids are the same person at different stages of their lives. Eva is enamored with the upstart who defeats the Philistines. Young David fights the establishment; King David becomes its symbol.

Hearing his name called, David, the apprentice, enters. This real David is neither a Goliath-killer nor a king, but a diligent student of cobbling and mastersong composition. His lengthy aria is a detailed catalog of master tunes and their appellations. Some critics, starting with Hanslick, suggest that the aria is "horribly boring," but they miss the point.[89] This aria needs to be annoying, even boring, because it is the product of rote learning and sets up a counterpoint for Walther's "natural talent."

The dichotomy between tradition (old product) and innovation (new product) reaches its initial climax at the meeting of the mastersinger guild which concludes the first act. The mastersingers are introduced as a body of stolid men dedicated to preserving tradition for its own sake, having lost sight of the fact that the tradition itself came about as a result of change. Enter Hans Sachs: the prodigious poet-cobbler and most respected of the mastersingers who ends up playing the role of moderator. Wagner considered the historical Sachs (1494–1576) to be "the last example of the artistically-productive *Volk* spirit,"[90] a direct reference to Herder, whose ideas are at the core of Wagner's drama. Herder lamented that "our pedants patch together and memorize everything ahead of time only to stammer really methodically." Praising the "poets of old" like Homer, Herder advocated improvisation, because "art," which he codes foreign (non-Germanic), "extinguishes nature," and requires memorization of "syllable quantities which ear and nature no longer let us feel, and to work according to rules which a genius would least of all recognize as rules of nature."[91]

For Herder, the existence of "art" reflects the advent of cultural demise which can only be reversed by the *Volk*, meaning "uncorrupted children, woman, people with good common sense." Hence Sachs's observation in Act I that "a woman's opinion, quite untutored, is equally valid with

---

[88] There is apparently no evidence that Dürer painted such a picture, see Volker Mertens, "Mittelalter und Renaissance," *Wagner und Nietzsche: Kultur – Werk – Wirkung*, ed. Lorenz Sorgner, H. James Birx, and Nikolaus Knoepffler (Reinbek bei Hamburg: Rowohlt, 2008), 79–105, here 86.
[89] Hanslick, *Moderne Oper*, 294.
[90] "die letzte Erscheinung des künstlerisch produktiven Volksgeistes" (*SSD* IV: 284).
[91] Herder, *SW* V: 182.

popular opinion."[92] Consequently, Sachs proposes that "the *Volk* be judges too, they will assuredly agree with the child" (i.e. Eva).[93] Sachs wants "to test the rules" to see whether the mastersingers "are still on the right track," which only "someone who knows nothing of the table of rules" will be able to determine.[94] Fearing that Sachs is "abandoning the rules to the *Volk*," Kothner, speaking for the masters, rejects his apparently demagogic proposal: "Art is threatened with downfall and disgrace / if it seeks the favor of the *Volk*."[95]

But Kothner and Sachs are talking about two different audiences. Kothner wants to protect his art from the "masses." By contrast, Sachs trusts the innate aesthetic good taste of the *Volk*. Kothner's *Volk* is actually the modern public; Sachs's *Volk* is Wagner's "audience of the future."

Given the different paradigms, there can be no meaningful exchange between Sachs and the others, so it is time to introduce the special guest, Walther von Stolzing, who is interviewed by the assembled group. He has left his aristocratic estate and intends to establish residence in Nuremberg. Walther seems to embody the transition from the rural feudal Middle Ages to a new town-centered modernity, while also turning his back on the aristocracy (coded French) in favor of a German-national bourgeois *Volk*. He also seems to be the opposite of the masters: he does not belong, is young, good-looking, and seems ignorant of the mastersinger rules and tradition. But is this really the case? When asked about his qualifications, he mentions that he has learned from a book of poetry by the thirteenth-century poet, Walther von der Vogelweide (lit. Walther of the Bird Meadow), known simply as "Walther." He may well be "long since dead" (*doch lang' schon tot*) as Beckmesser sneeringly remarks, but he is one of the so-called Twelve Old Masters whose memory the mastersingers are themselves dedicated to preserving. In other words, Walther von Stolzing (lit. "Proud to be Walther") is grounded in the same poetic tradition as the mastersingers themselves. Beckmesser's remark – motivated out of jealousy for the prospective rival that Walther turns out to be – thus lacks aesthetic legitimacy, especially since Kunz Vogelgesang points out that Walther has just sung "two nice verses" (*zwei artige Stollen*) i.e. that even when speaking informally Walther spontaneously communicates in traditional forms.

[92] Sachs: "Der Frauen Sinn, gar unbelehrt, / Dünkt mich dem Sinn des Volks gleich wert."
[93] Sachs: "So laßt das Volk auch Richter sein / Mit dem Kinde sicher stimmt's überein."
[94] Sachs: "Daß man die Regel selbst probier' … Und ob ihr der Natur / Noch seid auf rechter Spur … Das sagt euch nur, / Wer nichts weiß von der Tabulatur."
[95] Kothner: "Gebt ihr dem Volk die Regeln hin? … Der Kunst droht allweil Fall und Schmach, / Läuft sie der Gunst des Volkes nach."

Ex. 6. *Die Meistersinger von Nürnberg*, Act I, Sc. 3, "guild meeting" motif

Ex. 7. *Die Meistersinger*, Act I, Kothner calls the meeting to order

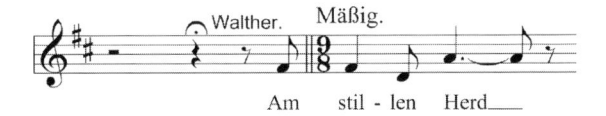

Ex. 8. *Die Meistersinger*, Act I, Walther's first aria

This deep connection between Walther von Stolzing and the mastersingers is emphasized musically. The motif used to signify the mastersingers' meeting – first heard at the beginning of the scene when the masters enter the church (Ex. 6) – is repeated in the same key when Kothner subsequently calls the roll (Ex. 7). His roll-call and explanation of the Tabulatur – set to a rich faux-Baroque contrapuntal accompaniment in the orchestra – reek of bloated pomposity and a marked datedness. In performance this is often sung with a smug cynicism, especially the richly melismatic rendition of the Tabulatur. But such readings miss the fact that, musically, Wagner in these passages presents the compositional foundation of the Western (German) art-music tradition of which he too was a product. Kothner may not represent the future, but he does embody solid origins. So it is clear why Walther's first aria, "Am stillen Herd," in which he talks about the influences on his writing and singing style, though in D major, begins with exactly the same melodic line in terms of interval relationships (Ex. 8).

Ex. 9. *Die Meistersinger*, Act I, Walther's "Trial Song" ("*Fanget an!*")

    Even if they do not want to admit it, the mastersingers and Walther come from the same place. However, the way they honor that heritage differs. The common origin and different path is stressed even more forcefully in Walther's so-called "Trial Song" ("Fanget an!") which follows. After his emphatic introduction that echoes Beckmesser's instruction to begin, Walther outlines the *identical* melody line from the meeting, this time even in the same key, F major (Ex. 9).

    Only then does he "stray from the path." While the F-major tonic triad of the meeting/roll-call motif is repeated over and over and over, turning in on itself – blinkered, self-absorbed, trapped in an endless loop, unable to move forward – Walther breaks free. Carried by rising chromatic waves in the strings, he moves rapidly up the F-major scale, ending on a massive dominant-seventh chord – which even hints at a ninth chord – that sets up the roller-coaster ride to follow. Walther's song has a kind of pulsating momentum and an undulating harmonic freedom not yet heard in the opera,

Ex. 10. *Die Meistersinger*, Act I, Sc. 3

Ex. 11. *Die Meistersinger*, Act III, *Abgesang* from Walther's "Prize Song"

so the rejection by the masters is quite understandable: they are shaken to the core. Significantly, Walther's words – filled with fluid metaphors and erotic suggestions – occasionally even echo Isolde's *Liebestod*.[96]

Like Isolde before him, Walther's song seems like gibberish to the masters who, led by Beckmesser, criticize him vociferously. When Sachs offers an alternative opinion, the orchestra plays a four-note descending chromatic figure (Ex. 10) from G to E that extends a three-note idea already introduced in the E-major section of the Prelude. With its extension and played in unison with only implied harmonies, this chromatic descent becomes a highly exposed inversion of the desire motif from *Tristan* (see Ex. 3), which Walther will repeat in the second half of his Prize Song's *Abgesang* (Ex. 11), albeit rendered harmonically harmless.

[96] Walther: "Das Blut, es wallt / Mit Allgewalt / Geschwellt von neuem Gefühle … / Mit Übermacht, / Schwillt mir zum Meer / … / Im wilden Wonnegefühle."

Walther's song may be "new," but it was not confused. He may have "left our path," says Sachs, but he strode with confidence.[97] Sachs's metaphor is both instructive and precise. He alone realizes that Walther was initially on the same path, but has taken a different route.

At the behest of Sachs, but over the chaotic objections of Beckmesser and his supporters, Walther continues his aria, comparing himself to a bird with golden wings, soaring above the scavenger birds (ravens, crows, magpies) who stay closer to the ground and feast on the remains of the day. He flies bravely away from the town and back to the meadows (*Vogelweid*) where he can once again commune directly with "Master Walther."[98] Walther von Stolzing has an unmediated connection to the old master whose very name embodies nature. Still, staying with the ornithological analogy, even though his species of bird may move with greater freedom than its more land-bound relations, it is nonetheless subject to the same universal laws of gravity.

Testing the competition

The bird analogy continues in the second act. Alone in his workshop, Hans Sachs broods over the day's events. As the warm evening breeze spreads sweet scents, the horns play a haunting version of Walther's aria accompanied by an ever-so-gentle shimmer in the strings. Removed from the noisy chaos that sought to drown out Walther at the end of the previous act, the essence of his song is now presented much slower and drawn out, its constituent parts separated like ingredients which Sachs can savor with gastronomic delight. He tries to grasp the elusiveness of inspiration: "it sounded so old, but was so new: like birdsong in sweet May."[99] Sachs has grasped the secret of Walther's art: its novelty is grounded in fundamental and tested aesthetic principles of composition, a song inspired, but not fettered, by tradition. It is not – as Katharina Wagner would have us believe in her well-intentioned but fundamentally misguided 2007 Bayreuth staging of the opera – that the originally rebellious Walther "sells out" in order to win his prize. Walther never seeks the destruction of the aesthetic system, because he is rooted in it.

The centerpiece of Act II – Beckmesser's serenade – relates retrospectively to the preceding act and prospectively to the third. Both structurally

---

[97] Sachs: "verließ er uns're G'leise, / schritt er doch fest und unbeirrt."
[98] Walther: "dahin zur grünen Vogelweid', / wo Meister Walther einst mich freit."
[99] Sachs: "Es klang so alt, und war doch so neu, – / wie Vogelsang im süßen Mai."

and aesthetically, it is Beckmesser's song (as opposed to the mastersingers *per se*) that is Walther's competition.

Retrospectively, the circumstances of the Act I "Trial Song" scene are replayed, but this time Beckmesser performs and Sachs is the marker. The structural repetition is underscored both musically and textually with exact references back to the first act. Prospectively, however, Beckmesser offers a test performance of what he expects to be the prize-winning song. Sachs offers aesthetic insights and critical commentary which transcend his job as marker, and prefigure the role he will play in the lengthy duet with Walther during the third act.

The riotous ending of the second act provides a form of sociological commentary on the aesthetic stakes of the opera, and serves as an exponential intensification of the discord (literally) which concluded the first. There, too, chaos had reflected the aesthetic turmoil evident in the theoretical rift between the masters and Walther. At the conclusion of the second act, this aesthetic discord becomes social, triggered by Beckmesser's song which literally drives people mad. If, in William Congreve's often misquoted words, "Musick has Charms to sooth a savage Breast," Beckmesser's offering has the opposite effect: it transforms people into savages.

Does Beckmesser's song mimic the Jewish cantorial style – as Marc Weiner argues in his substantial and thought-provoking book?[100] If Weiner is correct, that settles the thorny issue of Beckmesser as a caricature of the Jew.[101] Weiner emphasizes the melismatic qualities of Beckmesser's serenade, which he considers a marker for the cantorial style. However, Kothner's rendition of the Tabulatur in the first act had already used this musical-vocal device. Melisma *per se* stands for outdatedness and was considered "unsuitable for the presentation of serious, noble or deep feelings," by Wagner and the "New German School."[102] The significant difference is that Kothner's reading of the Tabulatur is supported by a rich orchestral accompaniment, while the town clerk is left to stand sonically naked with nothing but the twang of his lute. It is not the melismas (i.e. the vocal line), but the presence or absence of the orchestra which delivers the crucial commentary. Kothner may be pompous and obsolete, but he represents

---

[100] Weiner, *Wagner and the Anti-Semitic Imagination*, 117–27.
[101] The debate that flourished in the mid-1990s concerning *Die Meistersinger*'s possible anti-Semitic content is given a balanced presentation and appraisal by Hans Vaget, "'Du warst mein Feind von je': The Beckmesser Controversy Revisited," *Wagner's* Meistersinger, ed. Vazsonyi, 190–208.
[102] See Schneider, "Wagner, Berlioz und die Zukunftsmusik," *Liszt und die Neudeutsche Schule*, ed. Altenburg, 85.

core values of a tradition that the opera never disparages. Beckmesser is left all but cast out.

Product launch

If the first act serves to introduce the basic set of product possibilities (conventional works routinely produced, adhering to a rigid regimen of rules versus a naïve free-flowing creativity in harmony with nature), it also grants the theater audience an insider look at a guild meeting, where the body controlling the production of art reveals its disdain for the consumer – often the consequence of a monopoly. The second act centers around a public demonstration of the competing product (the leading brand). Given the experience, status, and reputation of its maker, this product should have received good ratings. However, Beckmesser's song fails at every level.

The third act introduces the advertised new product and at some length, beginning in the workshop itself, where the theater audience gets a behind-the-scenes look at the creative act with explanatory narration from Sachs. What will turn out to be Walther's prize-winning song is presented in its discrete segments: *Stollen, Stollen, Abgesang*, thus apparently laying bare its internal structure. We then hear the second *Bar* without interruption. The third and final *Bar* is delayed – to increase the suspense – only to be "improvised" later when Walther sees Eva. This will be Eva's first meeting with the song and, although Sachs whispers to her that this is a "mastersong," she clearly already senses this (intuitively). The suspense is ours – "will Walther manage to come up with the required third *Bar*?" – not hers. Like the *Volk* in the festival scene that follows, Eva *knows it when she hears it*. For the theater audience, this third hearing of the song represents a musical-emotional release that anticipates the catharsis of the fourth and final performance in the Festival scene. It is a consumer satisfaction, achieved through what Adorno would later describe as the new mode of listening to music, characteristic of the age of mechanical reproduction.[103]

Modern listeners hardly know any more what it is to hear a piece of music for the first time. Relationships with music are based on repeated listening. Knowing "how it goes" replicates a feeling of coming home – a sense of familiarity confirmed, and expectation satisfied. A half-century

---

[103] Theodor W. Adorno, "On the Fetish-Character in Music and the Regression of Listening," *The Essential Frankfurt School Reader*, ed. Andrew Arato and Eike Gebhardt (New York: Continuum, 1982), 270–99.

before recording technology would begin to offer consumers this possibility, Wagner creates its conditions in *Die Meistersinger*, a condition that also lies at the heart of Wagner's so-called "leitmotif" technique. Did Wagner sense that modern audiences are no longer open to that with which they are not already familiar? The constant replaying of the prize-song-to-be in *Die Meistersinger* anticipates mechanical and now digital reproduction which, like a form of brain-washing, lends music a sense of inevitability.

To aid the process of familiarization, Sachs provides pseudo-technical information to Walther, and in so doing delivers a short course in song appreciation to the theater audience. But it is only the appearance of technical information. The theater audience understands as little about the art of composition at the conclusion of the scene as today's ordinary consumer really understands how "High Definition" or "Bluetooth" or "fuel cells" work. In both cases, however, special terms and buzzwords are dispensed with a modicum of explanation sufficient to make the consumer feel empowered.

Walther also has no idea about composition. He asks Sachs naïvely: "how shall I begin according to the rules?" Sachs's much-quoted answer: "You set them yourself and then follow them" has been interpreted as Wagner's justification to ignore rules, and as a mandate to be original for its own sake.[104] Such a reading turns Wagner into an aesthetic anarchist, architect of a poetics that grant license to create with no regard to anything other than personal inclination. This is not, however, Wagner's theoretical position, nor is it the aesthetic agenda of either *Die Meistersinger* or even the more adventurous *Tristan*.[105] Wagner stands for the opposite of aesthetic anarchy: that true creativity, while based on inspiration, nevertheless adheres to forms that are (feel) natural.

Walther's song originates in a dream, which he "naturally" retells in *Bar* form, again suggesting that this structure is *per se* not the object of Wagner's aesthetic attack. This common heritage is depicted melodically in each *Stollen* which begins with a fourth drop (E-B), an echo of the mastersinger motif that starts the opera. Walther begins on the same path but, as in the first act "Trial Song," he strays by making the endings of the two *Stollen* different from each other, even though the rules stipulate that they must be identical. The first *Stollen* begins and ends solidly in C major, confirming the basic key. The second half of the second *Stollen*, filled with F♯s, sets up a move to the dominant G where it ends. The increased tension makes the release into the *Abgesang* much more irresistible and thus "satisfying." The

---

[104] Walther: "Wie fang' ich nach der Regel an?" / Sachs: "Ihr stellt sie selbst, und folgt ihr dann."
[105] On this point, see also Grey, "Magnificent Obsession."

Abgesang then begins not with the conservative drop of a fourth, but with a drop of a fifth (G–C) followed immediately with a drop of a sixth (E–G). Walther literally takes the tradition "a couple of steps further" and, as if to demonstrate this, he echoes Sachs's chromatic descent from Act I supported in the orchestra by the melody of the *Abgesang* (see Ex. 11).

Walther's song is an "organic" creation, a spontaneous and symbiotic combination of music and poetry welling from the depths of his being: supposedly a reflection of Wagner's own compositional method. Wagner did not actually compose this way, but he would have us believe he did. His theoretical works, his autobiographies, even the artwork itself, all press home this claim, which Walther enacts on stage. Wagner's art is thus genuine, not "artifice" like the competition.[106] What he meant by "the organic nature of a real artwork"[107] is perhaps most famously recounted in the "vision of La Spezia" when he describes how the beginning of *Das Rheingold* came to him in a half-sleep. That this "vision" was a carefully crafted self-stylization of the compositional process in order to present Wagner's music as something "more natural" and less calculated only underscores the significance of its echo in *Meistersinger*.[108] Wagner's (and Walther's) art comes directly from the sub/unconscious world, uncorrupted by calculation. It is superior because it is natural, a favorite advertising device of contemporary manufacturers who, as Adorno points out, mask the industrial labor that goes into production, much as the invisible orchestra of the Bayreuth Festival theater conceals the origin of Wagner's sonorities.[109] In the spirit of Herder, Walther's song also recalls the "purer" (Homeric) oral tradition, because he does not write it down. Instead, Sachs takes dictation, and thus – true to Wagner's description of him – represents "the last example of the artistically-productive *Volk* spirit" as it transitions to the less intuitive, written, logocentric modern culture.

Before this new product gets its final push, Wagner puts one more nail in the competition's coffin. Re-enter Beckmesser, who finds and steals the

---

[106] *SSD* V: 31. Hanslick attacks Wagner precisely on the grounds that *Die Meistersinger* is a "product of reflexion" and does not, as it should, originate in the "magical power of the unconscious" (*Moderne Oper*, 305).

[107] "der organische eines wirklichen Kunstwerkes" (*SSD* V: 32).

[108] Wagner first mentions his vision in a letter to Emilie Ritter, December 29, 1854, and later more fully in *My Life*. The veracity of Wagner's tale has been challenged in recent scholarship, see, for example, Warren Darcy, "Creatio ex nihilo. The Genesis, Structure, and Meaning of the *Rheingold* Prelude," *19th-Century Music* 13 (1989), 79–100.

[109] Adorno, *In Search of Wagner*, 83: "In this respect Wagner's oeuvre comes close to the consumer goods of the nineteenth century which knew no greater ambition than to conceal every sign of the work that went into them."

text of Walther's song. Because of the handwriting, Beckmesser wrongly concludes that it is Sachs's, an assumption Sachs slyly does nothing to rectify. Even though Sachs lets Beckmesser keep the poem, Beckmesser's forthcoming performance originates in a criminal act. This is crucial, because it foreshadows the aesthetic crime he is about to commit. Sachs even warns him that the song's "performance is not easy even if you find the right melody."[110] But Beckmesser pays no attention. He will take what he thinks are Sachs's words and marry them to his own pre-existing melody already heard in Act II, saying: "Friend Sachs, you are a good poet / But where tone and melody are concerned, admit it, / no one surpasses me!"[111] This is Beckmesser's greatest crime. Abandoning the aesthetics of the mastersingers – who composed both text and music – he articulates the divorce between music and word characteristic of modernity. Beckmesser transforms himself into the sole outsider of the drama, the foreign element in the work. By a quirk of the dramatic action, his song will replicate the aesthetic constitution of French and Italian opera because text and music originate from two different creators. Saved from being a common thief by Sachs's "generosity," Beckmesser ends up worse: an aesthetic fraud.

As if to embody Herder's disdainful comments about "pedants," Beckmesser scurries off to "memorize" his lines. He next appears on the Festival meadow, his efforts at memorization futile. Unaware of his fundamentally erroneous aesthetic judgment, Beckmesser blames the text, but consoles himself with the following remark to Sachs: "I'm sure no one will understand the song, but I'll rely on your popularity."[112]

Like Kothner before him, Beckmesser has not understood the special nature of the Nuremberg *Volk* and so misjudges the essence of Sachs's "popularity." Beckmesser is thinking of modern consumer culture – controlled by a conspiracy of critics, the media, and successful advertising – that more readily accepts new products from established sources with a familiar and trusted brand name. Perhaps the *Volk* won't understand the song, he thinks, but because of Sachs's reputation, that won't matter. The quality of the artwork is less important than the PR it receives: "appearance over substance" as Wagner elsewhere dubbed his competition.[113]

---

[110] Sachs: "sein Vortrag ist nicht leicht; / ob euch die Weise geriet."
[111] Beckmesser: "Freund Sachs, ihr seid ein guter Poet; / doch was Ton und Weise betrifft, gesteht, / da tut's mir keiner vor."
[112] Beckmesser: "Das Lied, bin's sicher, zwar niemand versteht; / Doch bau' ich auf eure Popularität."
[113] "Schale ohne Kern" (*SSD* V: 31).

But the *Volk* behave quite differently because they spontaneously reject an artwork that is clearly ludicrous even though it is composed and performed by a leading member of the community. This is how modern theater audiences *should* respond to the equally meaningless offerings of French and Italian opera, except that they don't. Beckmesser's debacle may be overdrawn – as is Walther's success which follows shortly – but Wagner's point is that bad art is self-evidently so. However, the forces of commodification have numbed the senses and good judgment of the modern consumer.

But this is all a ruse, because the *Volk* of Nuremberg is of course no pre-modern body reacting "spontaneously." It is a professional studio audience following a closely scripted and carefully choreographed scenario: Wagner could not have been any more modern. Far from invoking Arcadia, then, the Festival meadow replicates the conditions of modern consumer culture, and employs tactics now common to advertisers. The competing product is presented in a poor light, while the advertised product is shown under the most favorable conditions. Beckmesser: "walks unsteadily and wobbles" (*tritt unsicher und schwankt*) and, as he steps on the podium, exclaims "how shaky" (*wie wackelig*) i.e. he is not on solid ground. At the end of his performance, Beckmesser is jeered off the stage and "is lost amidst the crowd" (*verliert sich unter dem Volke*). On the other hand, Walther "walks from out from the *Volk*" (*tritt aus dem Volke hervor*) and "proceeds with firm steps" (*beschreitet festen Schrittes*). Beckmesser sings supported only by the grating sounds of the lute he holds – a devastating realization of what Wagner called the "monstrous guitar," his description of the role played by the orchestra in Italian opera.[114] By contrast, the full orchestra magically and invisibly accompanies Walther with ethereally expansive tones, an anticipation of the Bayreuth Festival Theater with the surround-sound acoustics of its hidden orchestra.

The audience reactions, too, are demonstratively choreographed. The stage directions call for Kothner – who together with the other masters is eagerly reading along while Walther sings – to let go of the text and just listen.[115] The *Volk* also makes clear it is on the same wavelength. Walther may be unknown, but his song is "self-evidently" beautiful, no pre-publicity necessary. More significantly, the *Volk* reacts not as passive consumers, but

---

[114] "der italienische Opernkomponist, in dessen Händen das Orchester nichts Anderes als eine monströse Guitarre zum Akkompagnement der Arie war" (*SSD* VII: 130).
[115] "An dieser Steller läßt Kothner das Blatt ... vor Ergriffenheit unwillkürlich fallen; er und die übrigen hören nur teilnahmvoll zu."

actively as a community of feeling.[116] Just as Walther had inserted himself musically and dramatically into the pauses between the chorale phrases at the very beginning of the opera, now, in a structural analogy, the *Volk* inserts itself into the pauses between the discrete sections of Walther's song. They extend the duration of the dominant seventh that ends the second *Stollen* by delaying its resolution. In self-generated euphoric waves, the *Volk* sits on the dominant, not only increasing the tension but literally propelling Walther into the *Abgesang*, magnifying the "satisfaction" of the release. They model Wagner's imagined "audience of the future," functioning as co-creators and singing along "like the congregation in the church."[117] Prepped with repeated hearings of the prize song, the theater audience approvingly watches the "spontaneous" reaction of the *Volk* with a sense of superiority that grants its own satisfaction.

Buy German = buy Wagner®

The antagonism suggested throughout the opera between tradition and innovation, between old and new, turns out to have been a false dichotomy. This is the crux of Sachs's closing monolog so misappropriated first by German nationalists in the early part of the twentieth century, more recently by Wagner critics who, sadly, have simply accepted and adopted the Nazi reading, using it as the noose to hang around Wagner's neck. Contrary to prevailing academic opinion, still so burdened by the perversions of history, Sachs's closing paean to the glories of "German" art is not at all a foreign or forced element in the work, but is an explication and summation of the preceding dramatic action.[118] It is about honoring the

---

[116] *Volk*: "doch ist es grad', als ob man selber alles miterlebt."
[117] Wagner's footnote in the score reads: "Von allen mitzusingen" (*Sämtliche Werke*, IX, 3: 342). For a full musical analysis of the *Preislied*, as well as its impact on the *Volk*, see Stollberg, *Ohr und Auge*, 228–31.
[118] In a January 31, 1867, letter to King Ludwig II, Cosima claims that, shortly before completing the composition, Wagner considered dropping Sachs's monolog, ending instead with the Prize Song. Cosima apparently disapproved and "made a face" ("ich machte ein so jämmerliches Gesicht dazu"), so he reconsidered. This story has been repeated in the Wagner literature to exculpate Wagner from what many consider a misjudgement and a nationalistic stain on the opera, laying the blame on Cosima. However, Sachs's closing monolog was always integral to the drama from its inception in 1845, though the gravity of the sentiments grew in time.
I contend that Wagner's hesitation was momentary. It is neither to Cosima's credit nor is it her fault that the monolog was retained. See Richard Graf du Moulin Eckart, *Cosima Wagner: Ein Lebens- und Charakterbild* (Munich: Drei Masken, 1929), 333–4, and Cosima Wagner and Ludwig II von Bayern, *Briefe: Eine erstaunliche Korrespondenz,* ed. Martha Schad and H. H. Schad (Bergisch Gladbach: Gustav Lübbe, 1996), 348–9.

Ex. 12. *Die Meistersinger*, Act III, Sachs's final monolog

old German masters who have provided the bedrock upon which the new can flourish. The gesture is clear: the new must respect the old, but does so by taking the tradition one step further. Nowhere is this message more deliberate than in the orchestral response to Sachs's exhortation: "Do not disdain the masters, and honor their art" (*Verachtet mir die Meister nicht, und ehrt mir ihre Kunst*). At this moment, the violins play the melody of Walther's *Abgesang* (with its drops of a fifth and sixth) while in the basses, the Mastersinger motif sounds with its characteristic drop of a fourth (Ex. 12): innovation quite literally supported by tradition, sounding magnificent together in perfect contrapuntal harmony (see box).

The choice is not between old and new, but between home-grown and foreign products. The lesson of the opera is to "buy German" which in this case means "buy Wagner®."

The commercial twist is hinted at the end of the Prize Song, when the *Volk* sings "no one courts as well as he does" (*keiner wie er so hold zu werben kann*), a line repeated by Eva who replaces "er" (he) with "du" (you). As opposed to Eva's use of it, *werben* is a curious word choice for the *Volk*, if we think of its most obvious meaning in this context: to court. But *werben* also means "to advertise."

"Nobody *advertises* as well as he does." Eva and the *Volk* both play consumers: one of Walther's body and person, the other of his artistic product: Walther commodified. But the relationship is reciprocal: Walther wants to acquire Eva, too. This transaction may take place independently from the world of money – indeed the pre-modern setting is indispensable to the drama's subterfuge – but it is nevertheless a commercial transaction, which Wagner spends the better part of the opera trying to mask with the argument that the great artwork, like Eva's "love," is "priceless." Such is the conundrum the opera presents. Pogner's gesture to offer his daughter as the prize to the victor of the song competition may be wholly immoral in its pre-modern disrespect for the dignity of the human being, but it is frighteningly modern in its brutal recognition of the prostitution embedded in the practice of commodification which traffics as much in the human body as it does in inanimate material wares. The opera works hard to shield us from this truth.

"No one *woos* as beautifully as you." Just as Sachs had predicted, Eva, naïve child, embodies the voice of the people by echoing their words and musical line: to be sure, a love between Walther and Eva, but also a love affair between artist of the future and audience of the future. The potential inherent in art can only be realized if both artist and audience are spontaneous and active, if the separation between them melts away. This is surely the vision *Die Meistersinger* is supposed to convey, modeled by the stage audience of the future to transform the theater audience of the present. The *Volk* of Nuremberg – the post-consumer, responding "naturally" to the *Gesamtkunstwerk*, which has healed the wounds of the riot and restored both aesthetic and social order: the greatest happy ending of all. When you buy Wagner®, you get everything: aesthetic pleasure, satisfaction, and social harmony as well.

But has the theater audience of the present finally been freed from the influence of marketing, PR, and advertising, transformed into exercising its own aesthetic judgment spontaneously, once again able to appreciate the authentic work of art? Hardly. Just as the on-stage audience is NOT actually the *Volk* of Nuremberg, but paid actors, so too the audience response to the rousing final moments is anything but spontaneous. Instead, it has been musically and dramatically prepared for over five hours, and follows slavishly the exuberance modeled by the on-stage audience.

Die Meistersinger is a metaphor for the paradoxical nature of Wagner's project, which disavows all association with the commercial world, yet employs techniques to defame the competition and highlight itself, all in an effort to create a distinctive brand and induce customer loyalty. It also demonstrates the importance of physical space in translating idea into experience. The festival meadow of Nuremberg in this sense is a rehearsal for the Bayreuth Festspielhaus, the vessel into which all the self-marketing efforts of the preceding three decades could be concentrated, a tourist location which would become synonymous with the Wagner brand and the hub of the Wagner organization.

5 | Hub

In his book about the history of the Bayreuth Festival, Frederic Spotts suggests that "Wagner without Bayreuth would have been like a country without a capital, a religion without a church."[1] Typically for Wagner studies, Spotts limits himself to political and religious analogies, though he could just as easily have written "a multi-national company without a corporate headquarters." Similarly incomplete is his claim that "Wagner invented the modern music festival."[2]

The idea of a music festival was not new when Wagner conceived and later realized his vision for one. London boasted a commemorative Handel festival in 1784 and, in the same year, Birmingham launched its Triennial Musical Festival which would become one of the longest-running such events. By the first decades of the nineteenth century, music festivals were also established in Germany. Such occasions combined the renewed idealization of ancient Greek traditions with the urge to articulate a coherent German national identity, with its special emphasis on music. The longest-standing such tradition in Germany was the so-called Lower Rhine Music Festival, launched in 1818 and running through most of the century. This three-day event was held annually in the late spring during Pentecost, rotating its venue between a group of cities including Düsseldorf, Cologne, and Aachen. It was organized by amateurs and, in the early years, many of the orchestral and choral performers were also dilettantes, replaced increasingly by professionals during mid-century.[3] Despite, or perhaps because of, the amateurs, the program consisted mostly of major works by canonical composers like Beethoven, Mozart, and Haydn and, not unlike Wagner's own subsequent version, promoted a holiday atmosphere in which the general public participated actively in the performance of the pieces.

---

[1] Frederic Spotts, *Bayreuth: A History of the Wagner Festival* (New Haven: Yale University Press, 1994), viii.
[2] *Ibid.*, 5.
[3] Cecilia Hopkins Porter, "The New Public and the Reordering of the Musical Establishment: The Lower Rhine Music Festivals, 1818–67," *19th-Century Music* 3.3 (1980), 211–24. See also Bonds, *Music as Thought*, 92–9.

Music festivals also functioned as special events to spotlight newer works that were not yet part of the regular repertoire. The journey, often to remote locations, to hear such works took on the quality of a pilgrimage.[4] On June 22–3, 1852, Liszt co-organized such an event in tiny Ballenstedt. The festival featured several of Wagner's works, especially the overture to *Tannhäuser* which not only had to be repeated but, as a result of its success, was chosen to replace the programmed work by Mendelssohn scheduled to close the festival. While Liszt and Uhlig had already begun the journalistic campaign for Wagner in 1850, Helmut Kirchmeyer has argued that it was the Ballenstedt festival that marked the turning point in Wagner's fortunes most notably in Germany, especially because of a major review-article published by the influential Adolf Stahr.[5] From the start, Wagner had demonstrated his own predilection for special events, perhaps an indication of his sensitivity to what has become our own event-driven culture: for example, the Palm Sunday concerts in Dresden, his public–private reading of the *Ring* text in February 1853, and the May 1853 music festival in Zurich of three concerts exclusively featuring his works (*Rienzi*, *Flying Dutchman*, *Tannhäuser*, and *Lohengrin*).[6]

Even though there were precedents for the music festival Wagner founded, Bayreuth became something entirely different from preceding models, and much more than just a music festival. Marketed as an event of national importance, it continues to claim international attention. In this context, the concurrent development of the Richard Wagner festival and the festival in Stratford-upon-Avon dedicated to William Shakespeare is significant. In 1875, the same year Charles Garnier completed the Paris Opéra, a Stratford brewer named Charles Edward Flower launched a campaign to build a theater in the town of Shakespeare's birth. The Shakespeare Memorial Theatre opened in 1879 with a performance of *Much Ado About Nothing*, three years after the Bayreuth theater's first run of the complete *Ring* cycle.[7] There is much that links the two endeavors both superficially and in terms of their deep significance.[8] Both Stratford and Bayreuth are

---

[4] See, for example, *NZfM* 36.10 (March 5, 1852), 115.

[5] Helmut Kirchmeyer, *Robert Schumanns Düsseldorfer Aufsatz "Neue Bahnen" und die Ausbreitung der Wagnerschen Opern bis 1856: Psychogramm eines "letzten" Artikels* (Berlin: Akademie, 1993), 39–49, esp. 46.

[6] See Chris Walton, *Richard Wagner's Zurich: The Muse of Place* (Rochester, NY: Camden House, 2007), esp. 58–61, and Hanke, *Wagner in Zürich*, 269–89.

[7] Source: Royal Shakespeare Company www.rsc.org.uk/aboutthersc/46.aspx (accessed April 2, 2009).

[8] See Ian Frederick Moulton, "Stratford and Bayreuth: Anti-Commercialism, Nationalism, and the Religion of Art," *Litteraria Pragensia* 6.12 (1996), 39–50.

small communities, away from metropolitan centers, fortuitously located in the geographic center, and thus the symbolic "heart," of their respective countries, a location instrumentalized by those who promoted the festivals as expressions of national significance. The Wagner festival remains linked, if not tainted, with nationalist associations, but Shakespeare and the Shakespeare festival were no less accompanied by colonialist, even racist, rhetoric well into the twentieth century.[9] In both cases, the notion of national superiority was accompanied by the assertion that their respective works contained universal truths and timeless values, and thus spoke to all humanity. This universality, accompanied by notions of "high" art and quasi-religious experience, as opposed to entertainment, fueled both the non-commercial aspirations of the festivals, and the demand for a form of pilgrimage to attend performances, a rhetorical veneer for what in both cases became an industry.

But the differences between the two festivals are perhaps even more relevant. Stratford just happened to be Shakespeare's birthplace; the selection of Bayreuth was made part of an agenda. Shakespeare – long dead – was appropriated and commodified for a variety of purposes. Wagner – alive at the founding – was in the first place the architect of his own commodification.

Thus, Michael Karbaum has missed an important point when he argues that "there is no direct causal line that leads from the Zurich festival idea of 1850, that Wagner sketched out many times, to Bayreuth."[10] Though what he means by "causal line" is unclear, it is true that neither Wagner's original idea of the non-repeatable event, nor the economic utopianism of the initial conception, were retained over the more than twenty years that represented "the path from the ideal to the pragmatic conception of the festival."[11] But Karbaum overlooks the ultimately more significant issue that Wagner's festival became the vessel into which he could pour all the disparate elements of his marketing activities of the preceding three decades, as Wagner himself admitted: "and so I happily seize on the name 'Bayreuth' … to express everything that has come together from the widest circles to bring the artwork I have conceived to life."[12] Despite the proliferation of summer festivals in the twentieth century, Bayreuth continues

---

[9] *Ibid.*, 44–6.
[10] Michael Karbaum, *Geschichte der Bayreuther Festspiele (1876–1976)* (Regensburg: Bosse, 1976), 9.
[11] *Ibid.*, 15.
[12] "so fasse ich nun den Namen 'Bayreuth' … willig auf, um in ihm Das vereinigt auszudrücken, was aus den weitesten Kreisen her zur lebenvollen Verwirklichung des von mir entworfenen Kunstwerkes sich mir anschließt" (*SSD* IX: 331).

to be unique. While Stratford became a shrine, Bayreuth functions as both shrine and hub.

Bayreuth and the production of meaning

Most histories of the Bayreuth Festival take 1876 as the starting point of an ongoing tradition and family business venture. But 1876 also represents the culmination of a long process that started in 1840 with Wagner's failed attempt to succeed in Paris. First articulated in the letter of September 14, 1850, to Kietz, Wagner formulated several versions of an idea for a "provisional" theater and for a festival exclusively dedicated to the performance of his works, in the first place his *Ring* drama.[13] His original location – somewhere along the Rhine – partly reflected the national significance he already then claimed for his undertaking, given the symbolic role played by that river in expressions of Germanness, especially against the French following the "Rhine Crisis" of 1841. During the 1850s, Weimar (under Liszt's control) and Zurich (where Wagner was residing) were also each considered as possible sites for the "provisional structure."[14] In 1851, Wagner drafted a complete plan for a Zurich theater built and staffed by the citizenry which would "no longer be an industrial establishment for the purpose of making money."[15] In 1859, towards the end of Liszt's tenure, the *Telegraf* of Vienna announced "A Wagner Theater and a Wagner Festival" for Weimar, their headline already marking the extent to which the undertaking had been successfully branded with the Wagner name.[16] He may indeed have wanted to erect a monument to his own ego – as critics since have noted cynically – but his rhetorical objective was to create a "Central Model Theater" (*Central-Mustertheater*) in and for Germany, a center of excellence that could compete with other operatically more established countries.[17]

With Ludwig II's accession to the throne of Bavaria in 1864 came the first concrete opportunity for Wagner to realize his idea, initially in the state capital, Munich. Had it succeeded, the Munich plan would have

---

[13] See also Heinrich Habel, *Festspielhaus und Wahnfried: Geplante und ausgeführte Bauten Richard Wagners* (Munich: Prestel, 1985).
[14] Hubert Kolland, *Die Kontroverse Rezeption von Wagners Nibelungen-Ring 1850–1870* (Cologne: Studio, 1995), 17.
[15] "aufgehört haben, eine industrielle Anstalt zu sein, die um des Gelderwerbes willen ihre Leistungen … ausbietet" ("Ein Theater in Zürich," *SSD* V: 49).
[16] "Ein Wagner-Theater und ein Wagner-Fest" (quoted in Kolland, *Kontroverse Rezeption*, 19).
[17] *SSD* VII: 91.

constituted the most radical break with Wagner's initial conception, given his abhorrence of the metropolis, and his desire that it require an effort to attend.[18] The Munich festival theater, designed by Gottfried Semper, would not have been a modestly conceived "provisional" structure, but a colossal and permanent edifice located on the east bank of the Isar River near the end of what is today the Prinzregentenstrasse at the Friedensengel, dominating the cityscape. Wagner concurrently pursued a plan for a temporary theater to be erected in a wing of the Munich Crystal Palace to test out ideas during the lengthy undertaking to build Semper's theater. The two-pronged plan ultimately failed, brought down by a combination of Wagner's self-destructive behavior and the mounting opposition to Wagner within Ludwig's cabinet, again forcing Wagner into a form of exile, again in Switzerland, this time just outside Luzern, in Tribschen.

In order to retain Ludwig's financial backing, Wagner needed to find a location in Bavaria and, ultimately, settled on "small, remote, unappreciated Bayreuth" – seemingly negative qualities which Wagner reframed to his advantage.[19] It turned out to be the perfect choice because it satisfied so many aspects of Wagner's original plan, a location which Wagner could and did monopolize, something impossible to accomplish in a metropolis.

Not only did Wagner take over the city physically, he took possession of it as an idea. He wrote into "Bayreuth" a collection of mutually reinforcing narratives, so that Bayreuth has become synonymous with the entirety of Wagner's project – both an ideologically laden sign and a company town. As if it had had no previous history, Wagner filled it with meaning, which began with bald acts of rhetorical erasure: "Bayreuth is still untarnished, genuinely virgin ground for art."[20] Again and again, he and his allies called Bayreuth "neutral ground" for the "entire German public."[21] Wagner even referred to the town as "a kind of Washington-for-the-Arts."[22] Reminiscent of the new land claimed from the sea at the end of Goethe's *Faust Part II*, Bayreuth, like Washington DC, was to have no previous history, no contentious past, to haunt it. Wagner's "thoroughly self-sufficient new creation"

---

[18] For a full account, see Habel, *Festspielhaus*, 23ff.
[19] "das kleine, abgelegene, unbeachtete Bayreuth" (*SSD* IX: 331).
[20] "Bayreuth aber ist noch unentweihter echt jungfräulicher Boden für die Kunst," Richard Wagner, *Richard Wagner an Emil Heckel, Zur Entstehungsgeschichte der Bühnenfestspiele in Bayreuth*, ed. Karl Heckel (Leipzig: Breitkopf & Härtel, 1912), 28.
[21] Letter to Emil Heckel, September 23, 1873: "daß ich an einem neutralen Orte eine Unternehmung für das ganze deutsche Publikum, nicht für das Publikum einer Hauptstadt in das Auge gefaßt habe" (*Bayreuther Briefe*, 137).
[22] "*eine Art Kunst-Washington*," Letter to Friedrich Feustel, June 14, 1877 (*Bayreuther Briefe*, 270).

would be performed "at a location which would only become meaningful via this creation."[23]

But the campaign to infuse Bayreuth with meaning began well before the first performance of the *Ring*. Blurring the distinction between fiction and reality, Wagner borrowed words he had put in the mouth of Hans Sachs to now describe Bayreuth, instead of Nuremberg, as "Deutschlands Mitte" (Germany's center). If Wagner's fictionalized Nuremberg in *Die Meistersinger* had functioned as a synecdoche for Germany, his rhetorical makeover was turning the real Bayreuth into nothing less. Arguably, Bayreuth was even better suited for this role than Nuremberg, given its geographic centrality and political remoteness: at once middle and out of the way, the proverbial German "nook" (*Winkel*).[24] As opposed to urban life – characteristic of France, England, even Turkey – Wagner explains, historically de-centralized Germany is all about the *Winkel*. The metropolis is unGerman, and German ones are the "worst copy."[25] Just as Bayreuth represents Germany, Wagner's "provisional" theater reminds us of the German state which has also always been provisional.[26]

But, if Bayreuth and Wagner's theater signify genuine German "normalcy," the pristine ordinariness of a bygone age, this same quality makes them extraordinary in the modern context. Since the metropolis constitutes the quotidian center of modern life – the new norm – going to Bayreuth constitutes a departure from it, a return to the "heartland." Wagner understood that audiences might "suffer" the "monstrous discomfort of Bayreuth,"[27] but he argued that its seclusion would enable performers to participate in an artistic undertaking which, in the "ordinary" running of things, was not possible.[28] Lying outside the established operatic circuit, this remoteness would liberate performers from obligations to conform.[29]

---

[23] "an einem Ort, der erst durch diese Schöpfung zur Bedeutung kommen sollte" (*Bayreuther Briefe*, 270).

[24] *SSD* IX: 332, see also *Meistersinger*, Act III.

[25] "schlechtester Kopie" (*SSD* X: 22).

[26] *SSD* IX: 329.

[27] "Man hat das Opfer der ungeheuren Unbequemlichkeit Bayreuth's einmal – mir zu gefallen (auch zum Theil aus Neugier) – gebracht," Letter to Feustel, June 14, 1877 (*Bayreuther Briefe*, 270).

[28] "de[r] örtlich fixirten periodischen Vereinigungspunkt der besten theatralischen Kräfte Deutschlands zu Übungen und Ausführungen in einem höheren deutschen Originalstyle ihrer Kunst, welche ihnen im *gewöhnlichen* Laufe ihrer Beschäftigungen nicht ermöglicht werden können" (*SSD* IX: 316) (my emphasis).

[29] *SSD* IX: 128: "Die Ermöglichung einzelner, in meinem Sinne korrekter, theatralischer Leistungen konnte hierfür nicht ausreichend sein, sobald diese nicht *gänzlich außerhalb der Sphäre des heutigen Opernwesens* gestellt waren" (my emphasis).

Wagner's extraordinary offering requires a commensurately extraordinary effort and commitment from all – what Gutman sneeringly but not without justification dubs "grand opera with obstacles."[30] Performers would receive little or no pay. Audience members would go out of their way to attend.[31] And, as an 1870 review already pointed out, understanding the works fully required "a devoted public, ready to sacrifice itself … in ways not found in contemporary opera performances."[32]

In the opera world, "ordinary" for Wagner meant the repertoire theater where – like the department store – a wide array of works are programmed on successive evenings to keep audiences returning and to maximize box-office receipts. The ornate architectural exterior and opulent interior of the "ordinary" theater emphasizes spectacle – both on and off stage – and reinforces social stratification. Ostentation and the ceremony of social display was and is as much a part of a night at the opera as any aesthetic enjoyment. The Bayreuth experience was to be different in every respect. Wagner actually borrowed and adapted many existing ideas, but the textual overlay he provided to accompany the festival was unique. For instance, the famed sunken orchestra pit could already be found in the Riga opera house where Wagner had worked decades earlier. The stunning effect of darkening the theater for the duration of the performance had already been practiced in London since about 1856.[33] Gutman, for one, tries to minimize Wagner's originality by pointing out such facts. But he misses Wagner's real originality in the ways he promoted ideas (and by extension himself) by ceaselessly mentioning them in the media, giving them meaning, and making them integral to the Bayreuth experience.

Wagner feared that a performance of the *Ring* outside Bayreuth would render "ordinary" what was "extraordinary," hence the enormous effort to construct an aura of "extraordinariness" around the town, the theater, and the festival to frame the work. And yet, as Richard Sennett suggests, the Bayreuth theater, which stands for the opposite of Garnier's lavish Opéra in Paris, actually "arrived at the same end," imposing silence to show respect for the work, and bestowing social prestige on those able to attend.[34]

---

[30] Gutman, *Wagner*, 358.
[31] Already in a January 9, 1856, letter to Franz Müller, Wagner writes "eigens zu diesem Feste zusammen kämen, und sich somit gänzlich von der breiigen Masse unterschied" (*SB* VII: 335).
[32] "erfordert ein hingebendes, opferwilliges Publikum … wie es bei unseren modernen Opernvorstellungen nimmer zu finden [ist]" (quoted in Kolland, *Kontroverse Rezeption*, 177).
[33] Gutman, *Wagner*, 351.
[34] Sennett, *Fall of Public Man*, 207 and 205–10.

But if Bayreuth was supposed to be the "German" answer to the Opéra, Wagner coyly rejected the idea that the Bayreuth theater should be considered a "National Theater" at all, asking "where is this 'nation' that would erect such a theater?" Wagner echoes almost verbatim similar comments made a century earlier by Lessing and Schiller about the absence of a German state and the impossibility of a "national" culture. In so doing, he removes his project from any contemporary and arguably transitory issues of German nationalism and embeds it instead in a discourse of tremendous historical depth.[35] In Wagner's hands, Bayreuth became a myth, just as Nike Wagner has suggested.[36] But this "mythic dimension" lends Bayreuth a mystique, a discernible image in the cultural marketplace, that endures.

Fundraising and fan clubs

But the myth needed cash to become a reality, and still does. The fundraising story is a revealing and early example of the new relationship between art and money in modern times, and a testament to Wagner's creativity and flexibility. Instead of the actual money flow, that other studies have already examined,[37] I focus on Wagner's strategies and the rhetorical effort to gather and maintain financial support.

In one of the most electrifying scenes from Goethe's *magnum opus*, Faust is seated at his desk, intent on translating the opening of the Gospel of St. John. With characteristic arrogance, he refuses to accept that it could all have begun with a mere "word" and, in a flash of inspiration, settles on a new version: "In the beginning was the deed."

Convinced that he would never live to see his *Ring* performed, Wagner decided to publish its text in 1862. In the "Preface," Wagner, like Faust, despairs that he must be content with words only, a protest that rings hollow, considering how effectively he promoted himself and raised funds

---

[35] "Wo wäre die 'Nation', welche dieses Theater sich errichtete?" (*SSD* IX: 328); compare with Gotthold Ephraim Lessing: "den Deutschen ein Nationaltheater zu verschaffen, da wir Deutsche noch keine Nation sind!" (*Hamburgische Dramaturgie*, 101–4; Stück, *Werke und Briefe*, 12 vols., ed. K Bohnen [Frankfurt am Main: Deutscher Klassiker, 1985], VI: 684), and Schiller: "Deutschland? aber wo liegt es? Ich weiß das Land nicht zu finden, // Wo das gelehrte beginnt, hört das politische auf" (*Xenien* #95, "Das deutsche Reich," *Werke*, I: 320).

[36] Nike Wagner, *Wagner Theater* (Frankfurt am Main: Insel, 1998), 11.

[37] Karbaum has published records of the Bayreuth financial accounts as well as other details for each festival between 1876 and 1976 (*Bayreuther Festspiele*, 149–55).

using them. Then he expresses the hope that some royal person will step forth to ensure the festival:

| *Wird dieser Fürst sich finden?* | Will there be such a Prince? |
| "*Im Anfang war die That.*"[38] | "In the beginning was the deed." |

He did not have to wait long. Just two years later, in 1864, immediately following his coronation, King Ludwig II of Bavaria initiated what became a lifelong sponsorship of Wagner the person and Wagner the project. While Ludwig was by no means Wagner's only funding source, his backing freed the composer from the recurrent existential crises, and his deep pockets guaranteed liquidity at crucial moments in the often tenuous process of building the Festspielhaus and founding the festival. The significance of his support cannot be underestimated, and it is hard to imagine that Wagner would or could have successfully mounted the first festival without him.

Nevertheless, having a king as a patron and benefactor in the second half of the nineteenth century was becoming outmoded, a throwback to the days of the *ancien régime*. For that reason, this arrangement was not in the first place what Wagner-the-progressive had sought.

In the same 1862 "Preface," Wagner proposed that, instead of a single aristocrat, "an association of wealthy art-loving men and women" should collect the necessary money to realize the festival.[39] Once again, Beethoven provided a model. Given the gradual erosion of aristocratic and ecclesiastical patronage not yet replaced by regulated and dependable state or corporate sponsorship, Beethoven bridged the gap by forming a consortium of patrons who, Wagner notes, did not pay for his works, but rather funded his person so he could compose unencumbered.[40]

In 1871, shortly before his untimely death, the German-Jewish pianist and Wagner devotee Carl Tausig, together with the wealthy socialite Marie von Schleinitz, came up with an idea based on that kind of model: to create a *Patronatverein* (Patrons' Association) whose members would purchase a total of 1,000 *Patronatscheine* (Patron Certificates) for 300 *thalers* each, to

---

[38] *SSD* VI: 281.
[39] "Eine Vereinigung kunstliebender vermögender Männer und Frauen, zunächst zur Aufbringung der für eine erste Aufführung meines Werkes nöthigen Geldmittel" (*SSD* VI: 280).
[40] *SSD* IX: 91.

raise the estimated 30,000 *thalers* needed to build the theater and launch the festival. The owner of each *Patronatschein* would be guaranteed a seat for all three of the *Ring* cycles planned for the first festival. Should three individuals share the cost of a single certificate, each of them could attend one complete cycle.

Wagner was delighted. This plan would allow him to "collect contributions for the realization of a national idea," charting a middle course between older and newer forms of funding: a conglomerate of small-scale patrons instead of a single benefactor or the mercantilism of selling tickets at a box office.[41] Tickets would be given to the "patrons" who – through their support – had earned the right to attend a performance, with remaining tickets given free of charge to those without financial resources, but deemed worthy.

Two circulars dated May 12 and 18, 1871, quickly followed this original idea. In the first, Wagner optimistically announced the forthcoming festival for the summer of 1873, proclaimed Bayreuth as the location, and declared the formation of a "Society of Friends" (*Verein von Freunden*) called the "Patrons of the Stage Festival in Bayreuth" (*Patronen des Bühnenfestspieles in Bayreuth*).[42] The second flyer explains the financial details for the "Patron Certificate" scheme.[43]

A Mannheim piano manufacturer by the name of Emil Heckel wrote to Wagner on May 15 in response to the May 12 circular. Heckel recalls in his autobiography that he was originally "outraged" (*empört*) by Wagner's "abominable" ("*entsetzlich*") *Tannhäuser*, which he had seen in 1853, but became a Wagner convert ten years later at a concert of excerpts conducted by the composer, a conversion confirmed in 1868 when he and his wife had journeyed to Munich for the premiere of *Die Meistersinger*.[44] Without missing a beat, Wagner replied on May 19 to his "energetic friend of my art and direction,"[45] thanking Heckel for his interest and instructing him to contact Tausig directly. Heckel then actually traveled to Berlin to meet with Tausig. Concerned that even a three-way split would prevent those with modest financial resources from participating in the venture and having a chance to go to Bayreuth, he proposed the formation of "societies" (*Vereine*) so that members could share in the cost of a *Patronatschein*. So the idea of the "Wagner Society" was born, allowing essentially unlimited participation

---

[41] "[I]ch wollte … Beiträge sammeln zur Verwirklichung einer nationalen Idee" (*SSD* XVI: 119).
[42] "Ankündigung der Festspiele" (*SSD* XIV: 131).
[43] "Aufforderung zur Erwerbung von Patronatsscheinen" (*SSD* XIV: 132).
[44] Heckel, *Wagner an Heckel*, 3.
[45] "thatkräftiger Freund meiner Kunst und meiner Tendenzen" (*SSD* IX: 324).

in the purchase of a certificate.[46] Attendance at the festival would then be decided by lot.

On June 1, 1871, less than three weeks after the original circular, Heckel and a group of fellow enthusiasts in Mannheim founded the first "Wagner-Verein," calling itself a "Society in Support of the Great National Undertaking" (*Verein zur Förderung des grossen nationalen Unternehmens*). Membership was restricted to "Friends and supporters of Wagner's artistic endeavors" who committed to pay a contribution in 1871, 1872, and 1873. The Mannheim statutes set the standard for all future Wagner societies.

Two weeks later, on July 16, Cosima wrote to Heckel, asking what he thought of the idea of "getting in touch with various cities and spreading the Wagner society throughout Germany."[47] Although she did not know it yet, Carl Tausig was already critically ill, and would die the next day of typhoid. So her fortuitous entry into the discussion insured a seamless transition in the expansion and further development of the Wagner Society network, while also paving the way for the managerial role that would eventually characterize her leadership of the festival and the Wagner legacy after her husband's death. Mannheim, she wrote, would remain the center of the organization.[48] If Heckel was interested, Cosima promised to put him in touch with all the right people in various cities.

Within five months of the Mannheim founding, Wagner societies were formed in Munich, Leipzig, and Vienna. The following year saw explosive growth: Dresden, Bayreuth, two in Berlin, Weimar, Nuremberg, Darmstadt, Mainz, Göttingen, Cologne, and an Academic Richard Wagner Society in Berlin. The same year, 1872, the Wagner Society also went international with franchises founded in Pest (Buda and Pest merged in 1873), London, and New York. By the 1876 opening of the Bayreuth festival, there were additional Wagner societies in Prague, Basel, Zurich, Riga, Paris, Florence, Milan, Boston, Cairo, Warsaw, Amsterdam, Stockholm, and Copenhagen.[49] While they all echoed the basic premise of the Mannheim society statutes – the national significance, the personal commitment to Wagner's art, and

---

[46] On the founding of the first Wagner Society in Mannheim, see Karl Heckel, *Die Bühnenfestspiele in Bayreuth. Authentischer Beitrag zur Geschichte ihrer Entstehung und Entwicklung* (Leipzig: Fritzsch, 1891).

[47] "sich mit verschiedenen Städten in Verbindung setzten, und von Mannheim aus der Wagner Verein sich über Deutschland verbreitete?" (Heckel, *Wagner an Heckel*, 10–11).

[48] See also the letter from Schleinitz to Heckel, August 17, 1871: "den geschäftlichen Theil des großen Unternehmens ganz und gar zu übernehmen und daß der von Ihnen gegründete Verein in Mannheim als Centralpunkt betrachtet würde" (Heckel, *Wagner an Heckel*, 13).

[49] See also the contemporaneous article discussing the "Richard-Wagner Vereine," their history, purpose, and current state in *NZfM* 72.16 (April 14, 1876), 167.

the realization of the *Ring* in Bayreuth – later Wagner societies added wording to their charters to underscore the expansionist, proselytizing and even ideological mission that became synonymous with Wagnerism. The Darmstadt branch, for instance, sought to: "Unite friends of progress in the area of music-drama."[50] They also circulated an "appeal" (*Aufruf*) which began: "Wagner's works are conquering Europe; his artistic direction has been recognized in distant corners of the world. There is no significant city in the civilized world in which Wagner's friends are not active; the number of his supporters grows ever larger."[51] The Dresden chapter's "appeal" refers to Wagner as "the greatest living musical dramatist of our people."[52] The student-based Academic Wagner Society of Berlin which differentiated itself from regular Wagner societies ("which only appeal to the wealthier friends of Wagner's art") was formed to "give the entire nation intellectual and practical access."[53] Their charter and its accompanying rationale – all published in the newspaper and thus public – aggressively calls for "lively agitation" (*lebhaften Agitation*). Wagner is linked to the nationalist movement in which students had played such a crucial role since the 1810s through to Hitler's Reich. Using phrases that fatefully anticipate the rhetoric of national-socialism in the 1930s, the document refers to the "triumph" of the "world-historical calling of the Germanic peoples" (*welthistorische Beruf des Germanen*) in the political sphere – meaning the recent victory over France and the unification of Germany. Now, students are called upon to turn their attention to the cultural sphere: "the spiritual victory shall be celebrated through the German festivals in Bayreuth."[54] Wagner is "the Bard of German greatness" (*der Sänger deutscher Grösse*). "The great poet-composer, whose unfailing reformatory impact in the art world can only be compared to Bismarck's political activities … has dedicated his life's work

[50] "Freunde des Fortschrittes auf musikalisch-dramatischem Gebiete corporativ zu vereinigen" (Statutes of the Richard Wagner Society, Darmstadt. *Richard-Wagner-Archiv* Nr.: A2584/VII-1).

[51] "Die Werke *Wagner's* erobern Europa; im fernen, verwandten Welttheile hat sich sein kunststreben Anerkennung verschafft. Es gibt keine Stadt von Bedeutung in der civilisirten Welt, in der nicht Wagner's Freunde wirken, und immer grösser wird die Zahl seiner Anhänger" (*Richard-Wagner-Archiv* Nr.: A2584/VII-1) (emphasis in original).

[52] "der größte lebende musikalische Dramatiker unseres Volkes" (Statutes of the Richard Wagner Society, Dresden, January 26, 1872. *Richard-Wagner-Archiv* Nr.: A2584/III-1).

[53] "welche sich nur an die bemittelteren Freunde der Wagner'schen Kunst wenden" / "welcher dem ganzen Volke die intellectuelle und practische Betheiligung ermöglichen … wird" (Aufruf u. Statuten of the Akademischer Richard-Wagner-Verein zu Berlin, April 1872. *Richard-Wagner-Archiv* Nr.: A2584/VII-1).

[54] "der geistige Sieg soll durch die deutschen Festspiele in Baireuth gefeiert werden" (Aufruf u. Statuten of the Akademischer Richard-Wagner-Verein zu Berlin, April 1872. *Richard-Wagner-Archiv* Nr.: A2584/VII-1).

to the Fatherland."[55] Membership in the academic society was free – i.e. they were not in the business of purchasing Certificates – but members had to pledge "that they would be advocates in all circles for Richard Wagner's artistic direction."[56] Their mission: to mobilize "the entire *Volk* to energetically support the national festival." In its §1, the academic society states its "basic mission is to foster and propagate knowledge and respect for Wagner's reformatory ideas and achievements in music and drama through discussions and lectures." Today, all Wagner societies follow this agenda, hosting lectures, private concerts and other events, to educate members about Wagner, his project, and enable a deeper understanding of his dramatic works.

The initial growth of the Wagner societies was unprecedented for a living artist and, in the realm of "serious" (as opposed to popular) art, remains unmatched. Perhaps paradoxically, at this moment of greatest personal recognition after three decades of tireless self-promotion, Wagner seems suddenly ambivalent when he writes about the *Patronat* and the societies which bore his name. He repeatedly distances himself from the organization, first sending Heckel to contact Tausig, then allowing Cosima and others to take care of business. He even acts embarrassed that his name was being used at all, insisting that the Wagner societies were independent, self-forming bodies. Nevertheless, he monitored their progress closely, complained when things were moving too slowly, and cajoled when insufficient money was raised. His correspondence even lists individual successes and failures of specific local Wagner societies in selling Certificates.[57] In one letter, he calls for "fully calculated publicity" because "the formerly hoped-for success through the efforts of individual very energetic friends of my art has turned out to be rather weak."[58] He envisions a network of Wagner societies all over Germany and welcomes Heckel's idea that these be controlled by a central German Wagner Society (*Deutscher Wagnerverein*) because he realizes that "only with a large general association can the enterprise be permanently and successfully secured."[59]

---

[55] "der grosse Dichter-Componist, dessen unbeirrtes reformatorisches Wirken auf dem Gebiete der Kunst mit Bismarck's politischer Thätigkeit verglichen werden kann … weihte das Werk seines Lebens dem Vaterlande" (Aufruf u. Statuten of the Akademischer Richard-Wagner-Verein zu Berlin, April 1872. *Richard-Wagner-Archiv* Nr.: A2584/VII-1).

[56] "Jedes Mitglied hat in allen Kreisen die durch Richard Wagner angebahnte Kunstrichtung zu vertreten" (Aufruf u. Statuten of the Akademischer Richard-Wagner-Verein zu Berlin, April 1872. *Richard-Wagner-Archiv* Nr.: A2584/VII-1,§§4 and 5).

[57] Letter to Heckel, November 9, 1871.

[58] "volle, weithin berechnete Publizität," Letter to von Löen November 3, 1871 (*SSD* XVI: 134).

[59] Letter to Heckel, November 9, 1871 (Heckel, *Wagner an Heckel*, 17–18).

The "Mitteilung an die deutschen Wagner-Vereine" (Communication to the German Wagner-Societies) that Wagner published on Christmas Day 1871 in the *Musikalisches Wochenblatt* is characteristic of his ambivalence. "It is thus very important for me to see these societies spread preferably over the entire German fatherland," centrally organized under the "Allgemeiner deutscher Wagner-Verein," a name Wagner himself has selected, "because it is concise and pithy, even if it seems a bit presumptuous."[60] But at the same time, he denies his involvement in what we would today call a "grass-roots" movement: "but I state first of all, that I have not, nor do I now call for the founding of a 'German Wagner-Society,' but instead that I, inasmuch as I address it, assume that it has formed itself and is turning to me for answers."[61]

By early 1872 – six months after the first society was founded – Wagner moved the central administration from Mannheim to Bayreuth, thus, in Heckel's words, "creating the long sought after hub [*Mittelpunkt*] for patrons and the activities of the societies."[62] Bayreuth, an out-of-the-way "nook" becomes the central point for a movement that has sprung up in all the various "nooks" of Germany: what could be more "truly German"?[63]

Public and press reaction in Germany to these various schemes were certainly colored by significant contemporary events. The lightning victory over France which abruptly ended the Franco-Prussian war early in 1871 was immediately followed by the long-awaited creation of a unified German nation state, and an unprecedented industrial commercial boom known as the "founding years" (*Gründerjahre*), funded in part by French war reparations.[64] Wagner and his friends capitalized on the national(ist) fervor with their incessant descriptions of the festival as a "national undertaking ... in the service of German art," a seamless continuation of Wagner's own self-association with Germanness that had been a cornerstone of his persona since the 1840s.[65]

---

[60] *SSD* XVI: 134. See also the *Aufruf, 23. Mai, 1872 der ersten Patronensammlung* which declares the objective "dahin zu wirken, daß die Vereine sich zunächst über ganz Deutschland ausbreiten" (Heckel, *Bühnenfestspiele in Bayreuth*, 29).

[61] *SSD* XVI: 137.

[62] Heckel, *Wagner an Heckel*, 39.

[63] *SSD* X: 23.

[64] See also Manfred Wegner, *Musik und Mammon: Die permanente Krise der Musikkultur* (Baden-Baden: Nomos, 1999): "Nicht zufällig ist Bayreuth in den Gründerjahren entstanden. Kein Wunder also, daß die Wagnersche Festspielidee zwischen einem Nation- und einem Aktien-Unternehmen oszillierte" (160).

[65] "[D]ieses nationalen Unternehmens ... im Dienste deutscher Kunst" (*SSD* XVI: 132).

While the national claims were broadly appealing, the public was more negative about the fundraising efforts, reflecting both the pervasive German suspicion of and resistance to investment in shares of stock that also characterized the boom, as well as the rejection of what appeared like Wagner's questionable mixture of commerce with a high-art project, which seemed to blur the treasured distinction between the two worlds, an effort made more distasteful by his aggressive efforts at promotion.[66] The Patron association was "mistaken for a group undertaking a risk venture"; Wagner felt stung that he was "so grotesquely misunderstood."[67] Insisting that his "enterprise eschews all profit," the Patron Certificate, though perhaps reminiscent of stock shares, offered artistic rather than financial dividends.[68] Nevertheless, adverse reactions did much to permanently stigmatize the Wagner name.

Wagner was not entirely blameless in provoking comparisons with business ventures. In a circular "To the Patrons of the Stage Festival in Bayreuth" (August 30, 1873) he dangled the possibility of transforming his non-profit venture into a "for-profit" festival where tickets would be sold "at arbitrarily inflated admission fees," profits to be distributed like "dividends for stockholders."[69] This in turn would enable the selling of Certificates "just like with public offerings of shares and state securities" in order to raise "outstanding capital."[70] The contents of the circular were leaked to the press which failed to note the subjunctive tone of Wagner's ruminations, much to his outrage and renewed dismay.[71] Of course, Wagner had only contempt for any form of "profit-making," but he did leave the door open for such a reversal of the original plan with his "ends justifies the means" revelation that "whatever the means, whatever the cost, I will only execute the completed performance of my artistic plan as I have conceived it, in order … to prove

---

[66] See also Großmann-Vendrey, *Bayreuth in der deutschen Presse*, esp. I: 17.

[67] "Assoziation zum Betriebe eines chancengebenden Geschäftes" (*SSD* XVI: 139). This wording "was mainly suggested by Nietzsche, who rightly worried, that the business propaganda would tarnish the idealism of the great undertaking" (Heckel, *Wagner an Heckel*, 35). See also Großmann-Vendrey, *Bayreuth in der deutschen Presse*, I: 27.

[68] "[M]einer, jeden Gewinn ausschließenden Unternehmung," from "Ankündigung der Festspiele für 1876" (August 28, 1875) (*SSD* XIV: 154). Karbaum observes: "Mit allem Nachdruck wehrte er sich damals gegen jeden Vergleich mit profit-orientierten oder Aktien-Unternehmungen" (*Bayreuther Festspiele*, 21, also 19).

[69] "An die Patrone der Bühnenfestspiele in Bayreuth" (*SSD* XII: 317–18).

[70] "[W]ie dies bei Aktienausschreibungen und Staatsanleihen geschiet" (*SSD* XII: 318).

[71] Letter to Heckel, September 19, 1873: "Da glaubt Ihr nun mich eindringlich davon abmahnen zu müssen, meine Sache auf dem Wege der Actien-Unternehmung durchführen zu wollen? Das scheint also der ganze Sinn meines Circular's gewesen zu sein? Nun, weiß Gott! Ich habe die Sache nicht so verstanden; was ich in diesem Sinne andeutete, war doch wahrlich nur zur Beschämung des germanischen Publikum's gesagt" (*Bayreuther Briefe*, 133).

the correctness of all that which – in the absence of existing proof – nobody can be fully convinced."[72]

Wagner's response to the PR debacle following the leaked circular of August 30, 1873, was to call for "an improved strategy." Writing to Heckel on September 19, he pushed for an "agitation" to bring the matter "to the public ... and indeed with awesome publicity [*furchtbarer Publizität*], so that no one can say: 'I don't know anything about it.'"[73] The result was a meeting in Bayreuth of delegates from the Wagner societies during the last days of October 1873. There, Friedrich Nietzsche presented an "Exhortation to the Germans."[74] Though Wagner liked Nietzsche's wording, the rest of the assembly considered it "inopportune," and so the version eventually distributed to 4,000 book-sellers and music stores, and printed in several newspapers was written by a Dr. Stern.[75] Stern's terse and shorter text addressed "the entire German public" and declared it "the honorable duty of the German people" to support Germany's "most famous living artist," with the means to realize the "greatest artistic idea, to which he has dedicated his life."

Businesses receiving this text as posters announcing the festival were asked to append two sign-up sheets below: one was for direct contributions to the fundraising effort, the other to indicate interest in joining the nearest Wagner Society. The results were miserable: there was no increase in Society membership and almost no one other than a few students in Giessen filled out the subscription lists.[76] The Academic Richard-Wagner-Society in Göttingen noted that there was "not a single signature on any of the two lists ... which had been posted for a long time in several Göttingen bookstores."[77]

Despite the exponential growth of the Wagner Society network, the effort to raise the necessary 30,000 *thalers* failed. Wagner had wanted to found a non-commercial venture where art was enjoyed for art's sake, where only the truly devoted would participate and attend. Had it worked, this idea would have sealed Wagner's public break with conventional theater

---

[72] *SSD* XII: 318.
[73] Letter to Heckel, September 19, 1873 (*Bayreuther Briefe*, 134).
[74] Nietzsche, "Mahnruf an die Deutschen" (in *Fall Wagner*, 13–17).
[75] Presumably Dr. Adolf (Ernst) Stern (1835–1907), a professor of literature in Dresden. (My thanks to Barry Millington for helping me identify the correct Dr. Stern.) Stern's text is reprinted in Heckel, *Bühnenfestspiele in Bayreuth*, 35. The resulting poster is available at the *Richard-Wagner-Archiv* (Nr.: A2584/I-3).
[76] Heckel, *Bühnenfestspiele in Bayreuth*, 35.
[77] Source: document titled "Deutsche Festspiele in Bayreuth" formally dissolving the Akademischer Richard-Wagner-Verein in Göttingen because the Bayreuth festival was funded, thereby fulfilling its stated mission (*Richard-Wagner-Archiv* Nr.: A2584/VIII-3).

and theatrical practice. In the end, however, he found himself engaged in a relentless effort to attract attention and raise operating capital which made his venture appear not that different from the kinds of "industry" he condemned. To make matters worse, Wagner societies outside of Germany were being formed to raise funds for travel and tickets, as if, once again, getting to Bayreuth was just a question of money. Wagner may have been proud that "beyond Germany's borders, in Pest, Brussels, London, even New York, societies have been founded bearing the same name and dedicated to the same goals,"[78] but he nevertheless insisted that his name not be used for such societies, because "they conform so little to the intention with which the originally German societies were formed."[79] Elsewhere, he would explain:

> My intention was to offer the public free performances, solely supported by individual contributions. But in Germany I did not find those thousand generous patriots. Worse still, the entire press opposed my idea and stood against me.[80]

Once again, Wagner was forced to seek help from Ludwig II. After his initial refusal – which compelled Wagner to consider abandoning the project, at least temporarily – Ludwig ultimately provided a loan facility to be repaid directly from any patron subscriptions. Reporting all this to Heckel, Wagner adds: "all this does, is allow us to go forward … but this enterprise will only be possible if the public participates."[81]

Wagner was forced to compromise and do whatever was necessary, even relenting on the last vestige of his utopian vision, by agreeing to charge admission for tickets. The theater was built and the festival was launched on August 13, 1876. Nevertheless, short term, Wagner seemed to have failed completely, capitulating to both medieval and modern forms of fundraising, and still posting a significant loss from the first festival. Long term, however, Wagner's unconventional fundraising schemes had laid the groundwork for a global, self-perpetuating network of fiscal and moral support that still has no equal and which continues to guarantee the survival of the festival, even if it does not cover all its operating costs.

Therein lies the paradox if not the hypocrisy of the Wagner enterprise. Though he was a tireless critic of modernity, Wagner depended on the disposable income of the modern bourgeoisie and made full use of advances in communication and transportation to advance his cause. The Bayreuth

---

[78] *SSD* IX: 324.
[79] *SSD* XII: 321.
[80] "An den Herausgeber der Amerikanischen Revue" (1874) (*SSD* XVI: 119).
[81] Letter to Heckel, March 5, 1874 (Heckel, *Wagner an Heckel*, 83).

festival would not have been possible without a developed train system to transport the largely metropolitan audience to the provinces. A global news media was needed to raise awareness of the festival and articulate its significance. Wagner scholars continue to ignore his innovation and flexibility in the business of marketing himself, every match for his pioneering aesthetics. But, in so doing, they merely follow Wagner's lead. He liked to call Heckel "the strategist" (*den "Strategen"*), while Heckel talks of Wagner's "purely artistic concept of life."[82] In other words, the piano manufacturer – his hands already dirtied by money – can be calculating, while the artist remains unsullied, a PR image Wagner had constructed in the 1840s and now confirmed by others. But surely it was Wagner who had been the ultimate "strategist."

The fiscal failure of the first festival prompted a lengthy appeal on January 1, 1877, in which Wagner suggested a two-pronged approach to maintaining the Bayreuth idea in the long term, an approach which reveals, yet again, Wagner's "tactical genius."[83] Part of the funding would come from the newly founded German Reich, which would provide an annual state subsidy of 100,000 *marks* to fund seats for those deemed worthy, but unable to pay. Wagner's plea for what he termed a "nationalization of the entire enterprise"[84] was accompanied by Martin Plüddemann's essay "State Subsidy for Bayreuth," a continuation of the effort to link Bayreuth to the German national project.[85] The remainder of the funds would be raised through a newly formed "Patrons Association." Wagner, widely ridiculed in the press for seeking state support, conceived of a public–private sponsorship that was yet again ahead of its time.

State support was denied, so Wagner turned his attention to the Wagner societies and pushed for a centralized Patrons Association to concentrate funds generated by the independently run local societies. This new central body would be different from the organization for the first festival because "clout and purposefulness need to be present."[86] So, from the allegedly reluctant bystander, watching the formation of Wagner societies at a distance, Richard Wagner now became the unconcealed architect of the centralization effort that would form the hub of the Wagner empire. At the meeting

---

[82] "rein künstlerische Anschauung des Lebens" (Heckel, *Wagner an Heckel*, 32).
[83] "taktische[s] Genie" (Großmann-Vendrey, *Bayreuth in der deutschen Presse*, II: 8).
[84] "An die geehrten Vorstände der Richard Wagner-Vereine" (*SSD* X: 15).
[85] Martin Plüddemann, "Staatshülfe für Bayreuth" (April 1877) (*Richard-Wagner-Archiv* Nr.: A2585–2 and -2a) (repr. in Großmann-Vendrey, *Bayreuth in der deutschen Presse*, II: 9–12).
[86] Letter to Heckel, February 11, 1877 (Heckel, *Wagner an Heckel*, 121).

of delegates on April 2, 1877, in Leipzig, the "General Patrons Association for the Maintenance and Preservation of the Stage Festivals in Bayreuth" (*Allgemeiner Patronat-Verein zur Pflege und Erhaltung der Bühnenfestspiele zu Bayreuth*) was formed, and assumed some significant goals, outlined in its charter:

§1 To maintain and preserve permanently the Bayreuth Festival according to Wagner's intentions.
§2 Accordingly, the association must act
   I To secure the funding for the annual recurrence of the Bayreuth Festival;
   II To spread better understanding of Wagner's artwork in general, and specifically the *Nibelung* tetralogy.[87]

The statutes of the new centralized society combined the original focus on funding with the educational and propagandist mission of the academic societies. In Wagner's words: "I always thought that the Wagner Society would be charged with promoting my direction. I consider this to be its most important function."[88] The basis of the future Wagner industry is contained not only in the mandate for an annual festival, but also in the requirement that Wagner's "intentions" be forever preserved. What exactly those "intentions" are has dominated academic and critical conversations ever since, providing much of the fuel that powers the Wagner industry.

On September 15, 1877, Wagner gave a thirty-minute speech to the assembled delegates of the newly formed *Allgemeiner Patronatverein*. Since he spoke freely, the only record is the rough transcription by Franz Muncker, one of the delegates and the official stenographer. The speech analyzes the failures of the 1876 festival in order to devise a plan for the future, having realized that "money is power."[89] Wagner was undeterred, despite the negative press concerning his decision to sell some of the tickets, and despite the fact that he felt financially abandoned after the festival even by his closest supporters. But his January 1877 appeal for state support – which had unleashed such scorn in the press – had reanimated the "friends of my art" to further "spread better awareness of my intentions [*meines Wollens*] through meetings, lectures

---

[87] Source: Hans von Wolzogen, *Grundlage und Aufgabe des Allgemeinen Patronatvereins zur Pflege und Erhaltung der Bühnenfestspiele zu Bayreuth* (Chemnitz: Schmeitzner, 1877).
[88] "Eine Rede Wagners," reported by Franz Muncker, *Richard Wagner-Jahrbuch* 1 (1886), 196–208, here 204. The speech is also reproduced without Muncker's introduction as "Ansprache an die Abgesandten des Bayreuther Patronats" (1877) (*SSD* XII: 324–32). I quote from the version in the *Richard Wagner-Jahrbuch*.
[89] "Eine Rede Wagners," 204.

and exemplary performances of extracts of my works."[90] As in 1840, here too failure becomes the precondition of success. Did Wagner realize that there is "no such thing as 'bad' publicity," or, to quote Karbaum: "paradoxically, in the end, criticism always helped more that it harmed Bayreuth."[91] Emboldened, Wagner asked the assembled delegates whether they were willing to undertake a project "with patience and perseverance" (*mit Geduld und Ausdauer*) to achieve a great artistic goal, or whether they just wanted to assemble occasionally in Bayreuth to experience something extraordinary. If the latter, "then we should part company."[92] Returning to an idea he already articulated in the 1850s, Wagner presented a plan to found in Bayreuth a "school for the education of singers, musicians and conductors for the correct performance of musical-dramatic works in the true German style."[93] This would safeguard the long-term health and "permanence" of the festival as a means for it "to ensure its own funding."[94]

To secure another funding source, Wagner sent out an appeal on January 15, 1878, asking local Wagner societies to become branches (*Zweigverein*) of the Central Society and to send their annual dues directly to Bayreuth. If they preferred not to do so, he asked that they at least send a certain percentage or surplus of the funds they raised to contribute to the cash reserves (*eisernen Fonds*) of the Society.[95] What had started as a "grass-roots" movement,[96] was now being swallowed up by the makings of a corporate giant. Ever the strategist, Wagner also saw that the advantages of centralization should not completely eliminate the possibility for local organizations – familiar with and responsive to local exigencies – from continuing to exercise some measure of autonomy. Hence Wagner made it clear that he did not want them to "give up their local independence which, in some cases, has proven itself to be justified."[97]

Long term, the result of Wagner's entrepreneurial efforts looks quite different from the financial failure of 1876. He had constructed a complex "institutional network"[98] consisting of the festival theater as the physical

---

[90] *Ibid.*
[91] "Immer hat die Kritik … Bayreuth am Ende paradoxerweise mehr genutzt als geschadet" (Karbaum, *Bayreuther Festspiele*, 8).
[92] "Eine Rede Wagners," 208.
[93] *Ibid.*
[94] *Ibid.*, 207.
[95] "An die geehrten Vorstände der noch bestehenden lokalen Wagner-Vereine" (January 15, 1878) (*SSD* XVI: 162–3).
[96] "Arbeiten die Andern von Oben nach Unten, so Heckel von Unten nach Oben" (Heckel, *Wagner an Heckel*, 100).
[97] *SSD* XVI: 163.
[98] I borrow the term from Voigt, *Richard Wagners Autoritäre Inszenierungen*, 208.

plant, his residence at the Villa Wahnfried as the business headquarters, and an expanding web of funding organizations and fan clubs. For Karbaum, this organization is nothing but a thinly disguised marketing and distribution machine with little else beyond its aesthetic dimension to separate it from the commercial world.[99] "Similarly to comparable establishments," he writes, "Bayreuth as distribution apparatus of select art-wares subjected the festival to the harsh laws of 'industrial' production."[100] No wonder Wolfgang Wagner apparently tried to stop Karbaum's book from appearing in print.

Preview of coming attractions

The job of securing financial support was inseparable from the equally crucial effort to attract and hold public attention for what would eventually be billed as the musical-cultural event of the century.

As we have seen, Wagner's public relations campaign began already in 1840 with the Paris essays and short stories well before there was a *Ring* project. The announcement of the *Ring* together with the idea of a festival performance was made formally in September 1850 with two substantial private communications to Kietz (September 14) and Uhlig (September 20), and accompanied that same month with notices in several journals, including the *Allgemeine Zeitung*, the *Signale für die musikalische Welt*, and *Der Freischütz*, declaring that Wagner was at work on a new composition derived from the Nibelung saga.[101] Over the next twenty-six years, preceding the first full performance of the cycle, the *Ring* was subjected to publicity and public-awareness campaigns "like no other work in bourgeois musical culture."[102] The *Ring* was a media phenomenon from the start, subject to growing speculation for the opinion-makers. In the absence of completed works, public discourse was shaped in the first place by Wagner's aesthetic manifestos examined in Chapter 3. Journalistic efforts, for instance Uhlig's 1852 essay titled "A Small Protest in the Matter of Wagner," helped to whet audience appetite with observations like: "Wagner's theories come not out

---

[99] "In wichtigen äußeren Gesichtspunkten der organisatorischen und betrieblichen Leistung hält das Bayreuther Unternehmen den Vergleich mit zeitgenössischen Industrie- und Wirtschaftsgründungen durchaus stand. Ohne das hochgesteckte künstlerische Ziel aus den Augen zu verlieren" (Karbaum, *Bayreuther Festspiele*, 23).
[100] *Ibid.*, 14. Karbaum was also in possession of a letter from Hitler to Siegfried Wagner.
[101] Kolland, *Kontroverse Rezeption*, 10–11; see also Kirchmeyer IV.
[102] "wie keinem zweiten Werk der bürgerlichen Musikkultur" (Kolland, *Kontroverse Rezeption*, 1).

of thin air, but relate to artworks we are yet to see."¹⁰³ Wendelin Weißheimer wrote a fifteen-part series of articles on *Tristan und Isolde* which the *NZfM* spread out between September 1860 and May 1861, four years before it would receive its world premiere. Billed as a "review" (*Rezension*), it is actually a "preview" which concludes with the following thought: "*Tristan and Isolde* is nothing less than a pinnacle in the genre of music drama, which the greats since Gluck have striven to reach. Because of its immense significance, the work will endure as long as the sense for true art and greatness has not been entirely extinguished."¹⁰⁴

But Wagner was no ivory tower scribe and the promotional effort took every possible shape. He performed the text on many occasions, most notably between February 16–19, 1853, on consecutive evenings at the Hotel *Baur au lac* in Zurich.¹⁰⁵ The event, which biographies describe in detail, was intended for a group of invited "friends," and anyone they wished to bring along.¹⁰⁶ Wagner's reading (there was no music) was apparently so captivating that the audience grew over the four evenings. Already in 1851, Wagner had read his recently written *Opera and Drama* over twelve evenings,¹⁰⁷ and had continued the next year in 1852 (December 18–19) with the freshly completed *Ring* text in the home of François and Eliza Wille, again to a small circle of "friends," including the author Georg Herwegh.¹⁰⁸ His audience at such occasions was often small but prominent, so that news of the event spread. As late as January 17, 1873, Wagner still used this method to publicize his work, reading the text of *Götterdämmerung* at the Berlin home of Marie von Schleinitz with notable members of political and cultural life in attendance.¹⁰⁹ These readings, isolated from their total context, forced audiences to imagine the missing elements – the music and staging.

Conversely, in 1862 and concurrent with the publication of the *Ring* text, Wagner began performing orchestral selections, this time divorced from their dramatic context. Between 1862 and 1875 he conducted such concerts

---

[103] "Theorien, welche Wagner allerdings nicht aus der Luft gegriffen, sondern aus den Ideen zu seinen erst noch zu erwartenden Kunstwerken geschöpft hat" (Uhlig, "Ein kleiner Protest in Sachen Wagner's," *NZfM* 36 [1852], 277–8, here 278).

[104] Wendelin Weißheimer, "'Tristan und Isolde,' Handlung in drei Aufzügen von Richard Wagner," *NZfM* 53.14 (September 28, 1860), 113–14. The article begins in *NZfM* 53.12 (September 14, 1860), 97–8, and ends in 54.19 (May 3, 1861), 165–7.

[105] For an example of an invitation, see Wagner's February 12, 1853, letter to Hermann Rollett (*SB* V: 265).

[106] See Gregor-Dellin, *Richard Wagner*, 370–1. Kolland refers to the events as "ein Werbemittel" (an advertisement) (*Kontroverse Rezeption*, 21).

[107] Gregor-Dellin, *Richard Wagner*, 321.

[108] *Ibid.*, 359.

[109] Kolland, *Kontroverse Rezeption*, 20–1.

in Vienna, Prague, Berlin, Munich, and Hamburg.[110] Extracts like "The Ride of the Valkyries," Siegmund's aria "Winterstürme," "Wotan's Farewell and Fire Music," "Siegfried's Journey Down the Rhine" all became hits long before the *Ring* was performed in its entirety, and prepared audiences for the complete cycles to follow. No other single musical work ever had so much attention focused on it before its premiere, "so that even before the first complete performance as a festival, a *Ring* literature emerged on a scale not seen after decades with even the most successful operas."[111]

Theodor Adorno was not the first to critique Wagner's practice of performing extracts with the argument that it undermined the aesthetic integrity of his project by making commodities out of selections which, as complete works, were intended to resist the process of commodification.[112] Contemporary opponents of Wagner were quick to seize on the paradox, if not disingenuousness, of these concerts, which with one stroke seemed to contradict all of Wagner's pronouncements about the organic nature of his "total work of art." Wagner tried to compensate for the fragmentariness of the musical extracts by continuing the practice he developed at the 1846 Dresden concert. He wrote program notes that explained the dramatic context of the music; their often detailed narrative an attempt to restore that sense (or at least the illusion) of totality.[113] This time, however, audiences needed to imagine not the music, but the staging that accompanied it. Sometimes this raised false expectations of the visual qualities of Wagner's dramas, given the limitations of the physical stage, then as now.

Nevertheless, Adorno's charge of commodification is not unjustified. Wagner's practice anticipates the marketing device common to the announcement of new films. Known as the "preview of coming attractions," the most intriguing, memorable, exciting moments of a film are sewn together, sometimes with a textual overlay or additional voice-over narrative, in an attempt to lure prospective audiences with the suggestion that the remaining unseen portions of the film are equally gripping. Not dissimilarly, Wagner isolated highlights of the *Ring*, gave these sections evocative names, and accompanied them with textual descriptions that place the musical sequences into the context of the entire work. Like its modern successor, such a practice can be misleading. Small wonder that these extracts

---

[110] Erich Kloß, "Richard Wagner als Konzert-Dirigent in Wien," *Der Merker* 1.9 (October 2, 1910), 366–76.

[111] Kolland, *Kontroverse Rezeption*, 1.

[112] See Adorno, *In Search of Wagner*, 106.

[113] Kolland, *Kontroverse Rezeption*, 74. Program notes were reprinted in newspapers and in Wagner's complete works.

continue to be among the most popular, memorable, and identifiable moments of the *Ring*. Still, given Wagner's publicly announced direction, his insistence on the "organic" unity of text, music and drama, and the through-composed structure of his works, it is hard not to think that these extracts represent an irreconcilable contradiction and, perhaps worse, revert to the operatic "numbers" that Wagner had declared dead.

Wagner never denied the marketing utility of extracts, but he was ambivalent, or at least presented himself as such. On the one hand, he admits, "If I chiseled some extracts out of my scores, I flattered myself with the thought that this way it might not be impossible to draw some of the desired attention onto my work and its associated path."[114] On the other, "how repulsive it was for me to have to continually put together concert programs from meager fragments of my dramatic works, as sadly the only way at my disposal to excite German urban public interest in my greater enterprise."[115] From the 1860s on, these concerts ignited a devotion to Wagner especially amongst the younger generation which, in their enthusiasm, are arguably "precursors of the fan-clubs of the 20th century."[116] Nor was Wagner alone in seeing the beneficial aspects of this practice. Shortly before his death, Carl Tausig wanted to organize an ensemble in Berlin to perform selections from the *Ring* both to whet audience appetite, and to gather a trained core of players for the forthcoming Bayreuth orchestra.[117]

These concerts were also carefully structured. For example, at Heckel's request, Wagner grudgingly agreed to perform in Mannheim: "if I must (in order to gain a few more small-time donors)."[118] Notwithstanding the apparent reluctance, Wagner crafted a highly symbolic program for the December 20, 1871, concert starting with his *Kaisermarsch*, followed by the Overture to Mozart's *Magic Flute*; Beethoven's Seventh Symphony; (Intermission), Prelude to *Lohengrin*; Prelude to *Die Meistersinger*; Prelude

---

[114] "Schnitt ich für eine Konzertaufführung aus meinen Partituren einige Bruchstücke zurecht, so durfte ich … mir wohl ebenfalls mit dem Gedanken schmeicheln, daß es ja vielleicht nicht unmöglich wäre, auch auf diesem Wege die mir nöthige Aufmerksamkeit auf mein Werk und die mit ihm verbundene Tendenz zu ziehen" (*SSD* IX: 312). Referring to "Wagners Pragmatismus," Kolland argues that performing selections from the *Ring* seems to have bothered the critics more than the composer (*Kontroverse Rezeption*, 68).

[115] "wie widerwärtig es mir sei, aus dürftigen Fragmenten meiner dramatischen Werke immer noch Konzertprogramme zusammenstellen zu müssen, um auf diesem, leider einzig mir zugänglich gelassenen Wege die Teilnahme des Publikums deutscher Städte für mein größeres Unternehmen anzuregen" (in "An den Vorstand des Wagner-Vereins Berlin," March 18, 1873 [*SSD* XVI: 112]). See also Kolland, *Kontroverse Rezeption*, 9.

[116] Kolland, *Kontroverse Rezeption*, 71.

[117] Heckel, *Wagner an Heckel*, 9.

[118] "wenn es denn sein muß," Letter to Heckel, November 25, 1871 (*Bayreuther Briefe*, 28).

and Conclusion of *Tristan und Isolde*. Excluding the *Kaisermarsch*, the pieces are arranged chronologically by composer. The first half is a historical prelude to the second, which is entirely devoted to works by Wagner arranged this time according to increasing aesthetic difficulty, switching the order of the more conservative *Meistersinger* with the earlier but musically more daring *Tristan*. The trajectory presents Wagner as the culmination of German music history and arranges his works as an evolutionary process that points to the future: the *Ring* to be performed in a special festival theater (for which the concert was a fundraiser).[119]

Spin

Public relations (PR) refers to the art and science of managing communication by individuals, companies, or other groups to build and sustain a carefully crafted image, or convey a favorable message to the public, usually relying on a creative presentation of facts. A recent term – "spin" – describes a more extreme form of this practice, usually associated with the interface between politics and the press, where aggressive and manipulative rhetorical tactics are used to promote an agenda and sway opinion. Not unlike propaganda, "spin" seeks to control public discourse by supplying the preferred vocabulary and phraseology to be used in the discussion.

From the 1840s, Wagner's writings – no matter their apparent purpose – also served a public relations function to fashion a persona, to brand his artworks and, more significantly, to shape the public and intellectual discourse about them. Perhaps his single most potent tool in this effort were his periodic autobiographies which exemplify his special rhetorical skill of interweaving fact and fiction to present a stylized yet sufficiently credible version of the truth.

His ongoing PR initiative to win hearts and minds took on the character of "spin" as the focus turned to the opening of the Bayreuth festival. Beyond the persona and the special aesthetic direction, Wagner (and his allies) began to interpret his project and, increasingly, the world itself according to a certain set of principles. These became integral to the Wagner brand, infusing the growing movement of Wagnerism with an ideology which, in turn, became implicated in the drastic turn of German politics in the twentieth century.

---

[119] See also Veit Veltzke, *Vom Patron zum Paladin: Wagnervereinigungen im Kaiserreich von der Reichsgründung bis zur Jahrhundertwende* (Bochum: Brockmeyer, 1987), 29.

One recurring mantra was Wagner's self-characterization as a victim, in the first place, of a hostile media. This aptly named "Bayreuth martyr propaganda"[120] had already been honed in the streets of Paris, and perfected during Wagner's days as "outlaw" and political exile. Using what has become a common tactic in politics and entertainment, Wagner blamed the press for the multiple failures and scandals which accompanied the fundraising for Bayreuth and the aftermath of the first festival. According to Wagner, the press consistently misunderstood and misrepresented his intentions: "we have been convicted as people who sell themselves for money, as people one can talk about however one wants to, without regard for the actual nature of their undertaking."[121] Wagner had agreed to the sale of tickets in the hopes of a positive result. But this failed, "because we had enemies among us, who felt no remorse spreading slanderous rumors about our performances … we had to battle against infamy."[122]

A crucial aspect of Wagner's victim-narrative is that he triumphs "nevertheless." The words "derision" (*Hohn*) and "in spite of" (*zum Trotz*) become leitmotifs in the Wagnerization of the Bayreuth story. For instance, he names it the *Richard Wagner Society* "despite all derision" (*allem Hohne zum Trotz*).[123] Friends who gave their support did so: "despite all derision."[124] Wagner's project to resist modernity was the subject of "derision and disparagement" from those for whom the "the basic idea would remain totally foreign."[125]

Nowhere is this "against all odds" discourse of bravery and self-sacrifice more tersely formulated than in Friedrich Glasenapp's introduction to his edition of the *Bayreuther Briefe*, where he describes the collected letters as presenting "a significant retrospective on the heated battles and hardships that accompanied the raising of the mighty fortress of German art on the Bayreuth hill, and the first victory that was claimed against the surrounding cultural world's ignorance, indifference, and stubborn ill-will."[126]

---

[120] "Märtyrer-Propaganda der Bayreuther Orthodoxie" (Großmann-Vendrey, *Bayreuth in der deutschen Presse*, I: 41).

[121] "Wir sind beurteilt worden wie Leute, die sich für Geld preisgeben, über die man reden kann, wie man will, ohne Rücksicht auf den eigentümlichen Charakter ihres Unternehmens" ("Eine Rede Wagners," 201).

[122] "weil wir nun Feinde unter uns hatten, welche sich kein Gewissen daraus machten, verleumderische Gerüchte über unsere Vorstellungen auszustreuen … Wir haben mit Niedertracht zu kämpfen gehabt!" ("Eine Rede Wagners," 201)

[123] *SSD* IX: 324.

[124] "jeder Verhöhnung zum Trotz" (*SSD* IX: 330).

[125] "Verhöhnung und Verunglimpfung" (*SSD* IX: 330).

[126] *Bayreuther Briefe*, 5.

Already in Paris, Wagner – who owed much of his initial public exposure to the press – nevertheless constructed an adversarial relationship with what some nowadays call "the mainstream media," as the embodiment of modernity's corrupt and corrupting opinion-makers. Großmann-Vendrey conclusively shows that there was no "uniform condemnation" of Wagner and the festival, and that this was actually a myth.[127] Karbaum similarly seeks to counter the distorted version of the Bayreuth story which presents it as a "titanic individual achievement against contemporary ignorance, as a 'nevertheless' and 'nonetheless' under the sign of cultural decline."[128] But the stark division of the world into minority friend and majority foe, and the studiously fashioned persecution complex that results, is crucial to Wagner's "outsider-hero" persona and continues to be a factor in Bayreuth self-fashioning today.

This self-fashioning started with the first festival, because control of the information flow became increasingly important for Wagner and his circle. For instance, Malwida von Meysenbug sent Emil Heckel a progress report, "because Wagner requests that you distribute this information (phrased better) in a few newspapers, in order to show the public that things are going ahead, and that the absurd, debilitating notices being spread all over the papers are false."[129]

Often, *ad hoc* efforts at publicity did not work as intended. Heckel reports that he missed the Bayreuth "Hebefest" on August 2, 1873, because "he and many others had not seen the public invitation to the patrons that had been posted in newspapers."[130] On the other hand, expressly private communications such as the August 30, 1873, circular, mentioned earlier, were leaked to the press where they become fodder for adverse speculation.[131]

The first organized effort to control the information flow began in the spring of 1876 as final preparations for the first launch of the Bayreuth festival commenced. J. Zimmermann, editor of the local paper, the *Bayreuther Tageblatt*, began a series of what ended up as twenty-three press releases to report on the events. Every fourteen days between May and August 1876, these articles under the heading *Bayreuther autographische Korrespondenz* were distributed by the Festival Board to approximately 180 press outlets

---

[127] Großmann-Vendrey, *Bayreuth in der deutschen Presse*, I: 43.
[128] Karbaum, *Bayreuther Festspiele*, 9.
[129] Letter from Meysenbug to Heckel, December 1, 1873 (Heckel, *Wagner an Heckel*, 72).
[130] Heckel, *Wagner an Heckel*, 61–2. A "Hebefest" is a celebration of the raising of a building's roof.
[131] Heckel, *Wagner an Heckel*, 62.

throughout Germany.[132] The releases covered a wide variety of topics: the arrival of the performers, preparations by the town for the anticipated massive influx of visitors, the progress of the final rehearsals, listings of the dignitaries in attendance and the various honors they bestowed on the performers. The press releases were capped by a description of the performances themselves and an account of the audience response. Approximately half-way through the series, as the full stage rehearsals (*Hauptproben*) began, the musician and critic Heinrich Porges – an integral member of Wagner's team – also began contributing to the reports, offering authoritatively written "behind-the-scenes" glimpses of the coming attractions.[133]

It is difficult to determine the success of this venture. The *NZfM* published the "Korrespondenz" in their entirety, without additional commentary, as "special supplements" (*Extra Beilagen*) to their regular issues, as did the *Musikalisches Wochenblatt* – both pro-Wagner journals based in Leipzig.[134] Some journals ignored the press releases completely, while others published extracts both with and without their own commentary. Some of the mixed reaction can be attributed to the novelty of this particular effort at public relations, though, even today, each newspaper outlet handles press releases differently.

Admittedly, Meyerbeer had already used the press effectively to promote his works and influence public opinion prior to the premieres of his operas.[135] However, Zimmermann's (and Porges's) effort was different in several respects. First, the regularity and the consistency of the press releases, stretching over a four-month period, was unprecedented, and in effect created an in-house press agency for the festival. Second, in addition to the basic "reporting" of events, both Zimmermann and Porges – from their different vantage points as "local correspondent" and "expert witness" – amplified their reports by commenting tirelessly on the historic significance of Wagner's work and the event itself. As with any PR campaign, they ignore real organizational problems and actively deny negative "rumors" circulating in the German-speaking press. In addition, they engage in spin by making grandiose claims that Wagner's *Ring* represents the rebirth of Greek

---

[132] In the following, I rely heavily on Großmann-Vendrey, *Bayreuth in der deutschen Presse*, esp. I: 44–6.

[133] For more on the "Bayreuther autographische Korrespondenz," including an annotated translation of three sample press releases, see Nicholas Vazsonyi, "Press Releases from the Bayreuth Festival, 1876: An Early Attempt at Spin Control," *Wagner and His World*, ed. Thomas S. Grey (Princeton University Press, 2009), 391–408.

[134] The *NZfM* published the twenty-three reports in thirteen *Beilagen* between June and September 1876.

[135] Großmann-Vendrey, *Bayreuth in der deutschen Presse*, I: 45, note 44.

tragedy, a work on a par with Shakespeare and Beethoven, and declaring the Bayreuth festival as an event of German national significance.[136] Clearly, the objective was to create the success before the event.[137] The "Korrespondenz" transcends previous promotional efforts by Meyerbeer, Liszt, Paganini, and other artists of the nineteenth century with a knack for publicity. It is a testament to the breathtaking modernity of the Bayreuth venture that Zimmermann's and Porges's techniques are best described using terms developed much later.[138]

It is unclear just how much Wagner knew about, or had a hand in, this initiative, even though Großmann-Vendrey attributes it to him. There is no mention of it in his published letters, nor in any of his numerous writings and declarations accompanying the launch of the festival, nor does Cosima mention them in her diaries. However, the "Korrespondenz" borrows heavily from Wagner's own stylization of his work. In addition, Wagner seemed fully aware that a chronicle of the festival's first days would have "importance for the future." As early as 1872, he had written to Porges asking him to take "intimate" notes during the rehearsals of the *Ring* in order "to create a fixed tradition" of its performance.[139]

This effort to "sell" high art aggressively was, then as now, problematic. The press releases constantly risked trivializing the project. Newspapers picked up on their increasingly propagandistic tone and reacted accordingly. However, their content and their very existence as a public gesture served to frame the Bayreuth festival as a unique and exclusive project, while at the same time fashioning it as an event that represented and thus belonged to the German nation.[140] This dual image of Bayreuth – first articulated for the media in the "Bayreuther autographische Korrespondenz" – has remained constant since its inception, and is a testament to the PR talents of Wagner and the consortium which continues to maintain a media presence.

---

[136] See, for example, Releases IX and X in *NZfM* 72.28 (July 7, 1876) and 72.29 (July 14, 1876).

[137] "Sie versuchten soger, den Erfolg im vornherein zu steuern" (Großmann-Vendrey, *Bayreuth in der deutschen Presse*, I: 45).

[138] Thorau, *Semantisierte Sinnlichkeit*, 138–9: "Bayreuth wurde damit zum ersten künstlerischen Unternehmen mit einer Art Pressebüro."

[139] Letter to Heinrich Porges, November 6, 1872: "ich [hatte] Ihnen für mein Unternehmen ein für die Zukunft allerwichtigstes Amt bestimmt. Ich wollte Sie nämlich dazu berufen, daß Sie allen meinen Proben … genau folgten, um alle meine, noch so intimen Bemerkungen in Betreff der Auffassung und Ausführung unseres Werkes, aufzunehmen und aufzuzeichnen, somit eine fixirte Tradition hierfür zu redigiren" (Richard Wagner, *Richard Wagner an seine Künstler*, ed. Erich Kloss, 3rd edn [Leipzig: Breitkopf & Härtel, 1912], 31). These rehearsal notes have been published as *Wagner Rehearsing the Ring: An Eye-Witness Account of the First Bayreuth Festival*, trans. Robert L. Jacobs (Cambridge University Press, 1983).

[140] Großmann-Vendrey, *Bayreuth in der deutschen Presse*, I: 45.

Given this, it is short-sighted of Großmann-Vendrey to describe the "Korrespondenz" as a PR "disaster," even if the releases did not achieve all the intended results.[141] At the least, it was the forerunner of the in-house journal that began monthly circulation on January 1, 1878, to broadcast the Bayreuth message. Originally called the *Monatsschrift des Bayreuther Patronatvereins*, the journal was founded and edited by Wagner apostle Hans von Wolzogen, this time with Wagner's open participation. After 1883, the journal changed its format and was renamed *Bayreuther Blätter: Zeitschrift zur Verständigung über die Möglichkeiten einer deutschen Kultur* (Bayreuth Papers: Journal for Understanding the Possibilities of a German Culture) and appeared quarterly, running continuously until Wolzogen's death in 1938. More than any other single instrument, the *Bayreuther Blätter* provided the seamless transition between Wagner's project and the Wagner industry – in its different aspects – after Wagner's death. The revised title publicizes its self-appointed role as an organ for the dissemination of an ideology with pan-German reach.[142]

Initially, the journal had been founded to excite interest in the proposed school, or "Stilbildungsanstalt" (Institute for the Advancement of Style) as he preferred to call it, since the word "school" evoked the image of existing and highly flawed establishments. Wagner's plan was comprehensive. The festival would be an annual event drawing a national and international public to Bayreuth. The school, in operation year round, would generate income and train a core of dedicated musicians, loyal to the Wagner brand, who could perform at the festival and elsewhere. The journal would fulfill several purposes: first, publish periodic updates about finances and other organizational issues as well as general announcements; second, provide a platform for essays on artistic, theoretical, and cultural issues to support the educational mission of the Wagner societies and, third, hold the Wagner societies together with Bayreuth as the operational and ideological hub.[143]

From its inception, the *Bayreuther Blätter* was intended to project the Bayreuth philosophy. Wagner's stipulation that circulation be limited to the membership of the Wagner societies in the hopes that the mainstream media would take no note of its existence (*Nichtbeachtung!*) or, at best refer

---

[141] "Die publizistische Wirkung [war] … verheerend" (Großmann-Vendrey, *Bayreuth in der deutschen Presse*, I: 45).

[142] In the "Statuten des Allgemeinen Richard Wagner-Vereins," constituted at the meeting in Nuremberg, May 14–15, 1883, the *Bayreuther Blätter* was termed the "Vereinsorgan" and, in §23 described as follows: "Sie dienen der literarischen Agitation im Sinne des Vereinszweckes," see Beiheft of the *Bayreuther Blätter* 2.iv–vi (1883).

[143] "Ankündigung der Aufführung des *Parsifal* (1877)," *SSD* XII: 333. See also "Eine Rede," 207.

to it as a "local rag" (*Winkelblatt*) was surely disingenuous, since he had claimed that "our little corners [*Winkel*] cover all of Germany."[144]

Ancillary markets

Commercially, Bayreuth then as now signified much more than just a music festival, which is why Karbaum is fundamentally wrong when he suggested that "the first festival was not consumed essentially differently than a world premiere at any court theater."[145] His assertion overlooks not only the marketing that accompanied the event, but more importantly all the supplementary materials and services for sale. Even if Bayreuth proved ill-equipped for the first onslaught of visitors in 1876, the town was transformed overnight into a tourist attraction, replete with Wagner memorabilia in the shape of trinkets, medallions, busts, and publications. In sum, far from being an ordinary world premiere, the first full performances of the *Ring* in 1876 can also be considered the official launch of the Wagner industry, meaning the moment when "Wagner" became a product from which others could secure a livelihood.

Again, Wagner led the way, again with the written word, this time with the publication of his collected works. The idea for a four-volume edition was already floated in Wagner's January 6, 1865, letter to Ludwig II which even includes a detailed table of contents. In the end, Wagner's *Collected Works* (*Gesammelte Schriften und Dichtungen*) first appeared in nine volumes between 1871 and 1873 with a tenth added in 1883 after his death. Wagner used the opportunity to edit the original versions of his texts, but there is perhaps an even more significant difference between the occasional and haphazard initial publication of Wagner's essays – written, as he yet again claimed, unwillingly and under various forms of professional or existential duress – and this later edition. Timed to coincide with publicity- and fundraising efforts for the Bayreuth festival, this republication allowed Wagner to continue his self-fashioning with the retrospective claim that his writings "deal with the renaissance of art itself" no less.[146] In Wagner's time, collected works were usually published post-mortem, if at all, but Wagner humorously counters the possible accusation of "vanity," by confronting the problem that "I'm still alive."[147] Since his works had previously

---

[144] *SSD* X: 24 and 22.
[145] Karbaum, *Bayreuther Festspiele*, 16.
[146] "es handle sich hierbei um eine Neugeburt der Kunst selbst" (*SSD* I: vi).
[147] "daß ich noch lebe" (*SSD* I: iii).

appeared sporadically and in a variety of different venues, Wagner now wanted to offer them in one place. Nevertheless, to avoid ordering them in such a way that might convey the impression of an aesthetic "system," he decided on ordering them chronologically, "like a kind of diary."[148] This arrangement does not distinguish between the different genres, but instead suggests a narrative of continuous development towards a(n inevitable) goal: the Bayreuth festival. The edition itself becomes a fiction that merges works with autobiography. For example, the edition begins with Wagner's Paris writings from the 1840s, the self-styled "major turning point" where circumstances "forced" him to become a writer.[149] This reinforces the link between the novellas about "a German musician in Paris" and Wagner's autobiographical experiences in Paris, between fiction and persona. In a larger sense, the collected works serve to annotate, explicate, and illuminate Wagner's autobiography, while the autobiography in turn functions as a sinew, a coherent narrative to contextualize and smooth over the inconsistencies of the collected works.

Recycling text for rhetorical purposes was a technique not limited to Wagner. In his 1855 preview article of *Rheingold*, Franz Liszt compares Wagner to Michelangelo and describes the developing *Ring* project using imagery reminiscent of Lohengrin's arrival: "Do you all see that shining spot far away on the horizon? It is the gigantic contour of a vast and majestic edifice the likes of which we have never seen before. Perhaps it will appear strange to you, perhaps you will find its style overly grand, the concept too vast, the design in its opulence too elaborate – but you will have to concede that it is the grandest of all existing monuments."[150] Twenty-one years later, Richard Pohl uses this paragraph in full in his multi-part report on the first Bayreuth festival.[151] What in 1855 had seemed audacious becomes prophetic with hindsight. It also reinforces the idea that Wagner's operas (in this case, the *Ring*) are best described using imagery from Wagner's operas (in this case, *Lohengrin*).

A similar pattern is repeated in 1872 when Ludwig Nohl presented "Five Popular Lectures on the German Music Drama" sponsored by the Wagner Society in Mannheim. The first four concerned Gluck, Mozart, Beethoven,

---

[148] "eine Art von Tagebuch" (*SSD* I: iv).

[149] "heftige Umkehr" (*SSD* I: 3), and "die erste Nöthigung zu schriftstellerischen Arbeiten" (*SSD* I: 1).

[150] "Seht Ihr den schimmernden Punkt fern dort am Horizont? Es ist der gigantische Umriß eines majestätischen, großen Gebäudes wie wir im ganzen Lauf unseres Weges noch kein ähnliches erblickten. Vielleicht wird es Euch befremden, vielleicht werdet Ihr den Styl zu erhaben, den Plan zu riesig, die Ornamentik in ihrer Fülle zu reichhaltig finden – aber Ihr werdet zugestehen müssen, daß es das Großartigste unter den bestehenden Monumenten ist" (Liszt, "Richard Wagner's *Rheingold*," *NZfM* 42.1 [January 1, 1855], 1–3, here 2).

[151] Richard Pohl, "Bayreuther Erinnerungen," *NZfM* 72.39 (September 22, 1876), 374–5.

and Weber respectively. The fifth lecture was devoted exclusively to Wagner and ended with a segment titled: "The German National Drama: *The Ring of the Nibelung*."[152] The lecture series replicates the sequence of Wagner's musical program for the December 1871 Mannheim concert, again suggesting that his work and specifically the *Ring* represent the culmination of German musical and cultural history.

Perhaps the most notable early example of someone who made a career off the Wagner name is Hans von Wolzogen. His *Thematischer Leitfaden*, announced in July 1876 and published to coincide with the festival, became a best-seller.[153] The book is a guide through the leitmotifs – a "musikalischer Bädeker"[154] as Hanslick referred to it, comparing it disparagingly to the popular travel guides still in use today. Even though he initially used the term "Leitfaden" (leading thread), Wolzogen popularized the concept and subsequent business of "leitmotif" guides.[155]

The technique of approaching Wagner's works through the idea of recurring musical motifs, pioneered as we have seen in the early 1850s by Liszt and Uhlig, and to a certain extent confirmed by Wagner's own somewhat tortured discussion of the subject, became more widespread by 1860, when Wendelin Weißheimer published his preview discussion and analysis of *Tristan und Isolde*, and amateurs like Baudelaire began writing about the composer and his works. In 1870, Gottlieb Federlein's study of *Rheingold* and *Die Walküre*, serialized in the *Musikalisches Wochenblatt*, again analyzed and named recurring motifs and their transformations.[156] Cosima was enthusiastic about Federlein's work,[157] and early Wagnerians like Heckel reported using the "leitmotif" system to orient themselves better.[158] By the

---

[152] "Das deutsche Nationaldrama: *Der Ring des Nibelungen*. Die Bühnenfestspiele zu Bayreuth," Poster announcement (*Richard-Wagner-Archiv* Nr.: A2584/IV-5).

[153] Hans von Wolzogen, *Thematischer Leitfaden durch die Musik zu Richard Wagner's Festspiel "Der Ring des Nibelungen,"* 2nd rev. edn (Leipzig: Edwin Schloemp, 1876).

[154] Eduard Hanslick, "R. Wagner's Bühnenfestspiel in Bayreuth," *Neue Freie Presse*, August 20, 1876 (quoted in Großmann-Vendrey, *Bayreuth in der deutschen Presse*, I: 175).

[155] See Thorau, *Semantisierte Sinnlichkeit*, for a thorough investigation of this often overlooked and – perhaps because of its perceived unseriousness – regrettably under-discussed aspect of the Wagner phenomenon.

[156] Gottlieb Federlein, "*Das Rheingold* von Richard Wagner. Versuch einer musikalischen Interpretation des Vorspiels zum *Ring des Nibelungen*," *Musikalisches Wochenblatt* 2 (1871), 210–13, etc., and the similarly titled work on *Die Walküre* (1872). See also Thorau, *Semantisierte Sinnlichkeit*, 107–8.

[157] Diary entry for October 23, 1870, Cosima notes: "Lektüre von Herrn Federlein's Abhandlung über *Rheingold*, die ich sehr gut finde und infolgedessen R. empfehle, sie in Artikeln drucken zu lassen."

[158] "Während der Theaterproben leisteten mir die von Federlein in München (jetzt in Amerika) zusammengestellten 'Leitmotive' aus *Rheingold* und *Walküre* gute Dienste. Ich hatte mir

1870 premiere of *Walküre* in Munich, press reports and reviews had widely adopted the habit of affixing labels to the most conspicuous recurring musical ideas.[159] In 1874, Wolzogen – apparently encouraged by Heckel – undertook to complete Federlein's project by tackling *Siegfried* through a similarly structured analysis.[160] His series, also for the *Musikalisches Wochenblatt*, became the basis for the subsequent book.

The taxonomy of leitmotifs seems to undermine Wagner's claim that all one needs to understand his works is common sense and a heart. Caught between rhetorical claims of simplicity, and the pragmatics of attracting and securing a customer base for a massive and unconventional work, this contradiction is reflected at the very start of Wolzogen's book. Bemoaning the widespread "prejudice" that Wagner and the *Ring* are "incomprehensible," Wolzogen pleads that "at first sight, one fears that … [text and music] might only be somewhat enjoyable with the aid of a course of study in each of the relevant academic disciplines."[161] However, he continues, since the *Ring* is based on myth, it should be "understandable to all without further ado,"[162] an assertion he immediately undermines by proposing that the key to Wagner's "self-explanatory" work is to understand the motifs (i.e. "buy my book"). Wolzogen's book marked the first time the world premiere of an opera was accompanied, in fact preceded, by a published commentary. An instant success, it had a second printing that same year and was translated into French and English shortly thereafter: Wagnerism was becoming a global industry.

For the sake of consistency, Wagner would have needed to distance himself from Wolzogen's primer, but his published objections radiate ambivalence.[163] On the contrary, Wolzogen's close association with Wagner, not to mention his editorship of the *Bayreuther Blätter* and, after Wagner's death, his leading role in the Bayreuth circle deep into the twentieth century, gave

---

dieselben aus dem *Musikalischen Wochenblatt* ausgeschnitten und an entsprechenden Stellen im Textbuch eingeklebt" (Heckel, *Wagner an Heckel*, 106).

[159] See, for example, Kolland, *Kontroverse Rezeption*, 169–70.

[160] "Ich machte Hans von Wolzogen den Vorschlag, anschließend an Federleins Arbeit auch die Motive aus *Siegfried* und *Götterdämmerung* zusammenzustellen" (Heckel, *Wagner an Heckel*, 107).

[161] Wolzogen, *Thematischer Leitfaden*, 1.

[162] *Ibid.*, 2.

[163] See *Über die Anwendung der Musik auf das Drama* (SSD X: 185), for Wagner's non-committal mention of analysis by "leitmotif" that addresses the dramatic but not the musical structure of his works. See also Cosima's diary entry for August 1, 1881: "Ich spiele mit Lusch 4händig aus der Götterdämmerung, R. sagt, es freue ihn das Werk. Leider kommen in dieser Ausgabe lauter Andeutungen wie: Wanderlust-Motiv, Unheils-Motiv etc. [vor]. R. sagt, am Ende glauben die Leute, daß solcher Unsinn auf meine Anregung geschieht!"

his *Thematischer Leitfaden* a "trademark" status as the authentic interpretational approach to Wagner's mature works, seemingly sanctioned by the composer himself.[164]

By the end of the nineteenth century, the "business of Wagner commentary"[165] fed the growing market for informational guides, companions, and aids in general, and specifically the interest in musical appreciation. By the twentieth, this was joined by the development of sound-reproduction technology, making the Wagnerian experience available to increasing numbers of middle-class homes. With Wolzogen's help, the "leitmotif" became the path of least resistance to understanding and enjoying the music dramas, and formed a core of Wagner commentary aimed especially at the dilettante, inextricably linking the work with its hermeneutics.[166] Wolzogen's book gave untrained readers the linguistic tools to discuss Wagner's works, and responded to the desire of the nineteenth-century bourgeoisie for cultural education as a means of social distinction (Bourdieu). His guide and its like offered "a feeling of self-assurance" based on the "impression that readers had understood the music"[167] – a feeling Wagner also induced through his autobiographical mystification of the compositional process, and promoted on stage by Walther in *Die Meistersinger*. But it also offered amateurs a "sense of superiority" over the less-informed and enabled snobs to "show off."[168] The highly lucrative explosion of commentaries led by Wolzogen not only coincided with, but was integral to, the growth of Wagnerism.[169]

Though Federlein and Wolzogen may have shared an approach to Wagner analysis, the book nevertheless transformed what appeared like Federlein's public service for educational purposes, published in a journal, into Wolzogen's venture for personal gain. The commercialism of Wolzogen's book was not lost on contemporary critics who used it to attack Wagner.[170] For example, Hanslick's "musikalischer Bädeker" comment implied by extension that the Bayreuth festival was nothing but a tourist destination. Not that this would have been the first time a music festival was also a venue for tourism. In August 1845, at the festival commemorating the unveiling of Beethoven's statue in Bonn, the composer's name and

[164] Thorau, *Semantisierte Sinnlichkeit*, 161: "daß der Titel … zum Markenzeichen des Bayreuthers geworden war."
[165] "wagnerianische Erläuterungsunternehmen" (*ibid.*, 181).
[166] *Ibid.*, 138.
[167] *Ibid.*, 129 and 274.
[168] "Wettbewerb der Besserwisserei" (*ibid.*, 120).
[169] *Ibid.*, 158 and 178.
[170] For a detailed account and analysis of this criticism, see Thorau, *Semantisierte Sinnlichkeit*, esp. Chapter 4.

image were exploited in the form of countless souvenirs – from Beethoven cigars to Beethoven trousers, striped like staves with musical notation. This practice represented yet another example of the emerging music industry, which exploited the "ascetic cult of great artists" (meaning dead ones) but also enabled the living to commodify themselves, as Wagner showed in exemplary fashion.[171] Since the departed could no longer reap the benefits of the commodification, the "seriousness" of their accomplishment was not in jeopardy. However the living were faced with the apparent choice of demeaning their art by seeking monetary success, or sacrificing themselves on the altar of eternal fame. Thus it was that the seriousness of the Bayreuth venture seemed compromised from the start by the commercialization that accompanied it. Quite contrary to Wagner's rhetorical position, Bayreuth was a tourist destination from its inception, and one for the very rich: "since who but the rich or the leisured can set aside six days in these hard economic times to experience the Wagner festival?" This same reviewer of the first festival further unmasks the reality lurking behind Wagnerian idealism, when he writes: "the Bayreuth festival is a new kind of travel amusement, which no one would deny for the rich patrons and patronesses, but let's call it as it is."[172]

Wagner's special skill was the ability to preserve the artistic integrity of his towering works amidst the blaze of commodification to which he in the first place had subjected them. Even his arch-critic, Eduard Hanslick, was forced to concede that Wagner had achieved "the greatest success a composer could ever imagine."[173] This book has illuminated only one aspect of his accomplishment.

---

[171] See Buch, *Beethoven's Ninth*, 135–6.
[172] Karl Frenzel, "Die Bayreuther Festspiele," *Nationalzeitung* (Berlin) August 27, 1876 (quoted in Großmann-Vendrey, *Bayreuth in der deutschen Presse*, I: 212–13).
[173] "den größten Erfolg, den ein Componist jemals träumen konnte" (Eduard Hanslick, "Wagner's Rheingold und sein Bayreuther Theater," in *Die moderne Oper*, 306–24, here 323–4).

Epilogue: the Wagner industry

The emphasis of the foregoing on specific episodes or examples of Wagner's self-promotional activities has necessarily meant that certain issues and key individuals in Wagner's life were not mentioned at all, or given only passing attention. Even the discussion of his self-marketing has been selective; to document and analyze every example between 1840 and 1883 would be a tedious exercise and would soon become annoying to read. For instance, only the fewest of Wagner's thousands of published letters contain no form of self-promotion. As his fame grew, along with the sense that these letters would become part of the permanent record, the self-stylization becomes ever more pronounced. Over a period of forty-plus years, self-marketing and branding became a daily exercise for Wagner to an extent that has no precedent, especially when juxtaposed with his equally insistent and sustained condemnation of the very social and economic conditions that encouraged and even required such behaviors.

Several important supporters of the Wagnerian cause, whose work falls into the chronological period covered by this book, have not been discussed in sufficient, or any, detail. I justify this in part because the impact of their contributions belongs more properly to the phase that followed Wagner's death, when his "undertaking" became an "industry."

Starting with the secretarial work of writing out Wagner's most extensive autobiography, *My Life*, not to mention the meticulous and self-effacing labor of her diaries, Cosima Wagner's increasingly archival and proprietary contribution to the Wagnerian image during the remainder of his life turned out to be the ideal preparation for the monumental role she assumed after his death to perpetuate and sustain – quite literally – the Wagnerian legacy, a role already anticipated by her active participation in the initial establishment of the Wagner societies.

If Cosima was the key figure in the establishment of a Wagner business, Friedrich Nietzsche was the intellect who first articulated a comprehensive cultural critique of Wagner. This work began in the early 1870s with the publication of *The Birth of Tragedy*, but it was not until Wagner's passing that Nietzsche penned his most trenchant and penetrating observations on the composer. Scarcely anything written since about the cultural significance of Wagner – including the main thrust of this book – is not somewhere mentioned or pondered by Nietzsche.

At a different level of discourse, there was Hans von Wolzogen, founding and sole editor of the *Bayreuther Blätter*. The direction of the journal was already evident in the five years it ran during Wagner's life. But its publication until Wolzogen's death in 1938 carried a continuous and fateful ideological coloring of the Wagner legacy deep into the heart of the Nazi period. If it was Cosima who oversaw the preservation and growth of a family that would eventually shake the hands of Adolf Hitler and, according to legend, provide him with the paper to write *Mein Kampf* in prison, it was in no small part Wolzogen and the circle that formed around him who fashioned the vocabulary of hatred and intolerance under the sign of Wagner's redemptive racist works, that continues to haunt his legacy.

Then there were musicians, like the singer and opera manager Angelo Neumann who, between 1882 and 1883, led his traveling "Richard Wagner-Theater" through Europe, performing the *Ring* interspersed with orchestral concerts of Wagner excerpts under the baton of Anton Seidl.[1] This was a breathtaking organizational feat which entailed moving an entire orchestra, singers, crew, and stage sets by chartered train, and setting up in a new town every week or so. Seidl, in turn, went on to New York in 1885 where he played a major role in establishing the Wagner repertoire in the United States.

Seidl and Neumann, whose entrepreneurial spirit seems second only to Wagner himself, provide welcome antidotes to the growing exclusivity, if not exclusionary world, of Bayreuth, exemplified also in 1882, by the premiere of Wagner's last work, *Parsifal*. From a marketing standpoint, *Parsifal* is in many ways Wagner's most interesting case. To emphasize its uniqueness, he dubbed it his "Bühnenweihfestspiel" (Stage Consecration Festival Play) and reserved for Bayreuth the exclusive right for its performance. The impact of this restriction, again felt most strongly after Wagner's death, remained a contentious issue until it lapsed in 1913. Wagner defended this restriction aesthetically with the argument that *Parsifal* was written specifically for the unique conditions of the Bayreuth theater, and that performance at an ordinary theater would desecrate the work by reducing it to mere entertainment. But these arguments masked the astute marketing strategy of limiting supply in order to increase or at least ensure demand: a guarantee for the initially uncertain survival of the Bayreuth concept. This notion of exclusivity and limited supply remains central to the waiting list for Bayreuth

---

[1] See Angelo Neumann, *Erinnerungen an Wagner*, 3rd edn (Leipzig: Staackmann, 1907).

tickets – artificially maintained, as some suggest – which currently extends to ten years.

It would be wrong to claim that Wagner was not sensitive to such issues of supply and demand. He made no secret of it, either. As the curtain fell on the last act of *Götterdämmerung* to conclude the first successful run of the complete *Ring* cycle on August 17, 1876, Wagner was encouraged to come forth to the Bayreuth stage and say a few words. His short speech ended with something like: "You have now seen what we can do; now it's for you to want! And, if you so desire we will have an art" (*Sie haben jetzt gesehen, was wir können; wollen Sie jetzt! Und wenn Sie wollen, werden wir eine Kunst haben!*).[2] Since his speech was improvised, and the theater was noisy, there is no reliable written record of what he said. Argument has raged over whether he said "*German* art" or not, while others thought he had suggested that there had been no art at all before Wagner. But what the debate missed entirely is Wagner's remarkable admission that the future of Bayreuth was dependent on "demand" (*wollen*). For an artist who worked hard to disassociate himself from the market, he seems to have been unusually attuned to its mechanics from the start. As I hope to have shown, it is no exaggeration to suggest that from 1840 on, Wagner dedicated his efforts to stimulating demand. Moreover, his last two decades were devoted to the establishment of a network that would continue this effort well after his death.[3]

Richard Wagner died on February 13, 1883. Less than one month later, the Wagner Society in Munich released a circular "To the representatives of the Former Bayreuth Patrons' Association."[4] Among their many suggestions was a call to combine and restructure the former *Patronatverein* and the Richard Wagner Societies into one General Richard-Wagner Society (*Allgemeiner Richard Wagner-Verein*) with the purpose of (1) maintaining the Bayreuth Festival "for all time to come" (*für alle Zeiten*) and (2) "to make both personal and literary efforts to maintain public interest."[5]

So far, the venture has succeeded.

---

[2] Großmann-Vendrey, *Bayreuth in der deutschen Presse*, I: 230. For different versions of what Wagner actually said that night, see also Paul Lindau, *Nüchterne Briefe aus Bayreuth* (Breslau: Schottländer, 1876), 42. The official version is: "Sie haben jetzt gesehen, was wir können; nun ist es an Ihnen, zu wollen. Und wenn Sie wollen, so haben wir eine Kunst!" (*SSD* XVI: 161).

[3] On this point, see also Thorau, *Semantisierte Sinnlichkeit*, 34–7.

[4] "An die Vertreter des früheren Bayreuther Patronat-Vereins," Munich, March 1883 (*Richard Wagner Archiv* Nr.: A2585–35).

[5] "durch persönliches und litterarisches Wirken die Theilnahme im Publikum rege halten" ("Statuten des Allgemeinen Richard Wagner-Vereins," Nuremberg, May 14–15, 1883 [*Beiheft* of the *Bayreuther Blätter* 2.iv–vi (1883)]).

Bibliography

Adorno, Theodor W. "On the Fetish-Character in Music and the Regression of Listening." *The Essential Frankfurt School Reader*. Ed. Andrew Arato and Eike Gebhardt. New York: Continuum, 1982. 270–99.

  In Search of Wagner. Trans. Rodney Livingstone. London: Verso, 1991.

Altenburg, Detlef, ed. *Liszt und die neudeutsche Schule*. Laaber: Laaber, 2006.

Ambros, August Wilhelm. *Culturhistorische Bilder aus dem Musikleben der Gegenwart*. Leipzig: Heinrich Matthes, 1860.

Anderson, Benedict. *Imagined Communities: Reflections on the Origin and Spread of Nationalism*. Rev. edn. London: Verso, 1991.

Bailey, Robert. "Wagner's Musical Sketches for *Siegfrieds Tod*." *Studies in Music History. Essays for Oliver Strunk*. Ed. Harold Powers. Princeton: Princeton University Press, 1968. 459–94.

Baudelaire, Charles. *Baudelaire as a Literary Critic*. Intro. and trans. L. B. and F. E. Hyslop. University Park: Pennsylvania State University Press, 1964.

Becker, Bernhard. "'Anonymität' der Wirkungsgeschichte. Phasen der Herder-Rezeption 1871–1945." *Johann Gottfried Herder: 1744–1803*. Ed. G. Sauder. Hamburg: Meiner, 1987. 423–36.

Beethoven, Ludwig van. *Briefwechsel Gesamtausgabe*. Ed. Sieghard Brandenburg. Munich: Henle, 1996.

  Ludwig van Beethoven: In Briefen und Lebensdokumenten. Ed. A. Würz and R. Schimkat. Stuttgart: Reclam, 1961.

Benjamin, Walter. *Charles Baudelaire: A Lyric Poet in the Era of High Capitalism*. Trans. Harry Zohn. London: NLB, 1973.

Berlioz, Hector. *A Selection from His Letters*. Trans. H. Searle. New York: Vienna House, 1973.

  Mémoires. 2 vols. Ed. Pierre Citron. Paris: Garnier-Flammarion, 1969.

Bernstein, Susan. *Virtuosity of the Nineteenth Century: Performing Music and Language in Heine, Liszt, and Baudelaire*. Stanford: Stanford University Press, 1998.

Besseler, Heinrich. *Das musikalische Hören der Neuzeit*. Berlin: Akademie, 1959.

Betz, Albrecht. *Der Charme des Ruhestörers: Heine-Studien – Ästhetik und Politik II*. Aachen: Rimbaud, 1997.

Bloom, Peter. "Berlioz and Wagner: Épisodes de la vie des artistes." *The Cambridge Companion to Berlioz*. Ed. Peter Bloom. Cambridge: Cambridge University Press, 2000. 235–50.

The Life of Berlioz. Cambridge: Cambridge University Press, 1998.

Bonds, Mark Evan. *After Beethoven: Imperatives of Originality in the Symphony*. Cambridge, MA: Harvard University Press, 1996.

Music as Thought: Listening to the Symphony in the Age of Beethoven. Princeton: Princeton University Press, 2006.

Borchmeyer, Dieter. *Das Theater Richard Wagners. Idee – Dichtung – Wirkung*. Stuttgart: Reclam, 1982.

Richard Wagner: Ahasvers Wandlungen. Frankfurt am Main: Insel, 2002; trans. Daphne Ellis. *Drama and the World of Richard Wagner*. Princeton: Princeton University Press, 2003.

Bourdieu, Pierre. *Distinction: A Social Critique of the Judgement of Taste*. Trans. Richard Nice. Cambridge, MA: Harvard University Press, 1984.

The Rules of Art: Genesis and Structure of the Literary Field. Trans. Susan Emanuel. Stanford: Stanford University Press, 1995.

Brzoska, Matthias. *Die Idee des Gesamtkunstwerks in der Musiknovellistik der Julimonarchie*. Laaber: Laaber, 1995.

Buch, Esteban. *Beethoven's Ninth: A Political History*. Trans. R. Miller. Chicago: University of Chicago Press, 2003.

Bürger, Peter. *Theory of the Avant-Garde*. Minneapolis: University of Minnesota Press, 1984.

Burnham, Scott. *Beethoven Hero*. Princeton: Princeton University Press, 1995.

Calinescu, Matei. *Faces of Modernity: Avant-Garde, Decadence, Kitsch*. Bloomington: Indiana University Press, 1977.

Campbell, Colin. *The Romantic Ethic and the Spirit of Modern Consumerism*. Oxford: Blackwell, 1987.

Chafe, Eric. *The Tragic and the Ecstatic*. Oxford: Oxford University Press, 2006.

Chua, Daniel K. L. *Absolute Music and the Construction of Meaning*. Cambridge: Cambridge University Press, 1999.

Dahlhaus, Carl. *Richard Wagner's Music Dramas*. Trans. Mary Whittall. Cambridge: Cambridge University Press, 1979.

Danuser, Hermann and Herfried Münkler, eds. *Zukunftsbilder: Richard Wagners Revolution und ihre Folgen in Kunst und Politik*. Schliengen: Argus, 2002.

Darcy, Warren. "Creatio ex nihilo. The Genesis, Structure, and Meaning of the *Rheingold* Prelude." *19th-Century Music* 13 (1989), 79–100.

De Nora, Tia. *Beethoven and the Construction of Genius: Musical Politics in Vienna, 1792–1803*. Berkeley: University of California Press, 1995.

Deathridge, John. *Wagner Beyond Good and Evil*. Berkeley: University of California Press, 2008.

Deathridge, John and Carl Dahlhaus. *New Grove Wagner*. New York: W. W. Norton, 1984.

Deaville, James. "The Controversy Surrounding Liszt's Conception of Programme Music." *Nineteenth-Century Music: Selected Proceedings of the Tenth International Conference*. Ed. Jim Samson and Bennett Zon. Aldershot: Ashgate, 2002. 98–124.

Devrient, Eduard. *Aus seinen Tagebüchern. Band 1. 1836–1852*. Ed. Rolf Kabel. Weimar: Böhlaus Nachfolger, 1964.

Döhring, Sieghart. "Meyerbeers Konzeption der historischen Oper und Wagners Musikdrama." *Wagnerliteratur – Wagnerforschung: Bericht über das Wagner-Symposium München 1983*. Ed. Carl Dahlhaus and Egon Voss. Mainz: Schott, 2000. 95–100.

Drüner, Ulrich. *Schöpfer und Zerstörer: Richard Wagner als Künstler*. Cologne: Böhlau, 2003.

Eichhorn, Andreas. *Beethovens Neunte Symphonie. Die Geschichte ihrer Aufführung und Rezeption*. Kassel: Bärenreiter, 1993.

Ellis, Katharine. *Music Criticism in Nineteenth-Century France: La Revue et Gazette musicale de Paris 1834–80*. Cambridge: Cambridge University Press, 1995.

Ellis, Katharine and Matthias Brzoska. "Avant-propos méthodologique." *Von Wagner zum Wagnérisme: Musik, Literatur, Kunst, Politik*. Ed. Annegret Fauser and Manuela Schwartz. Leipzig: Leipziger Universitätsverlag, 1999. 35–7.

Erb, Rainer and Werner Bergmann. *Die Nachtseite der Judenemanzipation: Der Widerstand gegen die Integration der Juden in Deutschland 1780–1860*. Berlin: Metropol, Veitl, 1989.

Fauser, Annegret. "Phantasmagorie im deutschen Wald? Zur *Freischütz*-Rezeption in London und Paris 1824." *Deutsche Meister, böse Geister? Nationale Selbstfindung in der Musik*. Ed. Hermann Danuser and Herfried Münkler. Schliengen: Argus, 2001. 245–73.

Finger, Anke. *Das Gesamtkunstwerk der Moderne*. Göttingen: Vandenhoeck & Ruprecht, 2006.

Finscher, Ludwig. "Weber's *Freischütz*: Conceptions and Misconceptions." *Proceedings of the Royal Musical Association* 110 (1983–4), 79–90.

Fischer, Jens Malte. *Richard Wagners "Das Judentum in der Musik": Eine kritische Dokumentation als Beitrag zur Geschichte des Antisemitismus*. Frankfurt am Main: Insel, 2000.

Flaubert, Gustave. *Sentimental Education*. Trans. and intro. Robert Baldick. London: Penguin, 1964.

Gibbs, Christopher and Dana Gooley, eds. *Franz Liszt and His World*. Princeton: Princeton University Press, 2006.

Glasenapp, Carl Friedrich. *Das Leben Richard Wagners in sechs Büchern dargestellt*. 4th edn. Leipzig: Breitkopf & Härtel, 1905.

Goehr, Lydia. *The Quest for Voice: On Music, Politics, and the Limits of Philosophy*. The 1997 Ernest Bloch Lectures. Oxford: Clarendon, 1998.

Goering, Theodor. *Der Messias von Bayreuth: Feuilletonistische Briefe an einen Freund in der Provinz*. Stuttgart: Richter & Kappler, 1881.

Gooley, Dana. *The Virtuoso Liszt*. Cambridge: Cambridge University Press, 2004.

Gramit, David. *Cultivating Music: The Aspirations, Interests, and Limits of German Musical Culture, 1770–1848*. Berkeley: University of California Press, 2002.

Gregor-Dellin, Martin. *Richard Wagner: Sein Leben – Sein Werk – Sein Jahrhundert*. Munich: Piper, 1980.

Grey, Thomas S. "Commentary: Opera in the Age of Revolution." *Journal of Interdisciplinary History* 36.3 (2006), 555–67.

Richard Wagner: Der fliegende Holländer. Cambridge Opera Handbooks. Cambridge: Cambridge University Press, 2000.

Wagner's Musical Prose. Cambridge: Cambridge University Press, 1995.

"… *wie ein roter Faden*: On the Origins of the 'leitmotif' as Critical Construct and Musical Practice." *Music Theory in the Age of Romanticism*. Ed. Ian Bent. Cambridge: Cambridge University Press, 1996. 187–210.

"Magnificent Obsession: *Tristan und Isolde* as the Object of Musical Analysis." *Music, Theatre and Politics in Germany: 1848 to the Third Reich*. Ed. Nicholas Bacht. Aldershot: Ashgate, 2006. 51–78.

Großmann-Vendrey, Susanna. *Bayreuth in der deutschen Presse: Beiträge zur Rezeptionsgeschichte Richard Wagners und seiner Festspiele*. Dokumentband I: *Die Grundsteinlegung und die ersten Festspiele (1872–1876)*; Dokumentband II: *Die Uraufführung des* Parsifal *(1882)*. Regensburg: Bosse, 1977.

Gutman, Robert. *Richard Wagner: The Man, His Mind, and His Music*. New York: Harcourt, Brace & World, 1968.

Habermas, Jürgen. *The Structural Transformation of the Public Sphere: An Inquiry into a Category of Bourgeois Society*. Trans. T. Burger. Cambridge, MA: MIT Press, 1989.

Hallman, Diana R. *Opera, Liberalism, and Antisemitism in Nineteenth-Century France: The Politics of Halévy's* La Juive. Cambridge: Cambridge University Press, 2002.

Hanke, Eva Martina. *Wagner in Zürich – Individuum und Lebenswelt*. Kassel: Bärenreiter, 2007.

Hanslick, Eduard. *Die moderne Oper: Kritiken und Studien*. Berlin: A. Hoffmann, 1875.

Heckel, Karl. *Die Bühnenfestspiele in Bayreuth. Authentischer Beitrag zur Geschichte ihrer Entstehung und Entwicklung*. Leipzig: Fritzsch, 1891.

Heckel, Karl, ed. *Richard Wagner an Emil Heckel. Zur Entstehungsgeschichte der Bühnenfestspiele in Bayreuth*. Leipzig: Breitkopf & Härtel, 1912.

Hegel, Georg Wilhelm Friedrich. *Vorlesungen über die Philosophie der Geschichte. Sämtliche Werke in 20 Bdn*. Ed. Hermann Glockner. Stuttgart: Frommann, 1961.

Hein, Stephanie. *Richard Wagners Kunstprogramm im nationalkulturellen Kontext: Ein Beitrag zur Kulturgeschichte des 19. Jahrhunderts*. Würzburg: Königshausen & Neumann, 2006.

Heine, Heinrich. *Lutezia. Historisch-Kritische Gesamtausgabe der Werke*. Vol. XIV.1. Ed. Manfred Windfuhr. Düsseldorf: Hoffmann u. Campe, 1973–97.

Herder, Johann Gottfried. *Sämtliche Werke*. 33 vols. Ed. Bernhard Suphan. Hildesheim: Olms, 1994.

Hobsbawm, Eric and Terence Ranger, eds. *The Invention of Tradition.* Cambridge: Cambridge University Press, 1983.

Holden, Raymond. *The Virtuoso Conductors: The Central European Tradition from Wagner to Karajan.* New Haven: Yale University Press, 2005.

Holoman, D. Kern. *Berlioz.* Cambridge, MA: Harvard University Press, 1989.

Huyssen, Andreas. *After the Great Divide: Modernism, Mass Culture, Postmodernism.* Bloomington: Indiana University Press, 1986.

Johnson, James H. *Listening in Paris: A Cultural History.* Berkeley: University of California Press, 1995.

Karbaum, Michael. *Geschichte der Bayreuther Festspiele (1876–1976).* Regensburg: Bosse, 1976.

Katz, Jacob. *Richard Wagner: Vorbote des Antisemitismus.* Königstein im Taunus: Athenäum, 1985.

Keiler, Allan. "Liszt and Beethoven: The Creation of a Personal Myth." *19th-Century Music* 12.2 (1988), 116–31.

"Liszt Research and Walker's Liszt." *Musical Quarterly* 70.3 (1984), 374–404.

Kietz, Gustav Adolf. *Richard Wagner in den Jahren 1842–1849 und 1873–1875. Erinnerungen von Gustav Adolf Kietz.* Recorded by Marie Kietz. Dresden: Carl Reissner, 1905.

Kirchmeyer, Helmut. *Robert Schumanns Düsseldorfer Aufsatz "Neue Bahnen" und die Ausbreitung der Wagnerschen Opern bis 1856: Psychogramm eines "letzten" Artikels.* Berlin: Akademie, 1993.

Situationsgeschichte der Musikkritik und musikalischen Pressewesens in Deutschland. Part 4: *Das zeitgenössische Wagner-Bild.* Vol. I: *Wagner in Dresden.* Vol. II: *Dokumente 1842–45.* Vol. III: *Dokumente 1846–1850.* Vol. IV [1st half]: *Dokumente 1851–1852/IV.* Vol. IV [2nd half]: *Dokumente 1852/V–1852/XII.* Regensburg: Bosse, 1967–72.

Kittler, Friedrich. "World-Breath: On Wagner's Media Technology." *Opera Through Other Eyes.* Ed. David Levin. Stanford: Stanford University Press, 1993. 215–35.

Gramophone, Film, Typewriter. Trans. with intro. by Geoffrey Winthrop-Young and Michael Wutz. Stanford: Stanford University Press, 1999.

Kloß, Erich. "Richard Wagner als Konzert-Dirigent in Wien." *Der Merker* 1.9 (October 2, 1910), 366–76.

Knittel, K. M. "Pilgrimages to Beethoven: Reminiscences by his Contemporaries." *Music & Letters* 84.1 (2003), 19–54.

Kolland, Hubert. *Die Kontroverse Rezeption von Wagners Nibelungen-Ring 1850–1870.* Cologne: Studio, 1995.

Kramer, Lawrence. *Music as Cultural Practice, 1800–1900.* Berkeley: University of California Press, 1990.

Kristeva, Julia. *Black Sun: Depression and Melancholia.* Trans. Leon S. Roudiez. New York: Columbia University Press, 1989.

Kropfinger, Karl. *Wagner and Beethoven: Richard Wagner's Reception of Beethoven.* Trans. P. Palmer. Cambridge: Cambridge University Press, 1991.

Kröplin, Eckart. *Richard Wagner: Theatralisches Leben und lebendiges Theater*. Leipzig: Deutscher Verlag für Musik, 1989.

Kürschner, Joseph. "Varianten und Ergänzungen zu Richard Wagners 'Autobiographischer Skizze.'" *Richard-Wagner-Jahrbuch*. Ed. Joseph Kürschner. Stuttgart, 1886. 286–92.

Lacoue-Labarthe, Philippe. *Musica Ficta: (Figures of Wagner)*. Trans. Felicia McCarren. Stanford: Stanford University Press, 1994.

Laube, Heinrich. *Gesammelte Werke in 50 Vols*. Ed. H. H. Houben. Leipzig: Hesse, 1909.

Levin, David J. "Randerlösung. Zur Dramaturgie der Figuration in Wagners *Tannhäuser*." *Figur und Figuration*. Ed. Gottfried Boehm *et al*. Munich: Fink, 2007. 263–71.

  "What Does Wagner Want? Thoughts on an Aesthetic (and Ideological) Vocabulary." *University of Toronto Quarterly* 74.2 (2005), 693–702.

Liszt, Franz. *Sämtliche Schriften*. Ed. Rainer Kleinertz. Wiesbaden: Breitkopf & Härtel, 1989– .

Locke, Ralph P. *Music, Musicians and the Saint-Simonians*. Chicago: University of Chicago Press, 1986.

Luther, Martin. *Sendbrief vom Dolmetschen*. Ed. Ernst Kähler. Stuttgart: Reclam, 1962.

Magee, Bryan. *The Tristan Chord: Wagner and Philosophy*. New York: Henry Holt, 2001.

Mann, Paul. *Theory-Death of the Avant-Garde*. Bloomington: Indiana University Press, 1991.

Mann, Thomas. *Leiden und Größe Richard Wagners*. Ed. H. Kurzke. Frankfurt am Main: Fischer, 1978.

Marx, Karl and Friedrich Engels. *The Communist Manifesto*. London: Penguin, 1980.

McKendrick, Neil, John Brewer and J. H. Plumb. *The Birth of a Consumer Society: The Commercialization of Eighteenth-Century England*. London: Europa Publications, 1982.

Mendès, Catulle. *Richard Wagner*. Paris: Charpentier, 1886.

Meredith, William. "Wagner's Beethoven: A Posthumous Pilgrimage to Beethoven in 1840." *The Beethoven Newsletter* 8.2 (1993), 46–53.

Mertens, Volker. "Mittelalter und Renaissance." *Wagner und Nietzsche: Kultur – Werk – Wirkung*. Ed. Lorenz Sorgner, H. James Birx and Nikolaus Knoepffler. Reinbek bei Hamburg: Rowohlt, 2008. 79–105.

Millington, Barry. *The New Grove Guide to Wagner and His Operas*. Oxford: Oxford University Press, 2006.

  Wagner. Rev. edn. Princeton: Princeton University Press, 1992.

Millington, Barry, ed. *The Wagner Compendium: A Guide to Wagner's Life and Music*. New York: Shirmer, 1992.

Miner, Margaret. *Resonant Gaps: Between Baudelaire and Wagner*. Athens, GA: University of Georgia Press, 1995.

Morrow, Mary Sue. *German Music Criticism in the Late Eighteenth Century: Aesthetic Issues in Instrumental Music*. Cambridge: Cambridge University Press, 1997.

Moulton, Ian Frederick. "Stratford and Bayreuth: Anti-Commercialism, Nationalism, and the Religion of Art." *Litteraria Pragensia* 6.12 (1996), 39–50.

Nattiez, Jean-Jacques. *Wagner Androgyne: A Study in Interpretation*. Trans. Stewart Spencer. Princeton: Princeton University Press, 1993.

Naumann, Emil. *Musikdrama oder Oper? Eine Beleuchtung der Bayreuther Bühnenfestspiele*. Berlin: Robert Oppenheim, 1876.

Neumann, Angelo. *Erinnerungen an Wagner*. 3rd edn. Leipzig: Staackmann, 1907.

Newcomb, Anthony. "Ritornello Ritornato: A Variety of Wagnerian Refrain Form." *Analyzing Opera: Verdi and Wagner*. Ed. Carolyn Abbate and Roger Parker. Berkeley: University of California Press, 1989. 202–21.

"Schumann and the Marketplace: From Butterflies to *Hausmusik*." *Nineteenth-Century Piano Music*. Ed. R. Larry Todd. New York: Schirmer, 1990. 258–315.

Newman, Ernest. *The Life of Richard Wagner*. 4 vols. London: Cassell, 1976.

Nietzsche, Friedrich. *Der Fall Wagner: Schriften, Aufzeichnungen, Briefe*. Ed. Dieter Borchmeyer. Frankfurt am Main: Insel, 1983.

The Birth of Tragedy and the Case of Wagner. Trans. Walter Kaufmann. New York: Vintage, 1967.

Pederson, Sanna. "Romantic and Enlightened German Music Criticism, 1800–1850." Ph.D. diss., University of Pennsylvania, 1995.

Perloff, Marjorie. *The Futurist Moment: Avant-Garde, Avant Guerre, and the Language of Rupture*. Chicago: University of Chicago Press, 1986.

Poggioli, Renato. *The Theory of the Avant-Garde*. Trans. Gerald Fitzgerald. Cambridge, MA: Harvard University Press, 1968.

Pohl, Richard. *Die Tonkünstler-Versammlung zu Leipzig am 1. bis 4. Juni 1859*. Leipzig: Kahnt, 1859.

Porges, Heinrich. *Tristan und Isolde*. Intro. Hans von Wolzogen. Leipzig: Breitkopf & Härtel, 1906.

Porter, Cecilia Hopkins. "The New Public and the Reordering of the Musical Establishment: The Lower Rhine Music Festivals, 1818–67." *19th-Century Music* 3.3 (1980), 211–24.

Prümm, Karl. "Berglinger und seine Schüler: Musiknovellen von Wackenroder bis Richard Wagner." *Zeitschrift für deutsche Philologie* 105.2 (1986), 186–212.

Puschmann, Theodor. *Richard Wagner: Eine psychiatrische Studie*. Berlin: Behr, 1873.

Revie, Ian. "Apollinaire and Cubist Innovation: Resetting the Frontiers, Changing the Paradigm." *European Avant-Garde: New Perspectives*. Ed. Dietrich Scheunemann. Amsterdam and Atlanta: Rodopi, 2000. 83–95.

Reynal, Philippe. "Richard Wagner als Pariser Korrespondent 1841: Neun *Pariser Berichte* für die Dresdener *Abend-Zeitung*: Reportage oder Vorwand?" *"Schlagen Sie die Kraft der Reflexion nicht zu gering an": Beiträge zu Richard*

Wagners Denken, Werk und Wirken. Ed. Klaus Döge, Christa Jost, and Peter Jost. Mainz: Schott, 2002. 21–31.

Rieger, Eva. *Minna und Richard Wagner: Stationen einer Liebe*. Düsseldorf: Artemis & Winkler, 2003.

Rose, Paul Lawrence. *Wagner: Race and Revolution*. New Haven: Yale University Press, 1992.

Sassoon, Donald. *The Culture of the Europeans from 1800 to the Present*. London: HarperCollins, 2006.

Schiller, Friedrich. *Werke. Nationalausgabe*. 50 vols. to date. Ed. Julius Petersen *et al*. Weimar: Hermann Böhlaus Nachfolger, 1943– .

Scholz, Dieter David. *Ein deutsches Mißverständnis: Richard Wagner zwischen Barrikade und Walhalla*. Berlin: Parthas, 1997.

Sennett, Richard. *The Fall of Public Man*. New York: Knopf, 1977.

Shaftesbury, Anthony Earl of. "*Soliloquy* or Advice to an Author." *Characteristics of Men, Manners, Opinions, Times, etc.* Ed. John Robertson. Gloucester, MA: Peter Smith, 1963.

Slater, Don. *Consumer Culture and Modernity*. Cambridge: Polity, 1997.

Solomon, Maynard. *Beethoven*. 2nd rev. edn. New York: Schirmer, 1998.

Spotts, Frederic. *Bayreuth: A History of the Wagner Festival*. New Haven: Yale University Press, 1994.

Stollberg, Arne. *Ohr und Auge – Klang und Form: Facetten einer musikästhetischen Dichotomie bei Johann Gottfried Herder, Richard Wagner und Franz Schrecker*. Munich: Franz Steiner, 2006.

Stumpf, Heike. "*… wollet mir jetzt durch die phantastisch verschlungenen Kreuzgänge folgen!" Metaphorisches Sprechen in der Musikkritik der ersten Hälfte des 19. Jahrhunderts*. Frankfurt am Main: Lang, 1996.

Talbot, Michael. "The Work Concept and Composer-Centredness." *The Musical Work: Reality or Invention?* Ed. Michael Talbot. Liverpool: Liverpool University Press, 2000. 168–86.

Tambling, Jeremy. *Opera and the Culture of Fascism*. Oxford: Clarendon, 1996.

Tanner, Michael. *Wagner*. Princeton: Princeton University Press, 1996.

Thorau, Christian. *Semantisierte Sinnlichkeit: Studien zu Rezeption und Zeichenstruktur der Leitmotivtechnik Richard Wagners*. Stuttgart: Franz Steiner, 2003.

Tusa, Michael C. "Cosmopolitanism and the National Opera: Weber's *Der Freischütz*." *Journal of Interdisciplinary History* 36.3 (2006), 483–506.

Vazsonyi, Nicholas. "Beethoven Instrumentalized: Richard Wagner's Self-Marketing & Media Image." *Music & Letters* 89.2 (2008), 195–211.

  "Marketing German Identity: Richard Wagner's Enterprise." *German Studies Review* 28.2 (2005), 327–46.

  "Press Releases from the Bayreuth Festival, 1876: An Early Attempt at Spin Control." *Wagner and His World*. Ed. Thomas Grey. Princeton: Princeton University Press, 2009. 391–408.

"Selling the *Ring*: Wagner's 'Enterprise.'" *Inside the* Ring, *Essays on Wagner's Opera Cycle*. Ed. John DiGaetani. Jefferson, NC: McFarland, 2006. 51–68.

Vazsonyi, Nicholas, ed. *Wagner's* Meistersinger: *Performance, History, Representation*. Rochester, NY: University of Rochester Press, 2003.

Veltzke, Veit. *Vom Patron zum Paladin: Wagnervereinigungen im Kaiserreich von der Reichsgründung bis zur Jahrhundertwende*. Bochum: Brockmeyer, 1987.

Voigt, Boris. *Richard Wagners Autoritäre Inszenierungen. Versuch über die Ästhetik charismatischer Herrschaft*. Hamburg: von Bockel, 2003.

Wagner, Cosima. *Die Tagebücher*. Ed. Martin Gregor-Dellin and Dietrich Mack. 2 vols. Munich: Piper, 1976–7. Trans. and annotated Geoffrey Skelton. *Diaries*. 2 vols. New York: Harcourt Brace, 1978.

Wagner, Cosima and Ludwig II von Bayern. *Briefe: Eine erstaunliche Korrespondenz*. Ed. Martha Schad and H. H. Schad. Bergisch Gladbach: Gustav Lübbe, 1996.

Wagner, Nike. *Wagner Theater*. Frankfurt am Main: Insel, 1998.

Wagner, Richard. "Eine Rede Wagners." Reported by Franz Muncker. *Richard Wagner-Jahrbuch* 1 (1886), 196–208.

Bayreuther Briefe. 2nd edn. Leipzig: Breitkopf & Härtel, 1912.

Das braune Buch: Tagebuchaufzeichnungen 1865 bis 1882. Ed. J. Bergfeld. Munich: Piper, 1975.

Der junge Wagner: Dichtungen, Aufsätze, Entwürfe 1832–1839. Ed. Julius Kapp. Berlin: Schuster & Loeffler, 1910.

Dichtungen und Schriften. Jubiläumsausgabe. 10 vols. Ed. Dieter Borchmeyer. Frankfurt am Main: Insel, 1983.

Mein Leben. Ed. Martin Gregor-Dellin. Munich: List, 1963; trans. Andrew Gray. *My Life*. Cambridge: Cambridge University Press, 1983.

Oper und Drama. Ed. and annotated Klaus Kropfinger. Stuttgart: Reclam, 1984.

Prelude and Transfiguration from Tristan and Isolde. Ed. Robert Bailey. New York: W. W. Norton, 1985.

Sämtliche Briefe. Ed. on behalf of the Richard-Wagner-Stiftung in Bayreuth by Gertrud Strobel and Werner Wolf. 18 vols. to date. Leipzig: Deutscher Verlag für Musik, 1967–2000; Wiesbaden: Breitkopf & Härtel, 1999– .

Sämtliche Schriften und Dichtungen. Volksausgabe. 16 vols. Leipzig: Breitkopf & Härtel, n.d. [1911].

Sämtliche Werke. Ed. Egon Voss and Christa Jost *et al*. Mainz: Schott, 1970– .

Richard Wagner an seine Künstler. Ed. Erich Kloss. 3rd edn. Leipzig: Breitkopf & Härtel, 1912.

Selected Letters of Richard Wagner. Trans. and ed. Stewart Spencer and Barry Millington. New York: W. W. Norton, 1987.

Wagner, Wolfgang Michael. *Carl Maria von Weber und die deutsche Nationaloper*. Mainz: Schott, 1994.

Walker, Alan. *Franz Liszt*. 3 vols. New York: Knopf, 1983–96.

Reflections on Liszt. Ithaca: Cornell University Press, 2005.

Walton, Chris. *Richard Wagner's Zurich: The Muse of Place.* Rochester, NY: Camden House, 2007.

Warrack, John. *Carl Maria von Weber.* 2nd edn. Cambridge: Cambridge University Press, 1976.

Weber, Max Maria von. *Carl Maria von Weber. Ein Lebensbild.* 3 vols. Leipzig: Ernst Keil, 1864.

Weber, William. "Mass Culture and the Reshaping of European Musical Taste, 1770–1870." *International Review of the Aesthetics and Sociology of Music* 8.1 (1977), 5–22.

  "Wagner, Wagnerism, and Musical Idealism." *Wagnerism in European Culture and Politics.* Ed. David C. Large and William Weber. Ithaca: Cornell University Press, 1984. 28–71.

Wegner, Manfred. *Musik und Mammon: Die permanente Krise der Musikkultur.* Baden-Baden: Nomos, 1999.

Weiner, Marc. *Richard Wagner and the Anti-Semitic Imagination.* Lincoln, NB: University of Nebraska Press, 1995.

Westernhagen, Curt von. *Wagner.* Zurich: Atlantis, 1968.

Wiesend, Reinhard. "Die Entstehung des *Rheingold*-Vorspiels und ihr Mythos." *Archiv für Musikwissenschaft* 49 (1992), 122–45.

Williams, Raymond. *Culture and Society: 1780–1950.* Harmondsworth: Penguin, 1963.

Wolzogen, Hans von. *Grundlage und Aufgabe des Allgemeinen Patronatvereins zur Pflege und Erhaltung der Bühnenfestspiele zu Bayreuth.* Chemnitz: Schmeitzner, 1877.

  Thematischer Leitfaden durch die Musik zu Richard Wagner's Festspiel "Der Ring des Nibelungen." 2nd rev. edn. Leipzig: Edwin Schloemp, 1876.

Woodmansee, Martha. *The Author, Art, and the Market: Rereading the History of Aesthetics.* New York: Columbia University Press, 1994.

Wordsworth, William. *The Prose Works of William Wordsworth.* 3 vols. Ed. W. J. B. Owen and J. W. Smyser. Oxford: Clarendon, 1974.

Zelinsky, Hartmut. *Richard Wagner – ein deutsches Thema: Eine Dokumentation zur Wirkungsgeschichte Richard Wagners 1876–1976.* 3rd edn. Berlin: Medusa, 1983.

Articles from the *Neue Zeitschrift für Musik* (chronological)

Uhlig, Theodor. "Die natürliche Grundlage der Instrumentalmusik im Hinblick auf Beethoven's Symphonien." *NZfM* 32.1 (January 1, 1850), 2–4.

  "Der Prophet von Meyerbeer." *NZfM* 32.11 (February 5, 1850).

  "Zeitgemäße Betrachtungen: Dramatisch." *NZfM* 32.34 (April 26, 1850), 173.

  "Zeitgemäße Betrachtungen: Reminiscenzen." *NZfM* 32.35 (April 30, 1850), 177.

  "Zeitgemäße Betrachtungen: Schön." *NZfM* 32.43 (May 28, 1850), 218.

"Zeitgemäße Betrachtungen: Außerordentliches." *NZfM* 33.7 (July 23, 1850), 29.

"Drei Tage in Weimar: Das Herderfest. Richard Wagner's Oper *Lohengrin*." *NZfM* 33.19 (September 3, 1850), 33.21 (September 10, 1850), 33.22 (September 13, 1850), 33.25 (September 24, 1850), 33.28 (October 4, 1850), and 33.30 (October 11, 1850).

Brendel, Franz. "Zum neuen Jahr." *NZfM* 36.1 (January 1, 1852), 4.

"Ein Ausflug nach Weimar." *NZfM* 36.4 (January 23, 1852), 37–40.

Uhlig, Theodor. "Ein kleiner Protest in Sachen Wagner's." *NZfM* 36 (1852), 277–8.

Brendel, Franz. "Zum neuen Jahr." *NZfM* 38.1 (January 1, 1853), 2.

Raff, Joachm. "An die Redaction der NZfM." *NZfM* 37.8 (February 11, 1853), 66.

Anon. "Zur Würdigung Richard Wagner's." *NZfM* 38.19 (May 6, 1853), 201.

Liszt, Franz. "Richard Wagner's *Rheingold*." *NZfM* 42.1 (January 1, 1855), 1–3.

Weißheimer, Wendelin. "'Tristan und Isolde,' Handlung in drei Aufzügen von Richard Wagner." *NZfM* 53.14 (September 28, 1860), 113–14.

Pohl, Richard. "Bayreuther Erinnerungen." *NZfM* 72.39 (September 22, 1876), 374–5.

Index

Abend-Zeitung (Dresden), 13, 36, 67, 74
Adorno, Theodor W., 4, 18, 106, 160, 162, 191
advertisement, 67–70, 74, 75–6, 77, 87, 88, 121, 192; leitmotif as, 107; Wagner's stage works as, 149, 150, 151, 160, 164, 167
aesthetics, 87, 93, 135, 161, 186, 189; of music drama, 65, 73, 79, 82, 88; in Wagner's stage works, 127, 128, 150, 159
Allgemeiner deutscher Musikverein, 108
Ambros, August Wilhelm, 103, 119
ancient Greece (*see also* drama), 83–5, 99, 104, 133, 169, 196
anti-Semitism, 9, 12, 18, 29–30, 79, 89, 90, 109, 138, 159
Apel, Theodor, 11
Arledge, Roone, 124
Arndt, Ernst Moritz, 54
Art & Revolution (Wagner), 78, 83–5
art for art's sake (*l'art pour l'art*, *see also* disinterestedness), 22, 25–7, 85, 90, 108, 109
Artwork of the Future (Wagner), 24, 39, 78, 85, 110, 112, 115, 132, 137
audience, 67, 90, 125, 131, 133, 151, 160, 186, 191; in Wagner's stage works, 128, 164, 167; Wagner's conception of, 128, 130, 133, 150, 174
Augsburger Allgemeine Zeitung, 115
Autobiographical Sketch (Wagner), 36, 42–4, 57, 63, 124
autobiography, 9–10, 30, 41, 59, 75, 82, 200, 205; used to shape Wagner's contemporary image, 12, 17, 44, 87, 123, 124, 162, 193
avant-garde, 3, 4, 24–5, 26–8, 34, 87, 123

Bach, Johann Sebastian, 6, 33
Baudelaire, Charles, 4, 23, 66, 69, 108, 121–2, 136, 201
Bayreuth, 83, 133, 182, 185, 186, 194, 206; significance of, 42, 84, 139, 173–4, 176, 199
Bayreuther autographische Korrespondenz, 195–8
Bayreuther Blätter, 198, 202, 206

Bayreuth festival (*see also* festival, idea of), 48, 99, 169, 170, 175, 177, 178, 180, 184, 185, 186, 187, 189, 193, 195, 197, 198, 199, 203, 204, 207; as national project, 171, 178, 179, 181, 182, 184, 185, 186, 194, 197, 198, 201; funding of (*see also* Patrons' Association and Wagner Societies), 176–81, 183, 185, 186, 188, 193, 194, 199
Beethoven, Ludwig van, 6, 21, 58, 66, 90, 119, 169, 177, 197, 200, 203; "blessed" by (*Weihekuss*), 34–5, 36, 38–40, 64; cult of, 32–41; Uhlig's discussion of, 110, 112; Wagner's appropriation of, 8, 42–3, 52, 64–5, 68–70, 73, 77, 98, 108; works by, Symphony no. 5 in C minor, 41; Symphony no. 7 in A major, 111, 192; Symphony no. 9 in D minor, 39, 55, 62–5, 68–70, 71–3, 90, 120; Wagner's performances of, 49, 62, 66–7, 68–71, 73–5, 76, 133
Benjamin, Walter, 4, 23, 84
Berlioz, Hector, 9, 13, 18, 24, 31, 33, 86
Bourdieu, Pierre, 4, 23–4, 26, 131, 203
Brahms, Johannes, 65
brand, 4, 7, 198, 205; Wagner's concept as, 86, 90, 101, 108, 125; Wagner's person as, 89; Wagner's works as, 1, 38, 81, 90, 150, 168, 193
Brecht, Betolt, 131
Brendel, Franz, 22, 79, 80, 93, 109, 120, 122
Bülow, Hans von, 116

camerata (Florentine), 99
canonization, 6, 8, 26–7, 33, 64, 114, 121
celebrity, 1–3, 102
Chopin, Frédéric, 29
chromaticism, 128, 152, 156
commodity, art as, 4, 16, 37, 85, 106, 130, 133, 138, 149, 167, 191, 204
Communication to My Friends, A (Wagner), 17, 21, 78, 83, 101, 124, 128
concerts, 6, 15, 66, 67, 70–3, 170, 190, 192
consumerism, 3–4, 102, 130, 134, 149, 164
consumers, 4, 6, 32, 106, 133, 149, 151, 160, 164, 167; Wagner's audience as, 9, 126

219

consumption, 4, 107, 108, 121, 130, 149, 160; in Wagner's stage works, 140, 141, 146, 149, 150, 167
criticism, music (*see* music criticism)
critics, music, 105
culture industry, 4, 14, 18, 23, 27

D'Ortigue, Joseph, 34
Dante, 71
Death in Paris, A (Wagner), 8, 35, 40–2, 125, 189, 200
Deutsche Allgemeine Zeitung, 56
Devrient, Emil, 56
diatonicism, 128, 134, 152
disinterestedness, in art, 16–19, 25–7, 37, 65, 86, 87, 109
drama, 84, 85, 146, 196
Dresden, 45, 46, 50–1, 79, 81, 89, 127, 170, 180, 191; 1846 Palm Sunday concert in, 62, 66; 1849 uprising in, 47, 81, 88, 93
Dresdener Anzeiger, 67, 68, 74, 75–6
Dresdner Abendzeitung (*see Abend-Zeitung [Dresden]*)
Dürer, Albrecht, 153

extracts, Wagner's performance of, 121, 123, 178, 188, 190–3

Fallersleben, Hoffmann von, 54
Faust (*see* Goethe, Johann Wolfgang von)
Federlein, Gottlieb, 201, 203
festival, idea of (*see also* music festivals), 84, 86, 101–2, 125, 133, 172, 189
Festival Theater (*see also* Bayreuth Festival), 1, 83, 133, 139, 162, 164, 168, 172, 173, 175, 177, 185, 188, 206
Fétis, François-Joseph, 28, 123
Feuerbach, Ludwig, 24, 131
Fischhoff, Joseph, 46
Flaubert, Gustave, 4, 23, 28–9
Flying Dutchman, The (Wagner), 88, 117, 125, 138, 170
friends, Wagner's definition of, 9, 121, 124, 128–9, 133, 179, 187, 190

Gade, Niels, 73
Gaillard, Karl, 46, 60
Gazette musicale de Paris, 28, 32
gender, 97, 98, 132, 137, 148; musical discourse of, 97, 137
Germanness, 17–21, 55, 89, 90–2, 132, 169, 172, 174, 182; ethical nature of, 25, 31, 37; in music, 11, 116, 117; Wagner as embodiment of, 8–10, 12, 29, 43, 44, 49, 65, 89; Weber and, 52–5, 56
Gesamtkunstwerk, 38, 65, 84, 85, 98, 102, 107, 127, 137, 167
Glasenapp, Carl Friedrich, 21, 75, 194
Gluck, Christoph Willibald, 99, 118, 119, 190, 200
Goethe, Johann Wolfgang von, 71–2, 73, 77, 131, 137, 173, 176
Grand Opera, 27, 29, 38, 89, 107, 127
Grillparzer, Franz, 33, 41, 58

Habeneck, François, 62, 64, 71
Habermas, Jürgen, 3
Halévy, Fromental, 30
Hanslick, Eduard, 136, 153, 201, 203, 204
Heckel, Emil, 178, 179, 181, 182, 184, 185, 186, 192, 195, 201
Heine, Heinrich, 14–15, 29–30
Herder, Johann Gottfried, 115, 132–3, 136, 153, 162, 163
Herwegh, Georg, 190
Hitler, Adolf, 55, 180, 206
Hoffmann, E. T. A., 32, 37–8, 41, 90

identity, German (*see* Germanness)

Janin, Jules, 32
Jewishness in Music (Wagner), 1, 79, 90–3, 95, 96, 97, 112
Journal des Débats, 114

Kant, Immanuel, 54
Kietz, Ernst Benedikt, 60, 61, 101, 172, 189
Kietz, Gustav Adolf, 61
Kulturindustrie, see culture industry

La Revue et Gazette musicale de Paris, 28, 36, 43, 50
Laube, Heinrich, 42–4, 91–2, 95
Leipzig, 35, 43, 187
Leipziger Zeitung, 56
leitmotif, 103–5, 106–7, 108, 113, 116, 117–18, 122, 161; guides for, 108, 113, 118, 201–3
Liszt, Franz, 24, 34–5, 46, 59, 60, 81, 108, 141; as virtuoso celebrity, 3, 5–6, 15–18, 28, 76, 197; as Wagner supporter, 78, 82, 108, 170, 172, 200; 1851 essay on *Lohengrin*, 114–20, 121, 122, 201; piano transcriptions of Wagner's works, 123
Lohengrin, 48, 88, 112–18, 120, 138, 170, 200; Prelude to Act I, 119, 121, 127, 192; 1850 premiere of, 82, 112–13, 116

Ludwig II, King of Bavaria, 172, 177, 185, 199
Luther, Martin, 18–20, 58

manifesto, 3, 4, 87, 189
Mannheim, 178, 179, 182, 192, 200
Marx, Karl, 25, 84
Mein Leben (My Life), 30, 59, 60, 62, 75, 124, 205
Meistersinger von Nürnberg, Die, 54, 126, 128, 133, 150–68, 174, 178, 192; characters in: David, 22, 152–3; Eva, 152, 160, 167; Hans Sachs, 36, 151, 153–4, 157, 158, 161, 163, 165, 174; Sixtus Beckmesser, 22, 66, 74, 151, 154, 157, 158–60, 162–4; *Das Volk*, 128, 133, 160, 163–5, 167–8; Walther von Stolzing, 36, 150, 152, 154–8, 161–2, 164–5
Mendelssohn-Bartholdy, Felix, 92
Mendès, Catulle, 2
Meyerbeer, Giacomo (Johann Liebmann Beer), 5–6, 11–12, 21, 52, 91, 127, 196, 197; *Le prophète*, 88, 109, 112; Wagner's campaign against, 27, 29, 57, 82, 89, 93–7, 103
Meysenbug, Malwida von, 195
Middle Ages, 85, 133, 143, 154
modernity, 1, 16, 26, 83, 130, 143, 149; Wagner as critic of, 6, 24–5, 29, 57, 83, 85, 134, 141, 150, 185
Moritz, Karl Phillip, 3
Mozart, Wolfgang Amadeus, 8, 33, 41, 43, 65, 99, 119, 169, 191, 200
Muncker, Franz, 187
Munich, 172, 178
music criticism, 32, 79
music drama (*see also Gesamtkunstwerk*), 38, 90, 99, 106, 108, 113, 120, 139, 180, 190, 200
music festivals, 73, 84, 115, 119, 169–70, 203
music market, 6, 11–16, 23, 37
music, instrumental, 11, 20, 39, 64, 65, 72, 90, 97, 110, 111, 122
Musikalisches Wochenblatt, 196, 201
Musiknovelle, 32
myth, 48, 105, 117

Napoleon I, Bonaparte, 50, 84
national socialism/socialist, 165, 180, 193, 206
Neue Zeitschrift für Musik, 21–3, 71, 73, 78, 79, 80, 93, 108, 109, 111–12, 122, 190, 196
Neumann, Angelo, 206
New German School, 159

Nietzsche, Friedrich, 2–3, 31, 44, 103, 146, 184, 205
Nohl, Ludwig, 200

Opera and Drama, 38, 88, 93, 96–100, 102, 113, 114, 116, 121, 123, 190
opera, Wagner's conception of, 96–7, 100

Paganini, Niccolò, 5–6, 15, 197
Paris, 26, 35, 40, 42, 44–5, 85, 94, 121, 131, 194; musical life in, 10–17, 40, 57; significance for Wagner of, 27–31, 36, 38, 41, 43, 48, 49, 81, 83, 87, 125, 172, 189, 195; Wagner's journalism in, 22–3, 58, 90
Parsifal, 48, 114, 206
Patron Certificate (*Patronatschein*), 177, 178, 181, 183
patronage, 129
Patrons' Association (*Patronatverein*), 177, 181, 183, 186–8, 207
piano transcriptions, 81, 123
Pilgrimage to Beethoven, A (Wagner), 8, 31–3, 34–40, 42, 64–5, 89, 125, 189, 200
Planer, Minna (*see* Wagner, Minna)
Pohl, Richard, 200
Pohlenz, Christian August, 63
Porges, Heinrich, 145, 196, 197
profit, 18, 26, 203; anti-Semitism and, 29; Germanness and, 8, 16, 37; music business and, 6, 11, 16, 18–19, 40, 65, 85, 204; Wagner's rejection of, 4, 13–14, 41, 183
program notes, 8, 67, 71–3, 76, 119, 121, 191
public image, 31, 193, 205; of Wagner as Beethoven's successor, 35, 66, 76; of Wagner as Romantic artist, 17, 48, 124, 195; of Wagner as most German, 20, 44, 108, 182; Wagner's creation of a, 1–3, 5, 8–9, 12, 25, 32, 41, 49, 78, 83, 87, 102, 186, 199
public relations, 189, 193–9
publicity, 15, 109, 118, 121, 123, 125, 192, 199; for 1846 Palm Sunday concert, 49; for 1876 Bayreuth festival, 181, 184, 189, 195–8; Wagner Societies as organ for, 181

Raff, Joachim, 78, 79, 80, 81, 82, 103, 114, 116
Reissiger, Carl Gottlieb, 46–7, 52, 66
Rellstab, Ludwig, 33–5
Revue musicale, 28
Rheingold, Das, 105, 125, 138–9, 162
Rheinische Musikzeitung, 79
Riefenstahl, Leni, 55
Rienzi, 46, 47, 117, 129, 170

Ring des Nibelungen, Der, 108, 118, 127, 172, 174, 175, 180, 191, 199, 207; announcements of, 101, 125, 176, 189, 196, 201; development of, 82, 88, 200; performances of the text, 170, 190
Romanticism, 7, 14, 17, 24, 65, 138, 149
Romantics, 4, 41, 80, 87, 124

Sachs, Hans (*see also Meistersinger*: characters, Hans Sachs), 153
Schiller, Friedrich, 3, 20, 53, 54, 65, 71–3, 77, 83–4, 85, 136, 176
Schladebach, Julius, 54, 66–7, 68, 74–5
Schleinitz, Marie von, 177, 190
Schlesinger, Maurice, 28–30, 31, 35, 48
Schopenhauer, Arthur, 141, 143
Schott & Söhne, 64
Schröder-Devrient, Wilhelmine, 51
Schumann, Robert, 21–3, 24, 68, 93
Scribe, Eugène, 11, 14
Seidl, Anton, 206
self-fashioning (*see* public image)
self-promotion, 2, 5–6, 9, 15, 27, 46–7, 49, 108, 121, 123, 168, 181, 183, 186, 187, 190, 205; in Wagner's letters, 60–2; in Wagner's prose works, 22, 35, 51, 59, 87
Semper, Gottfried, 173
Shakespeare, William, 170–2, 197
Stahr, Adolf, 170
Stern, Adolf, 184

Tacitus, Cornelius, 90
Tannhäuser, 88, 93, 114, 121, 127, 128, 170, 178
Tausig, Carl, 177, 178, 179, 181
Tieck, Ludwig, 71
tourism, 168, 199, 203
Tristan und Isolde, 82, 105, 126, 128, 133, 135, 139–50, 151, 161, 190, 193, 201; characters in: Isolde, 133, 134, 136, 140, 141, 146–9, 156; King Marke, 143; Tristan, 134, 140, 141, 143, 148, 156

Uhlig, Theodor, 73, 78, 79, 80, 88, 96–114, 116, 118, 122, 189, 201; campaign against Meyerbeer by, 93–6; review of *Lohengrin* by, 116, 118, 120
Urhan, Chrétien, 71

virtuoso, 14–16, 19
Vogelweide, Walther von der, 154, 158
Volk (*see also Meistersinger*: characters, *Das Volk*), 9, 53, 57, 84, 96, 105, 128, 132–3, 153–4, 162, 181

Wackenroder, Heinrich, 32
Wagner Societies, 129, 178, 179, 181, 182, 184, 186, 188, 198, 200, 205, 207
Wagner, Cosima, 129, 179, 181, 201, 205
Wagner, Katharina, 158
Wagner, Minna, 48, 81, 138
Wagner, Nike, 176
Wagner, Richard, works by (titles listed alphabetically)
Wagnerian(er), 49, 102, 129, 131
Weber, Carl Maria von, 9, 34, 43, 46, 49–59, 61–2, 89, 118, 199
Wedgwood, 3
Weihekuss (*see* Beethoven, Ludwig van, "blessed" by)
Weißheimer, Wendelin, 190, 201
Wesendonck, Mathilde, 135
Wiener Allgemeine Zeitung, 66
Wille, Eliza, 190
Williams, Raymond, 128
Wolzogen, Hans von, 108, 198, 201, 202–3, 206
Wordsworth, William, 3, 21

Young Germany, 84

Zeitung für die elegante Welt, 67
Zimmermann, J., 195
Zukunftsmusik, 24, 86, 124
Zurich, 78, 87, 88, 172, 190
 1853 festival in, 119, 170